Supertrends

Lars Tvede

Supertrends

**50 things you need to
know about the future**

WILEY

Library of Congress Cataloging-in-Publication Data

Names: Tvede, Lars, 1957- author.
Title: Supertrends : 50 things you need to know about the future / Lars Tvede.
Description: Chichester, West Sussex, United Kingdom : John Wiley & Sons, [2020] | Includes bibliographical references and index.
Identifiers: LCCN 2019040990 (print) | LCCN 2019040991 (ebook) | ISBN 9781119646839 (paperback) | ISBN 9781119646853 (adobe pdf) | ISBN 9781119646846 (ePub)
Subjects: LCSH: Economic forecasting. | Business forecasting. | Technological innovations—Forecasting.
Classification: LCC HB3730 .T899 2020 (print) | LCC HB3730 (ebook) | DDC 303.48/30112—dc23
LC record available at https://lccn.loc.gov/2019040990
LC ebook record available at https://lccn.loc.gov/2019040991

Cover Design: Wiley
Cover Image: © pialhovik/Getty Images

Set in 10/15pt Minion Pro by SPi Global, Chennai, India

Printed in Great Britain by TJ International Ltd, Padstow, Cornwall, UK

10 9 8 7 6 5 4 3 2 1

CONTENTS

ABOUT SOURCES AND CONTRIBUTORS

This book has so many sources that I and the Wiley team decided to put the approx 60-page source list online on www.larstvede.com. This also makes it easier for readers to link directly to the source material for closer inspection. For those reasons, there is no source list at the end of this book.

Apart from this, unlike most of my previous books, I wrote this one with some assistance, for which I am of course extremely grateful! I must add, however, that none of those who helped and inspired me can in any way be held responsible for the contents of the book. I had the final word throughout the entire process. Anyway, this was the team:

Jens Ulrik Hansen: Futurist and senior management coach who helps large companies develop working methods to cope with our rapidly changing world. Jens told me about the changes such companies face in terms of creating flexible, creative organisations without ending up in chaos.

Jørn Larsen: Founder and CEO of the Swiss software company Trifork, which currently employees a permanent workforce of about 800. In addition to developing software solutions for customers worldwide, Trifork holds about 50 conferences a year on future technologies. Trifork has also created some 100 spin-off companies, mainly within the software sector. I have developed the Supertrends app and supertrends.com website with Jens, Jørn, and Trifork.

Nicklas Brendborg: Nicklas managed to achieve the highest average ever recorded in a Danish high school and, together with Lars Horsbøl, wrote the bestseller *Topstudent*. He has just completed his bachelor's degree in Molecular Biomedicine at the University of Copenhagen and is the author of an upcoming book on anti-ageing.

Lars Horsbøl: Also a member of our Youth Board and co-author of the bestseller, *Topstudent.* Lars holds a bachelor's degree from Copenhagen Business School, where he was selected for the elite GLOBE (global learning opportunities in a business environment) programme. He is now studying Business Analytics and specialising in Artificial Intelligence and big data. He also runs two podcasts: *Ejendomsinvestoren* (Property Investor) and *Fremtidsfabrikken* (The Future Factory), the latter together with Eske Gerup.

Karl Iver Dahl Madsen: Engineer, former Vice Chairman of the Copenhagen Institute for Future Studies, and former member of the Board of Representatives of the Technical University of Denmark. Karl specialises in mathematical modelling and aquaculture. He also possesses an impressive ability to analyse issues open-mindedly and objectively.

Sune Aagard: MA (History and Journalism). I was introduced to Sune by the Danish Foreign Minister, Anders Samuelsen. Sune has worked at the Danish national newspaper, *Børsen,* and as Head of Communications and Director for the Liberal Alliance party.

Eske Gerup: Member of our Youth Board. Eske is a student at Copenhagen Business School, where he is on the elite GLOBAL SCLM (global supply chain and logistics management) programme. Together with Lars Horsbøl, he runs the podcast *Fremtidsfabrikken,* for which the two of them interview entrepreneurs and investors about trends in the start-up environment and the technologies of the future. Most recently, Eske was hired by McKinsey & Company.

Andreas Faarup: Also a member of our Youth Board. While at high school, Andreas won an EY Young Talent competition and went on to conduct a research project at the University of Copenhagen on Industry 4.0 and digitisation. He is now an International Business student at Copenhagen Business School and has worked for the likes of IBM, Barclays, Bloomberg, Goldman Sachs, and PwC.

Again, my heartfelt thanks for your contribution to this book. I know that you are all passionate about the fact that we humans can go through life with a great deal of knowledge and insight.

1.
FEELER, THINKER, HEDGEHOG, FOX – ON PREDICTIONS

'We're on the verge of the biggest bear market in 300 years.' This was the opinion of the famous financial analyst, Robert Prechter, in an interview in The New York Times *in summer 2010. A 'bear market' is a stock market with falling prices. In other words, Prechter was expecting a colossal downturn with depreciation of 'more than 90%'. This was not the first time he had predicted a disaster. Just one year previously, in June 2009, he had forecast a sharp fall; while in 2011, once again he predicted that 'the bear market is not over'. The markets would fall, fall, and fall again! Each time, his predictions spread like wildfire. The only problem for the people that listened was that the markets actually went up, up, and up again.*

In fact, this is what stock markets generally do. For example, in 100 years US shares rose by an average of 7% per year – in addition to inflation, which, with compound interest, would have increased a passive stock investor's purchasing power by approximately 80 000%. Up, up, up!

On account of his endless doomsday forecasts, Prechter has often been described as the biggest 'bear' on Wall Street. That is Wall Street slang for a person who thinks that the markets are heading down. How exactly did he arrive at his predictions? Well, he used the so-called 'Elliot Wave Theory'. He also claimed that he has never seen a market evolve in anything other than an Elliot Wave pattern.

I will not bore you here with the principles of Elliot Wave. However, despite my persistent quest, I have never been able to find a theory for why it is supposed to work. Not even in Prechter's own writings, where he merely refers to it as 'magical'. That makes it a bit odd that a leading newspaper such as *The New York Times* published his advice in 2009, 2010, and 2011, not to mention on many occasions both before and since. Doubly odd, because, according to the *Hulbert Financial Digest,* if an investor had systematically followed Prechter's recommendations from 1985 to 2010, they would have lost 98.3%. To put things into perspective, if that same investor had invested in a fund that passively followed the stock market index, and then had not touched his or her portfolio during the same 25 years, instead there would have been a gain of 857%. It seems to me that Robert Prechter is a man with a great idea, which is simply not substantiated by anything whatsoever.

Are you a feeler or a thinker?

When we hear the story of Prechter, the expression 'fact-resistance' springs to mind. Fact-resistance is a slang expression, but applies to a scientifically recognised type who crops up, for instance, in the much-used Myers–Briggs personality test. The test distinguishes between 'feeling' and 'thinking' personality types: in other words, people who are overwhelmingly 'emotional' rather than overwhelmingly 'analytical'. So, according to Myers–Briggs, what is a 'feeler'? A person who recognises him or herself in many of the following statements:

- 'I have a people or communications orientation.'
- 'I am concerned with harmony and nervous when it is missing.'
- 'I look for what is important to others and express concern for others.'
- 'I make decisions with my heart and want to be compassionate.'
- 'I believe being tactful is more important than telling the "cold truth".'
- 'Sometimes I miss seeing or communicating the "hard truth" of situations.'
- 'I am sometimes experienced by others as too idealistic, mushy, or indirect.'

Feelers are empathetic, concerned with a civil tone in debate and with following consensus, while cold facts and dry statistics mean less to them. They react strongly to emotional stories or what science rather drily calls 'anecdotal evidence'. In life, they mainly do what immediately *feels* right and good, and they set great store by other people's points of view, on the basis of whether they deem these people to be good or not. Try having a discussion with a strong feeler. He or she will often relate more to you as a person than to your arguments. Given that the Myers–Briggs test is particularly widespread, it is possible to quantify how the population is divided, and international studies have shown that approximately 44% of men and 76% of women are predominantly feelers. If we take the population as a whole, approximately 60% are primarily feelers.

According to the Myers–Briggs measurements, the remainder – in other words, 40% of everyone, and 56% of men and 24% of women – are predominantly thinkers. They can generally respond affirmatively to the following statements:

- 'I enjoy technical and scientific fields where logic is important.'
- 'I notice inconsistencies.'
- 'I look for logical explanations or solutions to almost everything.'
- 'I make decisions with my head and want to be fair.'
- 'I believe telling the truth is more important than being tactful.'
- 'Sometimes I miss or don't value the "people" part of a situation.'
- 'I can come across as too task-oriented, uncaring, or indifferent.'

Thinkers are most likely to make decisions on the basis of technology, science, and logic. They prioritise what data tells them, and are less concerned about opposing consensus or offending other people by acting accordingly. In a debate, it is logic rather than tone that counts. If logic conflicts with consensus, they usually follow it anyway.

My guess is that Prechter is predominantly a feeler, because for decades he has behaved in a somewhat fact-resistant way. The same applies to the renowned environmental activist, Paul R. Ehrlich, who in the course of a lengthy career has postulated an endless array of abortive doomsday predictions about the world's environment and resources. For example, in the 1960s, Ehrlich could not imagine that India would be able to feed 200 million people in 1980. However, today there are 1.2 billion Indians, and they are much better nourished than back then. In his book *The Population Bomb* (1968), he further stated that global population growth would be curbed by disease, war, and famine. The following year, he said of the United Kingdom: 'If I were a gambler, I would take even money that England will not exist in the year 2000.' He thought that the country was so over-populated that it could collapse completely as a result of pollution and lack of resources. This did not happen and, in my opinion, the UK culinary offering has improved a great deal since he wrote the book, and both its air and its water are cleaner.

And so it went on. He frequently made dramatic predictions about global famine, and added that even the United States, for all its wealth, would not be spared famine. In fact, he predicted, in great detail, that 65 million Americans would suffer starvation in the 1980s, and that by 1999 the population of the United States would be reduced to 22.6 million. Despite the fact that it actually increased to 273 million, and that obesity became a growing problem, he did not retract his views. The world was running out of resources. No dispute! In his book *The End of Affluence* (1975), he went on to predict that, 'before 1985 mankind will enter a genuine age of scarcity', in which 'the accessible supplies of many key minerals will be nearing depletion'. Today, about four decades later, we have not run out of any of the minerals he was concerned about. But this has not affected his attitudes either.

Ehrlich also believed that the world was running out of life. In 1993, he estimated that half of Earth's animal species would disappear in the next seven years, and that all of them (yes, every single one) would have disappeared by 2015. Nonetheless, there is still life on the planet (I just saw a bird flying by), and the scientific consensus is that approximately a total of one thousandth of all species became extinct over the past 400 or so years. That is why we probably still have 7.4–10 million species plus bacteria etc.

Popular poppycock

While these might seem like bizarre stories, there is worse to come. Because, despite their endless succession of misjudgements, both 'Wave Robert' and 'Honest Paul' have lived the lives of veritable rock stars. Prechter has featured constantly in the media and is regularly referred to as a leading financial analyst, while Ehrlich has received so many official honours that a simple list would fill a few pages of A4. For example, he has won awards from the Sierra Club, the World Wildlife Fund, the Royal Swedish Academy of Sciences (which is involved in nominating candidates for Nobel Prizes), Volvo, the United Nations, the Albert Einstein Club, the Ecological Society of America, the American Institute of Biological Sciences, and the Royal Society of London. Not, we must assume, because his analyses happened to be scientifically substantiated and correct, but because many people regarded him as a good, well-intentioned person. He apparently *felt* good in these circles.

But what did all those gentlemen think about the fact that they were just about never anywhere near right? From time to time, more thoughtful journalists and others have naturally asked questions about this embarrassing situation, but 'Wave Robert' and 'Honest Paul' have stuck to their guns. Maybe they were just a bit too premature sometimes, and that proved how visionary they were. Or they were right. Other people just did not know how to measure correctly.

We find something similar in religious doomsday cults. The most famous study of this features in the book *When Prophecy Fails* (1956) about the secretive, press-shy doomsday cult, The Seekers, which was led by a Chicago housewife by the name of Dorothy Martin. At one point, the psychologist Leon Festinger and two of his colleagues infiltrated the cult to reveal the members' reaction when their forecast of an upcoming Judgement Day on 21 December 1954 came to nothing. It should be said that, prior to this, the members of the cult had generally quit their jobs and said goodbye to their colleagues and friends. On the eve of the anticipated Judgement Day, they awaited telecommunication with the crew from outer space who, at midnight on 20 December, would show them the way to the UFO that, according to Dorothy, would save them and whisk them off to a planet called Clarion – a mere seven hours before Earth would be eliminated in a great flood.

So, what happened when a watch showed midnight and no one came to collect them? First, one member pointed out that another clock showed only 11.55 p.m. But when that clock also passed midnight, they simply sat in painful silence until 4.45 a.m., when Dorothy suddenly received a message from God, informing her that the cult had 'spread so much light' that He had decided to save Earth. But now comes the interesting bit. The incident (or lack of one) only served to convince the members of the group that they were right. The following day, for the very first time, they contacted the press in order to spread their message to the entire world. That is how fact-resistant people can be.

Hedgehogs and foxes – which are best at seeing the future?

I think Dorothy and her followers probably had a couple of screws loose. But what 'UFO Dorothy', 'Wave Robert', and 'Honest Paul' probably had in common is that they were what, in his famous essay *The Hedgehog and the Fox* (1953), the philosopher Isaiah Berlin termed 'hedgehogs'.

Err ... hedgehogs? Yes, it was in this essay that Berlin distinguished between hedgehogs, who view the world on the basis of a single, fundamental idea, and foxes, who view it on the basis of a myriad of different ideas and observations. Hedgehogs, he added, are not nearly as good at looking into the future as foxes (which he went on to document in comprehensive statistical surveys). We can collate thinkers, feelers, hedgehogs, and foxes in a simple table in order to illustrate their various approaches to looking into the future.

	Focused on a single, fundamental idea	Combining many ideas, models, and observations
Myers–Briggs 'feeler'	Fact-resistant hedgehog	Fact-resistant fox
Myers–Briggs 'thinker'	Data-driven hedgehog	Data-driven fox

Fact-resistant hedgehogs, who live by making erroneous forecasts, can win all sorts of accolades and awards because they have such an appeal for other fact-resistant hedgehogs, but there is a huge difference in how good the four types are at predicting the future. The cleverest are the data-driven foxes.

No! As in never!

Throughout the approximately 350 000 years of human history, the average individual has not noticed any significant changes in the society around them from birth to death. Therefore, it is no surprise that, over the years, many even highly knowledgeable people have underestimated the progress of the future. For example, in 98 CE, the famous Roman engineer, writer, and politician Sextus Julius Frontinus said: 'Inventions reached their limit long ago, and I see no hope for further development.' Of course! Opportunities for innovation were exhausted a few thousand years ago. That is what he thought, anyway.

Not only was innovation obviously over and done with, but soon resources would be depleted too. A few centuries after Frontinus's lament, Bishop Cyprian of Carthage complained about the fact that 'the mountains, worn away and exhausted, produce less marble. The mines are impoverished and supply us with fewer precious metals. The seams are spent, and they disappear daily.' In other words, resources were on the wane 1700 years ago, and that is what lots of people have believed right up to the present day. For a long time, one of the most famous doomsday preachers was Thomas Malthus. In 1798 he wrote: 'The eternal tendency of man to grow faster than his ability to feed himself is one of the laws of humanity, which we cannot expect to change.' He therefore predicted increasing famine in the world.

In 1908, US President Theodore Roosevelt convened a White House crisis meeting to discuss an acute problem: the United States running out of resources. 'The enormous stores of mineral oil and gas are largely gone,' he said, and 'more than half of the timber is gone.' He also added that 'many experts now declare that the end of both iron and coal is in sight'.

As we know, this was all wrong. But, particularly in the 1960s and 1970s, the belief in an acute scarcity of resources for the future prevailed again. For example, in 1969, the Nobel Laureate George Wald stated: 'There is every indication that the world population will double before the year 2000, and there is a widespread expectation of famine on an unprecedented scale in many parts of the world. The experts tend to differ only in their estimates of when those famines will begin.'

So, the experts only disagreed about the timing of the inevitable catastrophe – not on whether it would happen. But instead, after Wald's comment, the spread of famine *decreased* rapidly. Even though the resource sceptics were right that the global population would grow rapidly, they did not realise that our innovation and thus our capacity to supply ourselves would grow much *more* rapidly, as I have indicated with the graph.

The race between population and innovation

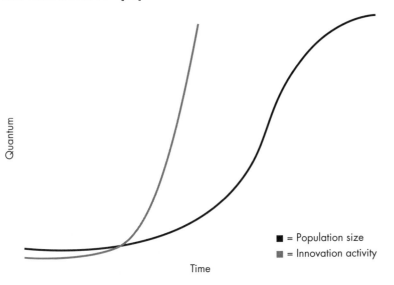

In purely psychological terms, it can be hard to imagine that the future will be dramatically different from today. Yes, we can see that up until now it has changed dramatically and become much better. But when we look forward, we tend to extrapolate the development in linear terms or not at all. Consequently, history is full of examples of prominent people, including some rather smart data-oriented foxes, who underestimated future development. Here is an example. In 1995, the futurologist Ian Pearson gave a lecture, in which he predicted that, in a few years' time, IBM's artificial intelligence (AI) computer, Deep Blue, would beat the world champion Garri Kasparov at chess. After the lecture, a member of the audience approached him and said that he himself had written that program and knew that it had limitations and would never be able to beat Kasparov. But just 18 months later Deep Blue beat Kasparov.

In fact, it is hard to name any major innovation that was not underestimated or rejected by leading experts. For example, on 9 October 1903, *The New York Times* published an article on 'Flying Machines Which Do

Not Fly', in which they ridiculed attempts to create flying machines and concluded that mathematicians and mechanics might succeed within 'one or ten million years'. A few weeks later, on 22 October, the famous physicist Simon Newcomb wrote in *The Independent*: 'The example of the bird does not prove that man can fly. The hundred and fifty pounds of dead weight which the manager of the machine must add to it over and above that necessary in the bird may well prove an insurmountable obstacle to success.'

Two things are worth noting. For one, Newcomb is still considered one of the most outstanding scientists of all time. In his time, he succeeded in becoming president of both the American Astronomical Society and the American Mathematical Society, and also made significant contributions to thoughts on national economy, including the famous quantity theory of money. But this leading astronomer, mathematician, and economist did not really believe in aeroplanes. That was one thing. The second remarkable thing is the date of the quote: 22 October 1903. At this very moment, the famous astronomer, physicist, and entrepreneur Samuel Pierpont Langley was experimenting with building an aeroplane. *The New York Times* had no confidence in this either. In their editorial on 10 December 1903, they wrote: 'We hope that Professor Langley will not put his substantial greatness as a scientist in further peril by continuing to waste his time and the money involved, in further airship experiments.'

What the newspaper's editors did not know was that the day before they published the leader, some hitherto-unknown brothers by the name of Wright were busy assembling parts for something they hoped would be an aeroplane. But perhaps the editors were inspired by the December issue of the *North American Review*, in which the prominent rear admiral and chief of the Bureau of Steam Engineering, George W. Melville also covered the pointless attempt to make aeroplanes, writing that there was 'no basis for hope'.

Now we know how that story ended and, if you happen to read this sitting in, say, a Dreamliner and flying over the rooftops at 800 km an hour, you will find it amusing. Especially when you consider that the

Wright brothers not only managed to build an aeroplane in a matter of weeks – if not days – following dismissals by the physicist, the admiral, and the editors, but also that they got it airborne just nine days after they had started assembling it. This took place on 17 December 1903, 'one to ten million years' earlier than *The New York Times* editor had expected.

So, people often underestimate what is possible. Furthermore, when it does work, they often say something indulgent along the lines of: 'It's pretty clear that there's no market for X.'

And then the whole world starts buying it like crazy. Take flights, for example. I just checked on FlightAware.com to see the state of the Wright brothers' invention. It informed me: 'FlightAware has tracked 113 646 arrivals in the last 24 hours.' I also learned that 10 710 aircraft were airborne at that moment in time. According to my calculation, this indicated that about 1.2 million people were actually sitting in flying machines at one time.

This tells us that, while people are often sceptical about innovation, they do tend to get their wallets out when it works. Yes, but when people start to buy lots of innovative things, the prophets of doom adopt 'Honest Paul's' point of view: 'If everyone buys X, we'll run out of resources.' However, we can state that, on average, commodity prices have *fallen* massively over the last few centuries, which in no way suggests that we are running out of resources – on the contrary. I will come to that at a later point.

The constant impossibility

Without getting bogged down in the matter, let me just give a few more examples of how often prominent doomsayers have got it wrong when it comes to development. For instance, in 1830 Professor Dionysius Lardner said that high-speed rail travel would be impossible because 'passengers, unable to breathe, would die of asphyxia'. Seven years later, the French physician and surgeon, Alfred Velpeau ruled out the possibility of anaesthesia and, after a demonstration of electric light at the Paris World Exhibition in 1878, yet another surgeon, Erasmus Wilson, assured the world that nothing more would be heard of this phenomenon in the future. In 1888, the aforementioned Simon Newcomb stated: 'We are probably nearing the limit of all we can know about astronomy.' Four years later, in 1894, in a speech at the inauguration of Chicago University, the physicist Albert Michelson said: 'The more important fundamental laws and facts of physical science have all been discovered, and these are now so firmly established that the possibility of their ever being supplanted in consequence of new discoveries is exceedingly remote.'

So, there was not much left to discover in the basic sciences and, according to Charles H. Duell, head of the US patent office in 1899, not in the areas of technology and commerce either. In fact, he more than earned his place in the technological book of dummies with the following quote: 'Everything that can be invented has been invented.'

And that is how things have gone on ever since. Highly esteemed specialists and scientists have rejected any future for the likes of military aircraft, television, home computers, nuclear power, etc. In 1957, the editor of Hall Business Publishing even wrote that computing was a mere fad that would not survive the year.

Let us put this all in a larger perspective. The species of Homo sapiens has existed for about 350 000 years and, during most of that period, innovation has been minimal. The beginning of the last Interglacial Period, which is said to have lasted about 11 700 years, saw intermittent development with gradually accelerating innovation, and about 5000 years ago the first actual civilisations together with their towns and cities started to emerge. Funny, isn't it? That means that for the first 350 000 or so years of the history of mankind, virtually nothing at all happened. But now there is no holding it back.

When it comes to those human accomplishments mentioned in international encyclopaedias, the first date back 3000 years. According to a major econometric study (econometrics means applying statistical methods to historical events), from that time until 1950 accomplishments developed as follows:

Human innovation/accomplishment from 1000 BCE to 1950

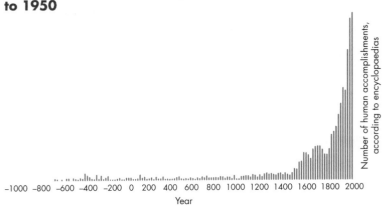

This shows us that, even though until around 1450 there was no significant overall acceleration in global innovation and performance, things were nonetheless accumulating. That linear accumulation of knowledge and capability, however, involves a lot of local ups and downs. At one point, Egypt flourished, then Persia, then the Greek city states, then China, then Rome, and then Spain or somewhere else. So, things went up and down on a local level, but with no overall *global* acceleration. Along the way, civilisations flourished and perished in long successions. Boom, crash, boom, crash, boom, crash . . . In fact, approximately 200 civilisations ended up in history's graveyard.

However, in or around 1450 there was a huge increase in innovation in Western Europe, in particular in a belt stretching from the north of Italy up through present-day Switzerland, and into Germany, parts of northern Europe, and eastern France. For several centuries, both before and during this creative explosion, this geographical belt consisted of thousands of competing city states. And from that time until 1950, when the above-mentioned study stopped, the West (in other words, Western Europe and areas colonised by Western Europeans such as North America, Australia, etc.) stood for no less than 97% of global innovation (but typically less than 10% of the global population). From 1950 to 2000, the Western contribution to innovation probably dropped to 95%. However, given the innovation boom of recent years in Asia, the West is likely closer to 90% and heading for 80% and 70%. For example, the Chinese and South Koreans are now storming ahead, which I happen to think is a good thing for everyone.

Our knowledge at double speed

How quickly are our creativity and innovation evolving now when compared to before? Very quickly. In fact, it appears to be hyperexponential, which means in a constant state of acceleration, *but with an increasingly shorter doubling rate.*

Let me just add a technical remark. A linear sequence is, for example, 2, 3, 4, 5, 6, whereas an exponential sequence such as x^2 can be 2, 4, 8, 16, 32, etc.,

If your stride length in a race is 1 m, the first stride is 1 m, the second is 2 m, the third is 4 m, etc. – the twentieth stride is 500 km. When you finish that stride, you will have advanced 1000 km from your starting point, and 26 strides would get you 1.5 times round the globe.

In other words, exponential is off the wall. Let me put it another way. Imagine that you place a few water lilies in a large lake, and they propagate exponentially to the power of 2, until after 20 years they will cover the entire surface. So how much do they cover by year 19? Just half. If we move on to double exponential, things go even faster, since the exponent also increase exponentially over time. That can give a sequence such as this: 2, 8, 512, 13 4217 728, etc. We shall see a potential example of that when we study quantum computing.

Let us put these thoughts into perspective. According to archaeologists, the stone axe was probably invented by *Homo erectus* about 700 000 years ago, and the first skin tent about 200 000 years later. Then, about

400 000 years ago, came sharpened spearheads. This means that our hairy ancestors came up with three inventions on the course of 300 000 years. However, then things really started to accelerate:

- 250 000 BCE: stone cutting
- 230 000 BCE: burials
- 200 000 BCE: knives
- 200 000 BCE: rope.

That makes four inventions in 50 000 years, during which *Homo erectus* – roughly simultaneously with the invention of knives and rope – evolved into *Homo sapiens*.

The next 30 000 years saw at least four more inventions: serrated blades, needles made of bone (90 000 BCE), and art and toys (70 000 BCE). As we all know, after that things went even faster, and in his book *Critical Path* (1981), the futurist and inventor R. Buckminster Fuller came up with an interesting statement. First, he estimated the total amount of human knowledge accumulated from the time of *Homo erectus* to the birth of Christ, calling this a single 'knowledge unit'. He then estimated that the next knowledge unit was created over the following 1500 years. In other words, the total amount of human knowledge doubled over approximately 1500 years. The next doubling from two to four knowledge units took only 250 years and was completed around 1750. By 1900, in other words 150 years later, things had doubled yet again to eight knowledge units. That means that the development was exponential, but with a decrease in the doubling rate. That made it hyperexponential.

Here is another calculation. The physicist John Ziman has estimated that for every scientific document or scientist that existed in 1670, there were 100 in 1770, 10 000 in 1870, and 1 million in 1970. Mind blowing! Let me take this opportunity to introduce the first of the 50 rules of thumb that we will use to facilitate our understanding of the past and help us investigate the future. Here we go:

1. **The global scientific activity doubles every 15 years. In a century this means growing by a factor of 100 (Ziman's Law).**

The point of this rule and the subsequent ones, most of which can be referred to as vectors, is that together they provide a fundamental sense of how the world evolves.

And applying rules is handy when contemplating the future. Alfred Marshall, one of the most influential economists of his time, had a fun way of working. Whenever he read other people's writings on the subject of economics, he transcribed their prose into simple mathematical formulas. He thereby sought to understand the underlying algorithms behind their argumentation, which often helped him understand whether their words actually made sense.

Ziman's Law is such a rule. It corresponds to an annual growth of approximately 4%, which, via the derived innovation, contributes to a combination of increasingly better, often cheaper products and a long-term growth in the global gross domestic product (GDP) of about 3% per year in total, and 2% per year per capita.

And just how fast are things going right now, not just in terms of scientific activity, but also in terms of innovation? It is very difficult to measure, but we know, for example, that the amount of digital data we store doubles approximately every third year, and that the amount of business-related data apparently doubles every 25th month, while a number of digital technologies double their performance around every other year. I will come back to that.

Now here is an interesting perspective. If Ziman's Law still applies, it means that by 2030 the world will have about 10 times more scientific activity than it had in 1980. That also implies that, by 2080, it will have 10 times more scientific activity than in 2030, and 100 times more scientific activity than in 1980. And that a person born in 1980 and dying in 2080 will personally witness a 100-fold increase in scientific activity. That is a pretty good rule to have in the back of your mind.

And now get this. If Ziman's Law remains in place for the next two centuries, it also means that our scientific activity will be 10 000 times greater in 200 years' time. That's interesting, isn't it? Just think of the prospects if by 2100 people will know about 100 times more than they did in 2000, and by 2200, 10 000 times more; which, by the way, would be possible as computers take over more and more scientific tasks from humans. What an amazing journey we are on!

The dynamics of innovation

It goes without saying that knowledge and its effects do not disperse equally amongst people, companies, industries, and nations. Instead, it spreads more like local clusters of water lilies in a very large body of water. It often involves one sector after another changing from, say, linear to (hyper)exponential growth, and through so-called co-evolution: in other words, phenomena in which breakthroughs in one technology stimulate corresponding breakthroughs in others. Knowledge thus creates more knowledge, just as success often leads to more success.

But do not some of the exponential processes come to a standstill again? That debate is relevant when it comes Moore's Law: the number of transistors or components in an integrated circuit (for example, a computer chip) doubles every one and a half years. At the same time, the cost of a processing unit is halved. The reason that I don't assign Moore's Law as one of the key rules in this book is that, in its literal sense, it seems to be running out. However, it has been amazing. If we imagine it had formed the basis for the development of cars, today cars would have a top speed of 675 million km per hour. So, we could drive round Earth in just over one-fifth of a second, which funnily enough happens to be the speed of light. On various occasions throughout most of my life, people have unsuccessfully attempted to bury Moore's Law. But now there is much to indicate that (in its original form) it is approaching its final call. This is because the effect of smaller components (so-called *Dennard scaling*) is decreasing. At the same time, there are some basic physical constraints in terms of how small the distances between the electronic gates can be before electrons can inappropriately jump between them. And we are stumbling more closely towards them.

But we will not notice this in the products. You see, manufacturers are beginning to incorporate a third dimension. Computer chips are traditionally flat, but when you also add extra layers to them, their performance improves dramatically. Such 3D chips already exist, for example, in Samsung's advanced hard disks. But in order to deliver on expectations, they need to cool down the systems, because they generate a great deal of heat per surface unit. IBM and others are currently exploring solutions.

However, there are other technologies that will support an experience of the fact that Moore's Law remains in force, including multi-core processors, cloud computing, optical computing, and quantum computing.

I would like to dwell a bit longer on computers, because they illustrate so well how our innovation takes place. In its book *Megatech* (2018), the UK magazine *The Economist* collated several other reasons for optimism vis-à-vis the future performance of computers, even though Moore's Law, in its original expression, will run out. For example, the magazine emphasises better programming and the design of more specialised chips with circuits specifically designed for particular tasks. The principle was demonstrated in 2017, when Google's AlphaZero chess program beat the StockFish 8 program, which until that moment had been the best chess program in the world after beating IBM's Deep Blue. What is interesting in this context is that the winning AlphaZero 'only' made 80 000 calculations per second, while StockFish 8 made 70 million – almost 1000 times more. And, while StockFish contained data from all kinds of professional chess games, AlphaZero had taught itself to play chess in four hours (yes, four!) by playing against itself at a mind-blowing pace. This goes to show how computers can get more efficient without necessarily being faster.

A more fundamental change is the fact that, in the future, computer power will be more of an external resource like plug-in electricity or tap water, which you switch on when you need it, as opposed to having it permanently placed on a server in your back room, in a box on your desk, or in a smartphone in your pocket. Apple's Siri feature is an example of that development. Siri does not answer your questions with the computer power and knowledge stored on your phone, because it is simply not big enough. Instead, your question is recorded and sent to an army of more powerful computers in one of Apple's numerous data centres. These data centres will always be abreast of the latest technologies, which in the future may involve optical computing, quantum computing, and much more. So, when your question gets answered, it may very well be that 10 000 computers together are helping you in one tiny fraction of a second. Once we are into this territory, Moore's Law becomes less important.

Life, designed on a computer

As mentioned earlier, we see one sector after another progressing from being subdued and maybe linear to becoming exponential. This also applies to large parts of biochemistry: in particular, to genes and proteins.

The Human Genome Project, which was launched in 1990 and scheduled for completion in 15 years – in other words, in 2005 – was the biggest ever joint biological research project to date. It set out to map the human genome: the molecular double helix that contains our genes and determines how we are created. For a long time, it was a source of great frustration, because initially things went so slowly that people estimated it would take another 693 years to complete. Consequently, in 1997 – after seven years – despite costs of about $1.4 billion and a number of productivity improvements, they had still only mapped 1%. At that rate, many people believed it would never get completed, or the cost might escalate to as much as $14 billion. Totally unacceptable.

However, the entrepreneur and futurist, Ray Kurzweil believed that they could stick to schedule. You see, he saw what many other people did not: that the mapping was developing exponentially. And he was right. The project was actually completed in 2003: in other words, two years *before* the deadline. That was thanks to new methods of chemical analysis combined with new methods of computer analysis. The cost of mapping genes has since continued to fall dramatically: cf. the next rule of thumb, which *The Economist* named after predictions by the physicist, Rob Carlson:

2. **Doubling of performance and decrease in price of DNA decoding technologies will evolve at least as fast as Moore's Law (The Carlson Curve)**

Carlson was right. In practice, the efficiency of these gene technologies has evolved much faster than Moore's Law, and today, as a result, the genes of more than 500 000 people have been mapped: a feat that in 1997 would have sounded ridiculously utopian – in fact, downright insane. But it happened, and consequently we have at our disposal an amazing resource for health diagnosis and prevention, which, by the way, is growing exponentially. No, sorry, *hyper*exponentially.

The success of decoding DNA is an example of first-class technological co-evolution. And there is lots more to come in the same area. Just look at 'Internet of DNA': a matchmaking platform sponsored by a variety of research institutions and companies, where you can share genetic profiles to enable doctors to discover genetic explanations to diseases. This phenomenon is also growing exponentially. If we combine it with AI and big data, which we will come to later, a hitherto hidden world is revealed to us.

We live in the future

The other day on Instagram I saw a photo of a Lamborghini parked in front of a medieval castle in Germany. It suddenly struck me to what extent we are living today in what for our ancestors would have been a totally crazy future. Just imagine how medieval people would have flipped out if they had seen a Lamborghini drive past. Or a plane passing in the sky. Amazing! Occasionally, I think we need to stop and think about the development we are experiencing. Living as we do in an era of exponential development, we can easily forget how far the world has come even in our own lifetime. For instance, today, scientists can program microorganisms, which, like self-replicating robots and with incredible precision, can create such products as complex proteins and drugs. In other words, life has now become our computing platform, and cells are now our robots.

3. As societies become more digitised, we increasingly code biological cells so that they will act as self-replicating robots that work for us.

This is a part of a much broader overall tendency, which involves making very small things work for us intelligently. Meanwhile, our computers have reached a stage at which they can also program themselves and each other. This will inevitably lead to super-intelligent versions with totally astonishing capability.

I mentioned before that our scientific activity increases 100-fold in 100 years and, even though I am not 100 years old, it is simply amazing how much it has obviously grown in my lifetime. Also bear in mind the following. As I write this, just 10 years ago we did not have Uber, Snapchat, Airbnb, Spotify, Instagram, Bitcoin, selfie sticks, and the iPad. If we go further back, say to 1970, we did not have the Internet, the personal computer, DNA decoding, Netflix, mobile phones, plasma screens, and a host of other technologies we take for granted today. These thoughts lead to something I think we should make our fourth useful rule:

4. **The challenges of the future are rarely solved with the technologies of today.**

Thank heavens for that. Because we do not solve many of today's problems with the use of medieval solutions. If we look forward, we must adjust to the fact that if today's technologies amount to about 10% of the technologies we will have in 50 years' time, and approximately 1% of those we will have in 100 years' time, could it not be that the 90% or 99% of entirely new technologies we will have developed in the meantime will often be smarter?

The creative design field

Innovation is chiefly about combining existing things in new ways. But here comes the thought-provoking aspect. All things being equal, such a process will become hyperexponential. For example, if we only have product types A and B, we can combine them in three, two-letter ways: AA, AB, and BB. But if we double the number of existing products to four (A, B, C, and D), the number of possible two-letter combinations increases from 3 to 14. This means that if the number of creative building blocks grows in a linear manner, it results in a hyperexponentially increasing number of possible combinations.

A piano is a good example. It has 88 keys. However, as we can see, what people can accomplish with them seems infinite. Chemistry is another example. There are 118 elements. If we assumed conservatively that molecules can only contain 10 atoms each, their order of appearance doesn't matter, they are always connected in a single string, and each can only appear once, in principle we could still combine them in 42 634 215 112 710 different ways (if we disregard the fact that certain atomic combinations do not work). However, in practice, there are countless molecules with far more than 10 atoms and, if we merely increase the number of atoms to 15, the combinations increase to 1 015 428 940 004 440 000 different kinds of molecules. The truth is, however, that if we remove my artificial restrictions, there are molecules with *billions* of atoms, which is why the combination options for the 118 atoms is totally mind blowing – and, needless to say, the combination options for the molecules coming out of it totally out of sight. Mathematicians call such phenomena 'combinatorial explosions'.

In his book *The Beginning of Infinity* (2011), the quantum physicist David Deutsch argued convincingly that, given such reasons, innovation can continue indefinitely. This is something I totally agree with. Hence the following rule, which I derive from the likes of Deutsch:

5. **Innovation is an infinite, exponential process – and once it gets started, apart from the laws of physics, there are no natural limitations in terms of it stopping.**

Some people will object: 'But lots of societies were innovative in the past, and then it all stopped.' True. Very true, in fact. But that had something to do with social changes such as tyranny, centralisation, or religion; because societies subject that those restrictions would indeed lose their innovative powers. But again: innovation has no *natural* boundary apart from physical limitations.

So, innovation is a phenomenon that is easily underestimated. But it is hugely powerful. Consequently, in the wake of the above-mentioned rule, I will immediately posit one more:

6. **What is fundamentally possible and desirable will probably happen. Just about everything, which does not conflict with the laws of physics, and for which there is a demand, will get done.**

It is a great rule; at least I think so. Great because the laws of physics are extremely generous: for example, the absolute speed limit of physics

– the speed of light – corresponds to flying seven times around Earth in one second. Or how about this. The energy potential of our deuterium and tritium, the ingredients of energy from nuclear fusion, are enough to provide us with clean, safe energy for between 30 million and countless billions of years. And quantum computers will be able to make certain types of calculations up to several billion times faster than the fastest traditional computers today.

Fantastic. Maybe that is why the famous science fiction writer and, as it happens, staggeringly brilliant forecaster, Arthur C. Clarke, can be credited with this rule: 'If an elderly but distinguished scientist says that something is possible, he is almost certainly right; but if he says that it is impossible, he is very probably wrong.' Incidentally, there is a phenomenon in technology that often prompts us to underestimate technological advances: the fact that their effect is sometimes *overestimated* in the short term (we have already seen that) and *underestimated* in the long term. This has been described, for example, by the futurist Roy Amara. That is why I now call it 'Amara's Law':

7. **We tend to overestimate the impact of a technology in the short term and underestimate the long-term impact (Amara's Law).**

I believe that the main reason for this phenomenon is that every great core innovation has few if no clients until derived applications have been developed. For instance, TV broadcast required development of live sport, talk shows, soap operas, etc., which all took lots of time to develop and get right. Time because its complex and because most applications on top of new core technologies are not just about technology but also about new business models and new kinds of companies.

Why am I so certain that innovation will continue hyperexponentially? Besides the reasons I have already mentioned, including the fact that recombining is in itself a hyperexponential process, I have some other reasons that I will explain here.

Firstly, today there are about 30 000 times more people than at the end of the last Glacial Period. Good ideas usually propagate exponentially. So, if a new idea has to reach 1000 times more people, it only takes twice as long. But 1000 times more people come up with at least 1000 times more ideas. So, population growth has put innovation on steroids.

At the same time, many societies have abandoned the belief that worldly events are remotely controlled by a divine power. Instead, they believe that they are driven by forces of nature that can be analysed. Call this enlightenment and science. In addition, we are increasingly closely connected with each other via travel, the Internet, inter-state trade, etc. So, we have far better opportunities to exchange thoughts, ideas, and inventions than previously. Urbanisation is also an important contributor, because the power of innovation grows even faster than the population of a town or city. The bigger the cities, the faster things happen. People even walk faster on the streets in big cities. In cities, people are also constantly meeting each other, working together, and exchanging ideas. It also goes without saying that the likelihood of meeting people who complement your own skills is also much greater when you are surrounded by lots of people. To put it bluntly, our rural areas are resource centres, and our urban areas are innovation centres. And it is the population of the latter that is growing. Paradoxically, this helps explain why we do not run out of resources and have less need for resource centres.

An additional reason for increasing innovation is the remarkable fact that we get wiser. This mechanism, which was first recognised in the 1980s, is now well-evidenced, and the basic rule is this.

8. **In countries with normal economic growth per capita, average intelligence increases by approximately 0.3 percentage points per year, or 3 points per decade until they become fully developed economically.**

At least, that has been the case in the West and Southeast Asia. In simple arithmetical terms, average intelligence as measured by standard IQ tests have risen 3 points per 10 years, which is the equivalent of 30 points per 100 years. That is an extremely high level. Such an increase can shift a population's average intelligence from what is referred to as 'stupor' to 'superior intelligence'. The causes are probably a combination of more racial mix – so-called outbreeding – and a lower level of inbreeding, better nutrition, fewer serious infectious diseases among infants, less prevalence of malaria and other chronic diseases, and better cognitive stimulation. The consequence is a positive spiral. As people get richer, they get wiser. And they get richer because they get wiser. However, it must be said that this process now seems to have stopped on the global level. But we made pretty good progress before, and the process is still working in poor countries.

In addition, an increasing number of people receive an education. For example, the number of people who start a university education now doubles about every 15th year. This is mainly due to two factors. First, the fact that many developing countries are becoming much richer, so they can invest more in education. Second, in purely educational terms, women are catching up with men, and in many countries overtaking them when it comes to higher education. In fact, in the prosperous world – the Organisation for Economic Co-operation and Development (OECD) countries – significantly more women than men are now engaging in a long education.

And finally, I would like to mention the fact that social media make it much easier for the world to discover good ideas and talented people, so inspiration and talent rarely go to waste. The result of all this is that the amount of innovation follows the number of people multiplied by a big factor. And this again explains why the amount of resources available *to each person* increases when the number of people becomes bigger – a conclusion that may seem totally counterintuitive, but that is extremely well documented.

The driving forces behind hyperexponential innovation

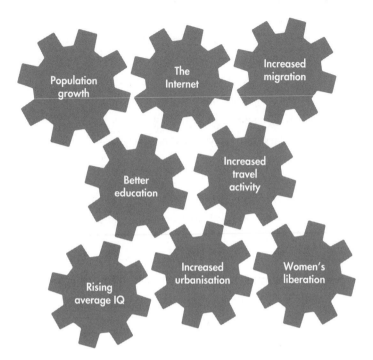

The world's a much better place than people think

So, the effects of innovation are far greater than many people assume. This has been proven, for example, by the Swedish doctor, statistician, and university professor Hans Roslin. Roslin achieved fame for his graphically animated statistics for world development, and in 2012 *Time Magazine* voted him one of the 100 most influential people in the world. Try reading his co-authored book *Factfulness* (2018), and watch him on YouTube. Sensational!

Roslin, who unfortunately died in 2017, was constantly invited to lecture on the world's true development to often prominent assemblies: students at elite universities, participants at Lindau Nobel Laureate Meetings, delegates at science conferences, top executives in the corporate world, etc.

Usually, in these contexts, he kicked off by asking some statistical questions, for which people could choose between three answers. The questions could relate, for example, to whether the world's future population growth is a result of more children or more elderly people (more elderly people is the right answer), or how large a percentage of the world's boys and girls attends primary school (92% and 90% respectively).

When choosing between three answers, a blind monkey will have a 33.3% chance of choosing the right one. But Roslin found that even the cleverest and best-educated experts were systematically worse at choosing the right answer than blind monkeys. Strangely enough, there was system in their ignorance. On average, they underestimated to a systematically huge extent how much progress goes on in the world. For example, 69% of Nordic healthcare scientists underestimated the proportion of the world's children that get vaccinated. And that was healthcare scientists! Blimey!

It gets worse. Roslin gave a presentation to an annual meeting of global finance executives at the headquarters of one of the 10 biggest banks in the world. One of the questions he asked was: 'What percentage of the world's 1-year-old children have been vaccinated against a disease today – A: 20%, B: 50%, or C: 80%?'

A staggering 85% of the 71 participants believed that the correct figure was 20%. So, the audience belonged to the ultimate elite of the global financial world and believed that the world was so wretched that only 20% of its children are vaccinated. Sad. But the correct answer was 80% – 80%! Go figure. Globally, we now manage to vaccinate four out of five infants. That tells us that the world's population is not made up of 80% poor people, on the one hand and, on the other, a small group living the good Western lifestyle. You see, the distribution of vaccines requires refrigerated containers, refrigerated warehouses, refrigerated vehicles, and a myriad of local refrigerators. And that costs money.

People – the elite included – are thus far too pessimistic. For example, far too few people are aware that the number of people in the world living in extreme poverty has dropped from approximately 50% in 1966 to less than 10% today.

Sometimes, people's ingrained, uninformed pessimism was enough to drive Roslin mad. For example, at an event, he would present a myriad of key statistics, all demonstrating the long-term, unbroken improvements in everything from health and average life expectancy to education, security, and prosperity. Then some fact-resistant audience member would come up to him and say something along the lines of: 'Even though things have gone well so far, I am sure it's going to be downhill from now on.'

This really got his goat. But after he had finished pulling out his hair, Roslin would think about why things were so. Part of his explanation lay in the many flaws in human information gathering and psychology. But also in the lack of searching for information. According to Roslin, the frame of reference for many people was knowledge they had acquired from teachers in their youth. But it was staggeringly obsolete knowledge, which perhaps reflected the far worse state of the world when those teachers received their education. In other words, people often remember figures from a worse world. For example, a majority of highly educated people believed that 60 must be the global average life expectancy. This answer would have been correct in 1973, but now the answer is actually 72.

According to Roslin, an additional reason for the excessive pessimism was the fact that the press concentrates on disaster stories. But disasters are typically exceptions in an everyday existence, in which a large majority of the global population now lives a kind of middle-class life. The debate may also be influenced by the fact that some feelers find it heartless to draw attention to facts about overall progress when something is still going badly. But, when all is said and done, the following holds good:

9. **The state of the world is generally better and generally develops better than the majority of the population – including the well-educated and the experts – believe.**

It is paradoxical that many people are regularly seized by a strong conviction that everything is about to go to hell. That Earth is nearing its end, and that humanity is facing a terrible future. Or so they say.

The more you study the phenomenon, the more striking the similarities between all the different doomsday prophecies are. Not their issues. After all, there is an undeniable distance from the feared next Ice Age to acid rain and forest decline, listeria, mad cow disease, Belgian dioxin, Iranian weapons of mass destruction, Y2K, bird and swine flu, global famine, DDT, nuclear power, mass extinction, vaccination autism, genetic modification, plastic islands in the Pacific Ocean, carcinogenic phones, etc., in which the world press often wallows uncritically. Yes, the topics are different, but the processes that lead to the hysteria are quite similar. If you care to learn more about this, I recommend the book *Scared to Death* (2009) by the journalist Christopher Booker and the scientist Richard North. The book goes into great, often shockingly embarrassing detail about the frequently vast difference between the statements about these impending crises by the media and so-called experts and what really happened in every case. The process is often grotesque. But it does not cause the press to cover the difference between the horrible forecasts and the subsequent reality, because each time a given panic fizzles out, the next one is already in the pipeline, and that is where the attention goes.

The mechanism described by Booker and North 10 years ago is still going strong. On average, in the past 40 years we have been seized by panic as a result of a specific, expected phenomenon about once every three years, and this will probably continue. For example, at the time of writing, an insect extinction panic is in progress. The story is the same every time: huge threats are around the corner and millions of people may perish. Every time there is an explosion of documentation in the shape of reports, experts and politicians expressing their doomsday visions, TV documentaries, and intense headlines. And then, when the disaster fails to happen, the focus quickly shifts from that particular case to the next impending disaster.

Unfortunately, very few people notice the pattern at all. The reason I became aware of it quite early on is probably that when I was quite young I read the splendid book *Extraordinary Popular Delusions and the Madness of Crowds,* written by the polyhistorian Charles Mackay in 1841: in other words, almost 200 years ago. The book suggests that human nature is evidently such that, at regular and frequent intervals, it needs to invent a narrative about everything going wrong or about Armageddon lurking around the corner.

One of the mistakes people have often made is to overestimate the development of analogue and underestimate the development of digital. I should point out that digital consists of unique codes and can be described mathematically. Everything else is sometimes referred to as 'analogue'. What people previously disregarded was the fact that mechanical things often develop linearly, whereas digital things normally develop exponentially.

Let us place this in a more practical perspective. A senior executive with a lifetime's experience of top management in the industrial world once gave me the following rule from traditional industry, where, to put it colloquially, they 'bend iron':

10.   In industrial production, productivity increases by an average of 5–10% each time the market doubles.

For example, aircraft and cars are now significantly more efficient than in 1970, let alone in 1903. But the rule nevertheless means that, even if the market develops exponentially for some time, the efficiency of mechanical technologies will only improve more linearly.

Digital technology chiefly involves almost everything to do with computer technology (microchips etc.) and genetic manipulation. Think of it as follows. Biological life is digital technology (DNA, RNA, enzymes, etc.) encapsulated in analogue technology (muscles, bones, fat, water, etc.). Overall, this combination develops through natural evolution and goes very slowly: partly because the improvements occur quite randomly; and partly because potentially fast digital change constantly must wait for slow analogue development (reproduction, life, and death). This combination takes time.

But if you can skip analogue inertia, directly intervening and transcribing the digital – and not randomly but with purpose – the friction is minimal. Then biological life suddenly becomes like computer technology: a dynamic programming platform. Meanwhile, the 'iron-bending industries' are actually becoming increasingly digital, so variants of Moore's Law are creeping in there too.

Incidentally, there are many variants of Moore's Law, which can be divided into three main groups. The first relates to *efficiency,* the second *price,* and the third *user-friendliness.* For example, computer technology or gene manipulation is improving exponentially, but it is also becoming rapidly cheaper and easier, and the price effect often proceeds more quickly than the performance effect. The business models of Walmart, Amazon, IKEA, Microsoft, and Alibaba are very much about making services cheaper, and also about making them more user-friendly, which also makes money.

Digitalisation often plays a big role in all three processes. Marc Andreessen, who invented the browser Netscape, and who is now a leading venture capitalist, once summed it up as follows: 'Software is eating the world.' Here is another rule, inspired by that thought:

11. An increasing number of sectors are evolving from the emphasis on (1) manual work to being (2) mechanical and finally (3) digital. This means that productivity changes from being (1) static to (2) growing linearly and then (3) growing exponentially.

So, we now have 11 rules to be getting on with. But, as I mentioned before, by the time we get to the end of the book, we will have 50. And along the way we will delve into what we might call the probable future. Let us begin with demography and prosperity.

2.
DEMOGRAPHY AND PROSPERITY

The vast majority of people reading this book have probably seen graphs depicting the human population explosion, looking pretty much like this:

The world's long-term population growth

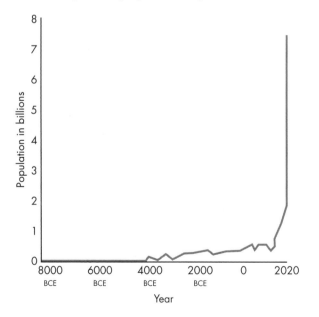

As we can see, the trend broke in an upward direction around 1500. The reason was that, at this point, Western civilisation had started to get hugely creative, consequently experiencing an explosion of prosperity, which reduced child mortality and made it easier to survive. According to estimates from the prominent economist Angus Maddison, a mere 500 years earlier Western Europeans had had the same standard of living as Native Americans, and actually lower than that of Africans and Asians.

The huge innovation explosion in the West gradually impacted other civilisations and, as a result, total global income rose about *320 times* between 1000 and 2000. That is quite a development, especially vis-à-vis the previous millennium, when the world's average per capita income actually remained unchanged. Yes, you heard right: 1000 years of nothing, and then everything suddenly took off.

Why did the West suddenly leave the others behind? Before answering, I should just point out that 'the West' was originally Western Europe, but later came to include areas that Western Europeans gradually populated and dominated: principally North America, most of Latin America, and Australia and New Zealand. But back to the question: *Why*? The reasons largely comprised the following series of processes:

- The Renaissance (c. 1200–1600), which advanced artistic activity, humanism, individualism, empirical experiments, and creativity.

- The Age of Discovery (c. 1500–1800), which involved the discovery by Europeans of most of the globe, and the colonisation of large areas of it.

- The Reformation (c. 1520–1650), which broke the dominance of the Roman Catholic Church, thus leading to its partial replacement with more liberal, individualistic religions.

- The Scientific Revolution (c. 1540 to the present day), which rediscovered and refined classical Greek concepts of science that led to a systematic empirical study of the world.

- The Age of Enlightenment (c. 1715–1800), which fostered freedom, democracy, science, religious tolerance, constitutional state, rationality, and common sense as Western core values.

- The Industrial Revolution (c. 1750–1850), during which mechanised mass production led to an enormous explosion of prosperity, large-scale urbanisation, and cultural upheaval.

- Women's Liberation (particularly from 1840 to 1920), which invested women with education, power, and political influence.

Note that the Age of Enlightenment, the Age of Discovery, the Reformation, and the Scientific Revolution all started in the period when the population was growing. By the time of the Industrial Revolution in or around 1750, the growth rate increased even further. There was a hitherto unprecedented boom in innovation and an explosion in international inter-state trade. As a result, between 1000 and 1800, the West's GDP per capita increased by approximately 300%, whereas in the rest of the world it only increased by approximately 30%. In order to facilitate Western growth, between 1470 and 1820, the merchant navy of Western Europe grew 17-fold.

The West versus the rest

However, we need to delve a bit more deeply. *Why* did these things happen in Western Europe, but not nearly as much (or at all) elsewhere? I addressed this question quite extensively in my previous book *The Creative Society*

(2016). The standard model I presented was that lasting innovation and growth usually require the following factors:

- A decentralised network of numerous small units – such as many companies and smaller communities.
- Local and international trade – for example, via rivers and seas.
- Competition – companies and states constantly compete on a number of levels. The competition then propagates the best ideas and obliterates the worst, while cooperation combines good ideas thereby creating new combinations.
- The creation and exchange of information through a common language code – knowledge, value, and ownership are respected and exchanged in ways that many people understand and accept. Examples include property rights, patent law, common units of measurement, money, and credit systems.
- Stimulants of change – for example, in the form of travel activity, expatriation, media, and, of course, inter-state trade.

The critical point – that which particularly distinguishes the West from the rest of the world – has been the first: i.e. *decentralisation*. In a decentralised system, the numerous small units will 'mutate' to create new thoughts, after which they compete and cooperate in changing patterns. This pattern was particularly pronounced in creative Ancient Greece, which in reality was a patchwork of 700–1000 city states, and not a country at all until Alexander the Great amalgamated these small states: an act that incidentally stifled innovation.

But let us return to what boosted Western creativity from the mid-fifteenth to the sixteenth century. After the fall of the Roman Empire, the next 500 years or so witnessed the emergence of a belt of thousands of very small city states in Europe. It stretched mainly from, and including, northern Italy through present-day Switzerland, Germany, and parts of northern Europe. And it was precisely in this *decentralised* belt that creativity exploded, just as it had done in the Greek city states before Alexander the Great merged them.

Population growth is actually decreasing rapidly

So, innovation led to the population explosion from the year 1500. Nonetheless, many people were concerned about the size of the population and, as mentioned earlier, expected it to lead to massive famine. However, as we have already seen, the exact opposite occurred: people's nutritional status gradually improved. But, since the 1960s, population growth has slowed down. In fact, percentagewise, this culminated in 1963 and, measured on the basis of absolute population growth figures, culminated in 1989. Since then, population growth (based on both measurements) has steadily decreased. According to the United Nations, we have now also reached *peak child,* meaning the point in time where the global number of children peaks. In other words, the number of children on the planet will remain more or less unchanged for the remainder of this century.

Global population of people who are 14 and younger

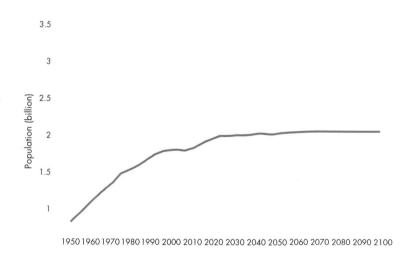

That means we are already more than half a century into a soft demographic slowdown process. This is evident in the following graphs.

World population growth, 1750–2100, according to UN 2015 revision

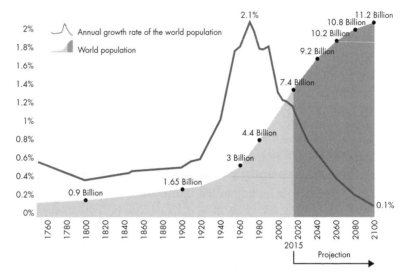

Why is the increase in the number of children stopping? Michio Kaku answers the question very well in his book *The Physics of the Future* (2012): 'the world's greatest contraceptive is prosperity'. And the effect progresses a long way up the income scale. So very rich countries have even lower child numbers than medium-rich countries. That brings us to our 12th rule:

12. When countries get richer, the population produces fewer children, and when the per capita GDP passes the $5000 mark, fertility generally starts to decline. When we exceed $10 000, the number of children (per woman) usually falls to below equilibrium level, after which the native population also begins to decline.

In fact, statistics show that the world as a whole exceeded $10 000 in GDP per capita in or around 2013. This in itself is pretty promising. The United Nations considers that the most likely future scenario will be a growth from approximately 7.5 billion today to just over 9 billion in 2050, and then maybe 11 billion by 2100. However, this estimate is based on the expectation of an unchanged population in the rich countries, and on the assumption that a number of African countries will not reach the demographic turning points. This may well be true, but is unlikely if prosperity grows significantly. And staff at the United Nations are aware of that. In fact, in its latest revision of 2019, the organisation reduced its population forecast for the year 2100 down from 11.2 billion in its 2017 revision to now 10.9 billion, citing observations that birth rates in Africa were dropping faster than they had previously expected.

UN population forecast per region, revised in 2019

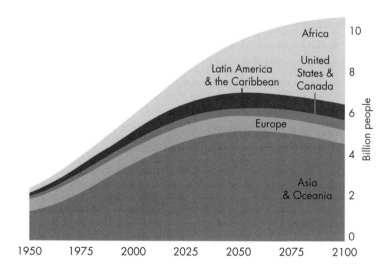

Even this revised estimate might be too pessimistic. In 2019, the journalist John Ibbitson and social scientist Darrell Bricker, in their book *Empty Planet,* predicted that global population would peak at around 9 billion people between 2040 and 2060. This would be a huge deal, or a 'defining moment', as they wrote:

> The great defining event of the 21st century – one of the great defining events in human history – will occur in three decades, give or take, when the global population begins to decline . . . Once that decline begins, it will never end.

A key reason for this forecast was the observed effect of giving women access to education. Once that happens – and it does all over the world – they tend to prefer just two children or less. Also, the authors cited results of polls amongst young women in 26 nations about how many children they preferred, and the respond was pretty similar all over: around two children.

It should be noted that when countries get richer, the birth rate can fall both substantially and rapidly. For example, from the end of World War II to around 1990, Iran had a birth rate of six to seven children per woman. In the course of a single generation, it then fell to 1.88. The following graph shows the recorded and predicted drop in fertility rates from six children per woman to around two for different nations. In many Asian

Total fertility rate, children per woman: Years from high fertility (around 6) to replacement fertility (around 2.1)

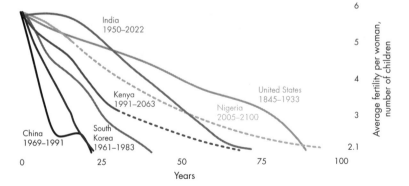

nations, fertility rates dropped extremely quickly in line with explosive wealth growth. In Africa, the drop is expected to be much slower, but not different from what was experienced in the West in previous generations.

And here is something else that is worth thinking about. What will be the consequence of the fact that China no longer has a consistent one-child policy? We find indications in Hong Kong, Taiwan, and Macao, which are Chinese and far richer than the rest of China. According to the World Population Review, in 2019 their expected fertility rates were respectively 1.3, 1.2, and 1.3, far below the 2.1 or so required for a stable population. And what was the fertility rate in Singapore, which is partly Chinese and extremely wealthy? Also 1.2, which corresponds to rapid depopulation, if we disregard immigration.

Huge growth in prosperity continues

Thus, even though it was an acceleration of innovation and prosperity that originally triggered the population explosion, innovation and prosperity are even more responsible for slowing it down again in one country after another. The reason, which Michio Kaku and many others have pointed out, is that prosperity leads to urbanisation, education, and a more exciting life, and all this leads to falling birth rates. That is why the fact that the world is getting increasingly wealthier is good not only for the people enjoying it, but also for the planet's longer-term prospects.

Most economists expect the world in 2050 to be approximately 2.5 times richer than in 2020 and perhaps 1.8 times richer per capita: tremendous growth in just 30 years. One of the effects will be that, by 2050, many countries that are currently poor will have the same standard of living as Germany today. However, there is a great deal of debate about what the growth rates will be in the rich countries. Italy, for example, has come to a complete standstill. Will many other Western countries experience similar stagnation? Some economists say this is a possibility. But a report by Accenture challenges pessimism with ammunition derived from artificial intelligence, or AI as I will refer to it from this point on. Accenture claims that AI has the potential to double the economic growth rate in rich countries as we head towards 2035. The report states that the majority are far too prone to regard AI as a traditional economic growth promoter in line with labour force and capital. Accenture disputes this. Their argument is based on the fact that AI is something new and essentially different from other technologies. It is a kind of previously unknown capital–labour hybrid. The development of AI implies, for example, that we can perform many tasks much faster, with greater uniformity, tirelessly, and under extremely difficult conditions, when compared to what human beings are capable of. AI can also acquire knowledge faster than humans, such as when AlphaZero taught itself to play world-class chess in four hours. Furthermore, it can take the form of physical capital: integrated, for example, with robots and other intelligent machines. Finally, it can make many services much cheaper than today. One example of the latter is so-called robo advisers, who provide financial advice for a low annual wrap fee, which even investors investing small amounts of money can afford to pay. So, all in all we have paved the way for intelligent automation, which provides much better use of existing labour and capital.

But – and this is important – AI also provides us with much better innovation distribution. Take driverless cars, for example. What each car learns from experience will be shared with the others etc. Moreover, when the number of accidents falls dramatically (which, in the long term, will make fully or partially self-driven cars one of the most significant health achievements in the history of mankind), resources will be freed up to solve other problems. At the same time, people who, possibly because of disability, were unable to transport themselves, will gain far more freedom.

Consequently, albeit with considerable differences between countries, Accenture's conclusion is that AI can independently and significantly increase economic growth compared to previous decades – and to what economists' standard macro models predict. In the United States, for example, from 2.6% annual trend growth rate in 2035 on the basis of standard models, to 4.6% on the basis of Accenture's adjusted model.

It is self-evident that calculations such as these are subject to extreme uncertainty. But we can see that AI is getting big, and it is interesting to contemplate whether AI will provide at least a temporary turbo boost to John Ziman's aforementioned law, which claims that the amount of scientific activity increases 100-fold approximately every 100 years. I think this is clearly possible.

Global GDP per capita, US dollars corrected for inflation

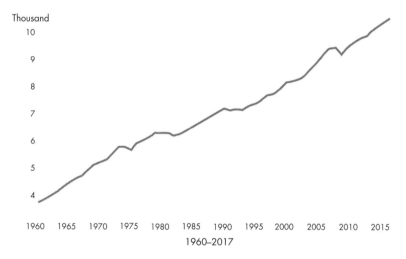

1960–2017

Regardless of whether Accenture's hypotheses are correct, it is obvious that the global economy and people's average prosperity will grow on a vast scale over the coming decades. Accordingly, it is also very likely that the global birth rate will fall – maybe even dramatically. Thus, rich societies typically experience exponential depopulation before immigration, and that will be the destiny of many societies if growth in prosperity continues.

A massive elderly boom

As mentioned before, we have reached 'peak child'. But, when it comes to the older generation, it is a very different story.

The global population of elderly 70+

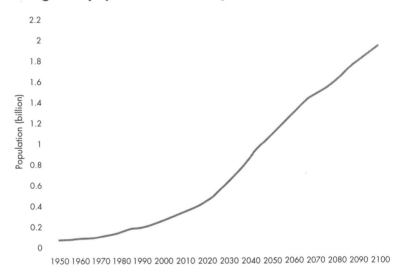

As the illustration shows, major achievements in the area of health and related fields mean that people are living longer. It is gratifying that we are no longer witnessing an endless exponential population explosion, but instead 'merely' a gigantic elderly boom driven by better health (which, moreover, provides large markets for products and services for the elderly – heh, heh). However, the development may exacerbate a democratic problem that already exists: a declining workforce in many places.

Depopulation of rural areas

We are also experiencing – and will continue to experience – an urbanisation boom. In fact, people are moving to cities to such an extent that we have already reached the stage in the history of mankind where the rural population is ceasing to increase after virtually uninterrupted growth for at least 1000 years. From here on, as far as we can see, the rural population will only go one way: down. That means that 97% of Earth's land masses are already beginning to be depopulated. So, if anyone thinks we will lack space for the people of the future to live, for example, in floating cities on the sea, they better think again. Where we are likely to witness even more lack of space than today is on the best beaches and in holiday resorts in general, which will receive far more visitors than today. Just take Venice on a summer's day!

Global urban and rural population 1950–2050

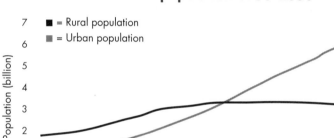

Increased global equality and local inequality – but will this continue?

Throughout my lifetime, a clear division between a handful of rich and a host of miserably poor countries has been replaced by a more normally distributed world with a huge middle class. That development is depicted here:

The world income distribution in 1820, 1970, and 2000

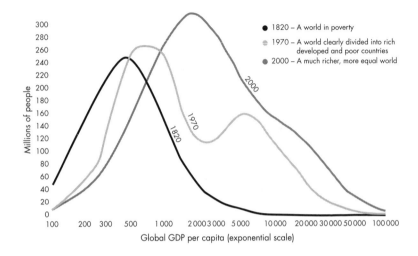

Note, moreover, that these figures show inflation-adjusted – in other words, comparable – incomes in the three periods, and that the horizontal scale is exponential. The latter slightly blurs the fortunate situation that the most common inflation-adjusted purchasing power level increased sixfold between 1820 and 2000.

Furthermore, the predominant reason for the development from 1970 to 2000 is that a large number of developing countries, in particular China, switched to a market economy and then rapidly caught up. In this respect, China has had the utmost importance. This country, which in 1980 had a similar standard of living to that of Somalia, after 1980 raised about 400 million people out of poverty and into the middle class. China's major importance for the size of the modern middle class is shown in the following diagram.

Global income distribution by regions

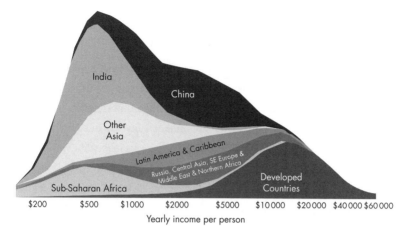

$200	$500	$1000	$2000	$5000	$10000	$20000	$40000	$60000

Yearly income per person

What about inequality? The most widely used measure for inequality is the so-called Gini coefficient. According to this method of calculation, global inequality has fallen quite a bit since 1970. This happy development is remarkable, and even more so when you take into account the fact that there were more children in the poorest countries (income and wealth peak when people are around 40–50, so countries with a very low average age may have misleadingly low average incomes).

However, in many places, inequality *within countries* has risen somewhat, which may account for the often propounded – but incorrect – claim that global inequality has increased. But there may be a correlation between these two trends, because rapidly rising income in the less prosperous countries is, for example, partly a result of the fact that the populations there via globalisation compete with people in low-income jobs in the prosperous countries.

By the way, just how much has inequality increased in the large, rich countries? Thomas Piketty's book, *Capital in the Twenty-First Century* (2014) provides us with a picture of this. The book contains an extremely thorough review of inequality in terms of income and wealth between 1810 and 2010.

It became a bestseller and is often promoted under the theme of increasing global inequality, which the book did not claim to exist. No, Piketty investigated inequality in four countries – the United States, the United Kingdom, France, and Sweden – and proved that inequality had remained unchanged or had fallen in the course of those 200 years. However, what he *did* regard as problematic was the fact that the inequality gap had declined particularly in the first 70 years of the twentieth century, but had then unfortunately increased. He then claimed that the initial reduction in inequality was due to temporary factors such as war, while the subsequent increase in inequality was due to the enduring situation that investment returns on capital exceeded economic growth rates. To my mind, this theory does not make sense. The graph on the next page shows Piketty's figures alongside an alternative version of these calculations, with certain errors corrected by an analyst from *The Financial Times*.

As I see it, the development of technical innovation is an important factor, so today, it often only takes innovators – especially in the IT sector – develop highly valued 'mini-multinationals': in other words, small start-up companies, which in a very short time will succeed in becoming multinational. Not only can this be implemented much faster now than before, but it can also be done with less capital than that needed in more traditional sectors such as industry and agriculture. This has meant that entrepreneurs today can often retain a larger share of their businesses than before, since they need less external capital. What is more, the founders are often young and do not yet have families, so they become sole owners of their fortunes. Previously, it could take generations to build a valuable business. That meant that ownership was divided between loads of children and grandchildren along the way. And let us not forget divorce. Finally, the fact that more women today benefit from higher education, so young men and women meet and become couples at university, contributes to capital concentration. This leads to polarisation, since the people who are best qualified to become rich are more likely to marry along the way.

At the same time, other factors have contributed to exerting downward pressure on the lower-measured incomes. The first is the frequent statistical error of measuring income per household. Because the fact is that the number of people in households has dropped. This in itself reduces household

Economic inequality in Europe and the United States 1810–2010, cf. Thomas Piketty and Chris Giles

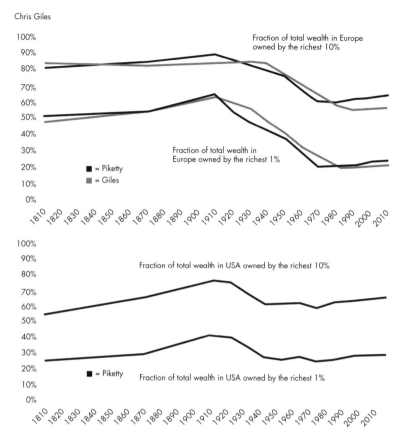

Chris Giles

Fraction of total wealth in Europe owned by the richest 10%

Fraction of total wealth in Europe owned by the richest 1%

■ = Piketty
■ = Giles

Fraction of total wealth in USA owned by the richest 10%

Fraction of total wealth in USA owned by the richest 1%

■ = Piketty

income without reducing personal median income, which actually increases. The tendency to study longer is also a contributing factor, because a large number of academic students are 'poor' in the technical sense of the word. One last factor is the fact that welfare states make a lot of people passive, and they then live their lives on the basis of low transfer income.

A more peaceful world

There is a widespread belief that the world is becoming increasingly violent. But it is not. It is persistently becoming *less* violent. Take, for example, the twentieth century, which featured two world wars, mass murders in Mao's China and the Soviet Union, and countless other bloody events. Nevertheless, this century was more peaceful than the nineteenth century, when it comes to the percentage of the world's population killed in war. In the Chinese Taiping Rebellion (1851–1864), just as big a proportion of the world's population were killed as in World War II, while Napoleon killed the same proportion of people as in World War I. Add to them the American Civil War, countless colonial wars – you name it – all of them made the nineteenth century far bloodier than the twentieth century.

And so it goes on. The further back in time we go, the more violent it gets. In fact, science now estimates that approximately a third of all Stone Age people were murdered or killed in war. Something similar applies to violence and brutality in general. So, the truth of the matter is that the extent of wars and crime falls when society gets richer. This phenomenon was originally described in Norbert Elias's classic *The Civilizing Process* (1939). It was later elaborated upon, on the basis of comprehensive statistical material, in the likes of Steven Pinker's *The Better Angels of Our Nature* (2011). The economist and development researcher, Paul Collier, also discovered that doubling the income level reduces the statistical risk of civil war by half.

It is not only the level of prosperity that is important in this context, but also the economic growth rate. On average, poor countries have a 14% risk of starting a civil war in any given five-year period. However, for countries with an annual growth rate of 3%, this risk drops to 12% and, if their economic growth rate reaches 10%, the risk of civil war drops to a mere 3%. Conversely, if there is a *negative* growth of 3%, the risk of civil war increases to 17%, which also increases the risk of even more negative growth.

There are also fewer wars and civil wars when the percentage of young men – particularly the percentage of *unemployed* young men – falls. This knowledge is used as a warning indicator by the likes of the CIA. One of the rules is that, if unemployed young men constitute more than 30% of a country's population, the risk of an outbreak of war or civil war rises to nearly 90%.

Another important factor is that, when a population is exposed to less uncertainty and stress, it becomes less religious/superstitious. The phenomenon was first described scientifically by the anthropologist Bronislaw Malinowski and was later confirmed by other studies. People whose life situation is stressed and insecure, often seek solace in superstition and religions – and in conspiracy theories. Accordingly, more fundamentalist religions with staunch, absolute truths about the good, the evil, and the saved usually gain ground in places and at times of major, prevalent uncertainty. Typically, however, the world has gone in an opposite direction. Here is the rule:

13. **High economic growth rates and a high level of prosperity lead to more rationality, peace, and tolerance, which in turn facilitate more economic growth.**

This self-reinforcing process can also work in reverse and thus lead to a negative spiral, in which a malfunctioning society becomes more irrational and violent, which in turn inhibits the possibility of growth. That is a serious problem, for instance, in parts of the Middle East.

The lost billion people – the world's biggest problem?

Oxford University's Paul Collier, the economist and development researcher referred to earlier, has published several excellent books on the subject of developing countries and their problems. One of them, *The Bottom Billion* (2007), tackles the phenomenon that, while 6.5 billion people live in countries that are either rich or well on the way to becoming so, approximately 1 billion live in nations that have been stagnating for decades. However, I have checked the countries Collier named as stagnating 11 years ago, and a number of them have actually achieved relatively high growth since then. That said, the likes of Afghanistan, Haiti, North Korea, Kyrgyzstan, and a large number of countries in Africa are still stagnating.

As far as the many African countries are concerned, some people might think that this continent as a whole is a total lost cause. Nevertheless, the fact of the matter is that a number of African countries have achieved extremely high economic growth rates: for example, Ethiopia, the Ivory Coast and Djibouti, Senegal, Guinea, Tanzania, Burkina Faso, Rwanda, and Sierra Leone. Not only that, but in 2018 the World Bank estimated that 6 of the world's 10 fastest-growing economies were African. So, even though some African countries are stuck in the swamp, others have shown that it is possible to achieve high growth in Africa.

3.

THE BIOTECHNOL-OGICAL REVOLUTION – LIFE AS COMPUTER TECHNOLOGY

The completion of the Human Genome Project in 2003 provided us for the very first time with insight into what a programmer might call 'life's machine code': in other words, the deepest software program layers behind our lives. I found this hugely interesting. But it was not until a few years later, when on holiday I read the book A Life Decoded *(2008) by J. Craig Venter, that my interest turned into profound fascination. It must be said that Venter is not just anybody. Deploying revolutionary technologies, this scientist made the greatest contribution to accelerating the decoding of the human genome. What's more, it was his own genome he decoded.*

He is also a serial entrepreneur and has given some amazing talks on how we can now accomplish the most incredible things using genes: creating a reproductive virus from pure chemicals; changing a living bacterium from one species to another by replacing its DNA, while it is still alive; etc.

DNA contains the code for creating proteins, which then create everything else in the body. Interestingly, there is a staggering similarity between the DNA of different species. For instance, human DNA is approximately 50% identical to that of a banana (!) and 96% identical to that of a chimpanzee. The individual genetic differences between people are due to pretty minimal differences in our genetic structures.

The work on decoding the genome triggered a revolution in the field of DNA sequencing, which has since knocked the price right down. Today, we can decode a single genome for less than $1000, while there are services such as 23andMe, which, by sequencing only selected, significant areas, can provide anyone with a good picture of their own genome for less than $200. This is because, on average, the rate at which we can decode a DNA sequence is halved every 10 months. This has already sparked a revolution in the field of biomedical research. DNA sequencings, which might previously form the basis for PhD projects lasting several years, can now be performed in just a few hours and for very little money.

On 13 July 2013, I backed my yacht with my family and friends aboard into the harbour of Villa Marina on the island of Capri. I then lay down on the front deck to read a fascinating book: *Before the Dawn* (2006) by Nicholas Wade. Shortly after, a 55-m yacht glided into the harbour basin and turned slowly, before reversing in next to us. Apart from the fact that it was one deck higher than mine and blocked the sun, I noticed it had a pretty weird name: *Gene Machine*. It did not take long before I suddenly heard a voice coming from the yacht's front deck. 'Is that Nicholas Wade you're reading?' asked a man who was standing up there. 'Yes,' I answered. 'Why do you ask?' 'He's a friend of mine,' he said. I got talking to the man, who turned out to be Jonathan Rothberg. I learned that Jonathan had named his yacht after his invention, the Personal Genome Machine or Gene Machine, which he developed in his company, 454 Life Sciences. Incidentally, when I Googled it later, I discovered he had sold the company in 2007 for $155 million. The Gene Machine could decode 10 million base pairs in a DNA sequence in a couple of hours. This was helpful, for instance, in terms of quickly and cheaply coming up with ways to attack cancer cells in a specific patient. In 2010, he had then sold another genetic coding company, Ion Torrent Systems, for $375 million. And there he was now, sailing around in the Mediterranean in a brand new mega yacht.

You certainly could not accuse him of being dull! Later I thought how hugely satisfying it must have been to develop this type of machine. The improved speed and reduced price of genetic analysis and genetic manipulation have already triggered entire scientific disciplines which never would have been possible before. So, a number of organisations are now in the process of sequencing as many personal genomes as possible. When this information is linked to information about its owner's life and health, then the real DNA revolution begins. We will be able to understand more fully the differences in our DNA sequences that underpin our individual properties, including diseases etc. This is generally done by using so-called polygenic scores. It has turned out that most human traits are due to a large number of genetic variants, each of which in itself has little or no effect. In other words, there is no single height gene, but thousands of genetic variations, each of which has a small influence on your height, and which together determine that height is in fact a hereditary issue. If you add up all these variants for a given feature, you can therefore collate them into a so-called polygenic score for an individual.

However, the connection between the polygenic scores and people's biological characteristics is far from fully charted. In other words, even though height and many other properties are easy to predict, we still have a lot to learn. For some features, including height, in the vast majority of cases, individual variation is due to genetic differences.

Work is also being conducted on polygenic scores that can predict our risk of various diseases. In the future, we will be able to use them to initiate preventive treatment many years before a disease might occur. We could use similar scores to predict patient-specific side effects in relation to different types of treatments, and to determine the optimum dose of a particular medicine etc. The possibilities are infinite. We simply need to decode enough genomes to discover the billions upon billions of tiny correlations.

CRISPR – the new genetic word processing

Following the first decoding of DNA, one of the greatest breakthroughs in gene technology resulted from a discovery made by Japanese researchers in 1987. Here they found repetitive sequences in the DNA of bacteria but could not detect their purpose. 'The biological significance of these sequences,' they wrote, 'is unknown.' In the course of time, other scientists found the sequences in DNA from other bacteria and named them 'Clustered Regularly Interspaced Short Palindromic Repeats', which has fortunately been abbreviated to CRISPR (pronounced 'crisper'). But the reason for their presence remained a mystery for many years.

It was only in 2007 that their function was revealed. Food technologists were studying *Streptococcus* bacteria for use in yoghurt production, but unfortunately, the bacteria were constantly attacked by bacteriophages – a kind of virus that attacks bacteria. However, it turned out that CRISPR acted as part of the bacteria's immune system against this. When, by means of enzymes, bacteria had destroyed a virus, the enzymes chopped its genes into pieces. They were then encapsulated in the bacteria's CRISPR sequence, and thus in the bacterium's own DNA.

But why? If a burglar broke into your home, you probably would not chop him into pieces and stash the pieces in your fridge. Let's hope not, anyway. But the bacteria saved the DNA of the attackers, because they needed to use them as templates to make special attack enzymes called Cas9s. Each of these contained fragments of the aforementioned viral genes from previous attacks, and if a Cas9 enzyme found a matching DNA sequence within the bacterium, it would recognise it as a virus and cut it into pieces. In other words, it had 'written down' how to recognise the enemy.

Brilliant, isn't it! Scientists then discovered that the Cas9 system could be used in artificially introduced DNA. Once this was established, research groups tried converting CRISPR/Cas9 into a functional tool that could process genes in organisms other than the bacteria from which the system originates. And it turned out to be possible. In fact, the system works much better than the methods hitherto used to artificially alter the DNA of organisms. In short, it is just like when, say, you instruct a word-processing programme to correct all occurrences of the spelling error 'ded' to 'did'. And that can be done on all the trillions of cells in a living organism (the adult human body typically has about 70–100 trillion cells).

Immediately after the discovery of the huge potential of CRISPR/Cas9, several leading scientists in the field created companies. Controversy over the ownership of intellectual property rights to the system resulted in a huge court case in the United States between two groups of scientists and their affiliated institutions. But in spite of all the lawsuits and personal disputes, the CRISPR technologies quickly made their mark in the scientific world and the pharmaceutical industry, where there is a myriad of opportunities. One of the most obvious is the curing of so-called monogenic disorders, which, unlike polygenic ones, are merely due to a single base change in an individual's genetic code. It is a bit like when a software program crashes because a single character in the code is wrong. If CRISPR/Cas9 can be transported into the cells of patients with monogenic diseases and change the individual 'spelling' of billions of cells back to the correct base, those patients can be cured. There are hundreds of such monogenic diseases that can all be cured in this way. For some of them, including Duchenne Muscular Dystrophy, no treatment is currently available, but experiments with mice have shown that CRISPR can eliminate the disease. Similarly, CRISPR has contributed to a huge increase in the growth of genetically modified (GM) crops, which now cover about 10% of the world's agricultural land. GM crops are modified for improved shelf life (to avoid food waste), improved resistance (to reduce spraying and wastage), improved resistance to weather (to increase yield per unit area), improved health, etc.

Global agricultural land sown with GM crops, 1996–2017

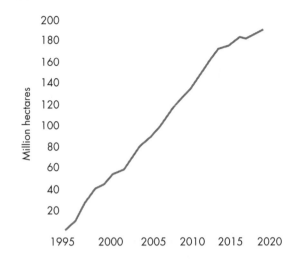

They are attempting to use CRISPR/Cas9 in agriculture too. In 2018, the US Department of Agriculture ruled that crops processed with CRISPR/Cas9 could not be considered GM crops, since they contained no foreign DNA. This ruling makes the bureaucratic work considerably simpler and has paved the way for crops processed with CRISPR/Cas9 to hit the shelves of US shops in the not too distant future. In Europe, however, the ruling was the opposite, so the crops have to go through the same complex authorisation procedure as GM crops.

Nevertheless, some scientists do not believe that in the future CRISPR/Cas9 will play a crucial role in major genetic projects. That is because the system can introduce errors into the genes being processed, and it will be impossible to use it for projects that require too many changes because the possibilities of error increase with the number of changes. Instead, researchers such as George Church from Harvard University hope to improve the techniques for synthesising DNA from scratch, one base pair at a time. In other words, instead of repairing a strand of DNA, you create a brand new one – the exact one you want.

The DNA chain is first designed on a computer. Then, just as when designing computer chips, it is physically produced and put into use. And that leads to a general rule:

14. Having decoded human genes, the development of biology will follow the main trends in the development of computer technology.

Not only has our ability to decode and synthesise genes evolved exponentially, the same exponential development will occur in relation to the number of practical applications we will produce as a result of this ability. This means *we are the first and only species among the Earth's several million that is able purposefully to change genes in both other species and ourselves.* And this process we have now triggered will continue to develop exponentially.

What concepts could we imagine? Let us start with the fact that, for the first time in the history of humankind, we can create a real Noah's ark. Obviously, with around 8.5 million extant species on the planet and the demand for a minimum population of maybe 50 of each (to prevent major inbreeding problems), we cannot create an actual Noah's ark as a realistic biological backup. It would have to accommodate millions of animals and plants, which would have very different and mutually-dependent growth conditions, and would immediately gobble up each other. But we can actually create some kind of Noah's ark by storing the DNA codes for all life on computers. This to some extent could be used to recreate extinct species. But more on that subject later.

In addition, we can manipulate animals and plants. In fact, we have already done so for millennia and on a huge scale. Take the 160 or so species of dog, which were bred by humans on the basis of the grey wolf. That means that, without humans, no dogs would exist. Likewise, almost everything we eat has been genetically modified radically, and for a long time. Ever since agriculture was introduced shortly after the last Ice Age ended about 11 700 years ago, by means of both targeted and unconscious selection humankind has developed many of nature's plants and animals to such an extent that it would be hard to spot their similarity to their original. Modern maize, for instance, originates from a species of grass known as teosinte. The latter still grows wild, but there is no visible indication that they are related. Wheat is a cross between three different species of grass, which were also genetically manipulated – for example, through irradiation – and it cannot grow without our assistance. Modern bananas are sterile and cannot develop seeds. The fruit we eat today is usually much larger, more lasting, and often juicier than it was in its natural state. So, we have genetically manipulated most of our food this way – even the food we refer to as 'organic'.

But now we can manipulate genes directly, the question is: What is the point of genetically modifying animals and plants? Perhaps to make plants that require less water, fertiliser, and pesticides. Or plants that are more resistant to wind, rain, frost, or saltwater, and that grow faster and get bigger, taste better, and are healthier. Or, for instance, we can genetically modify organisms to produce specific proteins that are used in medicines and a variety of raw materials. You name it.

New genetically engineered species

Another possibility is to make species of nuts that do not trigger fatal allergies in humans and contain fewer natural toxins (cassava, for instance, contains some natural cyanide). If we do this, it might be important to make them new species, not variants of existing species, and to give them visual characteristics so that users will not confuse them with their dangerous cousins. In fact, I would be surprised if over the coming decades and centuries we don't see an explosion in genetically engineered new species. The scientific consensus seems to be that a new species on average is created by nature every 400 years, but perhaps we shall soon see many new ones created every year.

Recreation of extinct species – the real Jurassic Park

One of the more radical ideas is to recreate extinct species and, of course, as with many other advances, the idea encounters many sceptics and opponents. The main claim of the opponents is that humankind should not play God and try to intervene in nature. However, the environmental activist Stewart Brand, founder of the Long Now Foundation and author of books including the excellent *Whole Earth Discipline* (2010), has devoted much time and in-depth work to this 'de-extinction' possibility, and his response to the sceptics is that actually we will simply be repairing what has been destroyed. That is my view too.

Brand uses the passenger pigeon as an example. The last of the species, Martha, died in 1914. A few decades earlier, there were more passenger pigeons in the world than any other bird. They lived throughout the continent of North America and moved in flocks up to 1.5 km wide and 650 km long. The passenger pigeon was also the American continent's cheapest source of protein, so was eaten to the point of extinction by the Americans. The positive thing was that the fate of the passenger pigeon made people aware of the extinction issue, which probably saved the American bison from suffering the same fate.

Many of the creatures we now think of recreating are major species that died out during the end of the last Ice Age about 11 700 years ago, when people migrated to hitherto uninhabited areas and probably hunted these species until they had wiped them out. For example, when the first native Indians arrived in North America some 11 500 years ago, three quarters of the region's large mammals died out. About 7000 years later, when they had also populated South America, five of the continent's large mammals disappeared. Altogether, North and Latin America lost wild horses, mastodons, mammoths, lions, sabre-toothed tigers, giant condors, and various types of musk oxen, bison, bears, wolves, wild boar, llamas, and giant beavers. When humans arrived in Hawaii, 50 of the island's original 98 bird species disappeared. And when they arrived in Madagascar 2500 years ago, 29 bird species died out, including all types of wingless birds – and that was *before* the Europeans arrived.

So Stone Age people were pretty detrimental for the environment, and in North and South America, and Australia, human immigration led to a total eradication of between 74% and 86% of local megafauna (animal species with a body weight of more than 44 kg). The scientist Storrs L. Olson has estimated that the extinction of a quarter of all bird species on islands in our seas was caused by tribal people – and again before civilisation came in on the act. In other words, tribal people wiped out a myriad of species, and thanks to fires they also transformed vast areas of forest into savannah and prairie.

We should also note that, because many of the species that were wiped out shortly after the end of the last Ice Age lived in the polar climate of the Ice Age, any future Jurassic Park will probably be located in Greenland, Siberia, Canada, Chile, or Argentina, all of which today have a suitable climate. So, the correct name will not be 'Jurassic', but maybe 'Pleistocene Park'. We will come back to this shortly.

It may be hard to imagine, but the wilderness of Europe was once full of animals that we now mostly associate with Africa. There were European lions, woolly rhinos, hyenas, and mammoths. There were also a number of extant animals that were reminiscent of today's animals – just with growing pains. Similar giants populated all the continents of the world before the Stone Age people immigrated, deliberately setting fire to forests and hunting with great efficiency. All these animals are now missing from our ecosystems, and we can actually still see traces of this. One good example is the pronghorn of the American prairie, which has a top speed of about 80 km an hour. That is a huge capacity vis-à-vis the region's predators – mainly wolves and is probably due to the fact that the prairie was once home to a cheetah-like predator that was as fast as the pronghorn. The evolutionary race that followed resulted in the lightning-fast pronghorns, who now run from everything imaginable with excessive speed.

Another example comes from South America: the favourite fruit of all millennials – the avocado. Usually fruit is propagated by animals who, having eaten the fruit, secrete the seeds in their excrement. But the avocado has a huge stone, so it is hard to imagine any animal swallowing it in Central and South America, where the avocado comes from. But that was not always the case. Once a particular creature lived in the region. Its favourite food was avocado, and it had no problem with the big stone. In fact, the stone acquired its size in order to fit this particular giant. The creature was the so-called ground sloth, which measured 6 m tall when standing on its hind legs.

Many of the animals we are now thinking of recreating are large species such as these. It was we who killed them, leaving countless gaps in our ecosystems. And now we have the technology to remedy the matter. In addition, sheer curiosity is also a bigger reason than most advocates of de-extinction will voluntarily admit. The zoo experience could at least scale new heights.

So how will we do it? There are several methods, but the least demanding in technical terms is the old-fashioned method: selective breeding. Here, over a number of generations, we breed a present-day species in such a way that it becomes roughly like the species we want to recreate. This was done, for example, with the quagga, a subspecies of the zebra that died out in the 1880s. It has since been recreated via the selective breeding of zebras. However, given that the new animal is not genetically identical to the quagga, its replacement is called 'Rau quagga'.

This kind of selective breeding can be quite effective and close the gaps in the ecosystems – and in the future may also provide us with new pets, exactly as we created dogs. There is an amusing example of this in Russia. When Russia was still part of the Soviet Union, a number of scientists decided to conduct research into the process known as domestication, which was responsible, for example, for turning the wolf into the dog (or rather the 160 or so different dog breeds), the wild ox into the cow, and the wild boar into the pig. In other words, the genetic changes that resulted in the fact that the dog is now generally submissive and happy, rather than aggressive and shy like the wolf. To investigate the process in greater depth, the scientists bought a huge number of foxes from local fur farms. The foxes were still wild by nature and therefore shy of humans, and they became aggressive if they were crowded into a corner. Now, for many generations, the scientists only bred the foxes in each generation that were friendliest towards humans, and relatively quickly, from generation to generation, the new litters began to change. The foxes they bred became increasingly relaxed in human company and even began to seek it out. Eventually, they bred foxes that were totally tame by nature and behave like dogs. They even wagged their tails and barked delightedly at the sight of humans. Pets!

However, selective breeding is not a high-tech method and is better suited to the last century. Church has come up with a more modern approach to de-extinction. Church's research group is working on a project in which they will use CRISPR/Cas9 to modify the genome of Asian elephants to make them more like mammoths. It is impossible to introduce all the differences between mammoth and elephant DNA. But it is not necessary anyway. Instead, Church and his group are focusing on using CRISPR/Cas9 to introduce limited changes that will invest the elephant with mammoth features such as fur growth, smaller ears, and layers of fat beneath its skin. The modified elephants can then be reintroduced as stand-in mammoths into ecosystems, where they historically belonged – until hungry people probably eradicated them thousands of years ago.

The third method for cloning an extinct animal involves inserting its DNA into an egg cell from a similar animal, which has already had its own DNA removed. This was the method used in the film *Jurassic Park,* where dinosaur blood was found in the stomachs of mosquitoes, which were enclosed in amber that was millions of years old. It goes without saying that the DNA must not be damaged, which it almost inevitably will be after millions of years, but often not particularly after thousands of years in a frozen state in the likes of Siberia.

However, we do know the complete genome, the complete DNA sequence, for many extinct species. So, one variation on the method involves synthesising a strand of DNA on the basis of the code that has been reconstructed by studying numerous DNA fragments from the species, thereby filling in the gaps in each DNA strand. However, currently both methods also require a living animal to serve as a surrogate mother or waiting for sufficient progress in the development of an artificial uterus that can be adapted to the species.

Now I bet you are thinking that, even though recreating extinct animal species sounds pretty exciting, you would probably rather not be attacked by a huge lion on your morning walk or see a herd of mammoths devastating Piccadilly Circus while hunting for food. So, what do we do with the animals once we have them?

Of course, zoos are the first option. This is where you will certainly be able to see prehistoric animals in the future. But it would be a bit sad to resurrect large numbers of prehistoric animals simply to lock them up in an enclosure. Fortunately, one particular man has come up with a possibility. Sergey Zimov is a Russian scientist who, together with a number of others, has bought a large plot of land in Siberia and named it Pleistocene Park. Zimov's plan is to use the park to recreate the old ecosystem that prevailed in the area 10 000 years ago in the form of grassy plains – somewhat similar to the savannahs of present-day Africa, but, of course, considerably colder. The project has already been underway for a number of years and the park is currently home to a large number of animals such as bison and yaks imported into the area. Once the mammoth and other extinct giants have been recreated, the plan is to incorporate some into the park to assume the role they used to have in the old ecosystem.

It is, of course, important that our ability to implement de-extinction in the future does not mean that the protection of species today is unnecessary. Conversely, experience shows that people become defeatist if they only hear doomsday sermons and bad news about the development of the world, whereas triumphs in terms of recreating extinct species can create enthusiasm and hope.

We cannot know what potential obstacles will occur, and it is far easier, cheaper, and safer to protect living animals than to recreate them later. For example, we have witnessed skilled work related to the protection of the mountain gorilla. In the early 1980s there were as few as 254 left, but now there are more than 1000. Another example is the Californian condor. There were only 22 extant birds back in 1987. Today there are more than 400, and half of them live in the wild. Hopefully in the future we will hear similar stories with regard to other endangered species.

Deliberate specicide

Now, having said that we can create new species and recreate extinct ones with genetic engineering, it should be mentioned that we may also use this technology for deliberately driving some species to extinction. Before

I carry on, let me just provide this statement which I just saw on the World Health Organisation's website:

> *Mosquitoes are one of the deadliest animals in the world. Their ability to carry and spread disease to humans causes millions of deaths every year. In 2015 malaria alone caused 438 000 deaths. The worldwide incidence of dengue has risen 30-fold in the past 30 years, and more countries are reporting their first outbreaks of the disease. Zika, dengue, chikungunya, and yellow fever are all transmitted to humans by the Aedes aegypti mosquito. More than half of the world's population live in areas where this mosquito species is present.*

Globally, there exist approximately 3500 species of mosquitoes, out of which about 30 spread malaria, and another few cause dengue fever, Zika, chikungunya, and yellow fever. Just getting rid of one single mosquito species out of the 3500, namely *Anopheles gambiae*, would provide huge benefits to mankind, since this is responsible for the vast majority of all malaria infections. Scientists now believe that they can do this via a so-called gene drive, which is an artificial gene that can force itself into 99% of an organism's offspring instead of the usual half. Scientists working in a project called Target Malaria have developed such a drive, which causes female *Anopheles gambiae* mosquitoes to become sterile. Experiments combined with calculations show that the spread of such a gene can drive the entire population to extinction within 11 generations. As I write this, Target Malaria is led by Imperial College in the United Kingdom with participation from Italy, Mali, Burkina Faso, and Uganda. The current plan aims for release of mosquitoes carrying this drive by 2029, after which malaria might become history.

Tomorrow's genetically modified humans

Even humans can be recreated. If we have intact knowledge of the full genetic sequence of a dead person, we can make a clone. Incidentally, that makes me wonder whether, in principle, we could clone the likes of the embalmed pharaohs and popes in museums and churches (that was not a suggestion – just a thought!).

On the subject, our own species is undergoing rapid change. The so-called International HapMap Project has revealed that today the genetic development of humankind is approximately 100 times faster than it was just 10 000 years ago. We do not yet understand the consequence of many of the more recent mutations, but what we do know is that a number of them relate to changes in metabolism and digestion, repair of DNA damage, reproduction, the central nervous system, and defence against diseases. So that has happened spontaneously, albeit largely as an adaptation to our changing lifestyle. But do we want to change ourselves *voluntarily*?

Yes, I believe that gradually this urge will become widespread, because people have always had the urge to change their own bodies. Take tattoos, for instance. The oldest tattoos we know of are 14 000 years old. Since then, people have deliberately deformed girls' feet, mistreated children and adolescents to create artificially long necks and flat foreheads, pierced ears, noses, and other body parts – you name it. Modern examples include pacemakers; Botox; liposuction; artificial corneas; hips, knees, and teeth; transplantation of kidneys, liver, heart, spinal cord, etc.; dental fillings; hair operations; hearing aids; contact lenses; and plastic surgery. Whatever we might think of each of these measures, we must conclude that the ability to change the human body via physical intervention is extremely popular.

But we have proceeded beyond that, because we also produce a large number of test tube children. The first child conceived in this way was born in 1978. At the time, critics claimed that these children would turn into psychological monsters. But that did not turn out to be the case, and now it is just something we do. Since 1978, nearly 5 million children have been conceived using the test tube method. We also conduct prenatal diagnosis to check for chromosome abnormalities or other known hereditary diseases in a foetus. If the result shows that this is the case, not infrequently parents opt for abortion, which, of course, over time helps change the human gene pool. We have also seen gene transplants in people with serious genetic diseases. The first successful gene transplantation was performed in 1989.

But what more do we want to see? In 1993, Darryl Macer from the Eubios Ethics Institute in Japan conducted a survey in Australia, Japan, India, Thailand, Russia, and the United States on attitudes to the following questions:

What is your opinion about changing genes in human DNA to:

- Reduce the risk of developing a fatal disease later in life?
- Prevent children from inheriting a non-lethal disease such as diabetes?
- Improve the level of intelligence that children will inherit?

To the first question (prevention of a fatal disease) between 75% and 82% of the countries' inhabitants responded positively. In terms of preventing non-lethal diseases, 62–91% again responded positively – the Japanese were the least positive and the Thais were the most positive. But what is interesting is that a majority in *all* the countries included in the survey responded positively to these two issues. Regarding the last question (about improving children's intelligence by means of genetic manipulation), 70% of Indians and 72% of Thais responded positively, whereas the proportion of positive responses in Australia, Japan, Russia, and the United States was 'only' 27%, 26%, 35%, and 44% respectively. Overall, we can conclude that large proportions of the populations were actually supporters of genetic manipulation of humans in different circumstances. So how could this proceed in the future? Here is a guess:

- Egg screening for genetic defects before implantation, and sometimes even of female egg cells before fertilisation. It happens today and is widely used.
- Cloning of people's pets. This has already started, but rarely happens.
- Genetic manipulation of pets; for example, to develop dogs with particularly high intelligence and long lives. This would not be inherently different from selective breeding, which we have already used to create approximately 160 dog breeds from the grey wolf.

- Designer children via egg screening – we screen not only to dese-lect serious diseases, but also to select certain features such as intelligence, health, etc.

- Designer children via embryo manipulation – we genetically manipulate an embryo to advance certain characteristics.

- Biohacking of adults – for example, in vitro alteration of hair col-our, eye colour, or skin colour, and/or genetic removal or addition of hair. One of the frontrunners in this field was the biohacker Josiah Zayner, to whom we will return later.

- Insertion of genes from other organisms into human DNA – for example, to delay ageing processes.

So yes, just as we hack nature, we are now well on the way to hacking ourselves and, in my opinion, this is one of the most important milestones in the history of the world. What is more, in 2015 it was discovered that human DNA already contains fragments of genes from 'at least' 145 other species, including flies, worms, bacteria, and plants that were transferred by means of so-called horizontal gene transfer (HGT), which in practice can be caused by viral infections. So, nature has already done this for us – frequently. The big difference is that nature's spontaneous computer has now acquired a programmer: us. And that leads to this rule:

15. **In the future, humans will use genomics to deliberately elimi-nate existing species (specicide), make extinct species reap-pear (de-extinction), change existing species, and create new ones. And humans will re-engineer their own species.**

A healthier, safer world

Our health is perhaps the area in which the greatest changes are under-way. Average life expectancy has already increased dramatically: pri-marily because we have succeeded in reducing child mortality, but also because we have improved the likes of nutrition and become much better at combating infectious diseases. There are some African countries where they succeeded in increasing the average life expectancy by 10 years – in 10 years.

We also keep ourselves fit and healthy longer. Previously, even commonplace disorders could be extremely painful and unpleasant, which of course also contributed to the fact that people did not live as long. Much has now been done about this, and the question is just how far we should go. Certain scientists believe that we can live to the age of 1000. But that gives rise to a number of ethical issues: for example, whether we should bring children into the world. But even if we do not get to that point, we should still contemplate a future Super Aged Society, because we are certainly going to grow older than previous generations.

We will also have the capacity to take even more care of our health and appearance. Of course, this development has been in force for a long time, but now technology is at hand to help us look good. Maybe you will soon have a mirror you can talk to, which will use AI to analyse your skin and provide you with tips on how to look good, even if you went to bed late the night before.

Beauty and health are areas in which we are going to see an increasing number of individualised, bespoke solutions. Maybe you will simply get your own shampoo and your own skin products and eat a muesli for breakfast that has been mixed optimally to suit your particular body.

Revolutions in the fight against cancer

Following the great success of the Americans with their moon landings, tremendous faith in humanity's ability to solve our greatest problems prevailed. So, it was natural that cancer became a major issue, because it was also a major killer at the time. When President Nixon officially started the war on cancer in 1971 by signing the National Cancer Act, he said: 'The same kind of concentrated effort that split the atom and took man to the moon should be turned toward conquering this dread[ful] disease.' Unfortunately, as we all know, it was not that easy, and in general, in contrast to many other technologies, cancer treatment has moved more slowly than we previously expected – despite a huge, professional effort on the part of scientists and developers. Cancer is actually many things and very complex. But, while some types of cancer are still just about as fatal as in 1971, the many small advances we have nonetheless made mean that the chance of survival vis-à-vis most types of cancer has significantly improved.

But those advances are nothing compared to what the future will bring. We now have more new treatments in the pipeline than at any time since 1971. The most promising include biopsies on blood or other fluids, which can chemically detect indications that a person already has cancer at a stage where the tumour is 1/100 of the smallest that can be seen in an MRI scan.

Another one, which in 2019 was described by scientists as being effective in mice, was to genetically modify non-pathogenic *Escherichia coli* bacteria to specifically lyse within the tumour microenvironment and release an encoded nanobody antagonist of CD47. What that meant in plain English was to genetically modify harmless bacteria so that they would specifically attach to tumour cells because they contained a protein called CD47. After they had done this, human T cells – a part of our natural defence system – would be able to attach to the tumour cells further and thus stimulate rapid tumour regression and prevent metastasis, which enables long-term survival.

However, currently, what is most interesting on the cancer front is immunotherapy, which utilises the body's own immune system to attack the cancer cells in a number of different ways. The method counteracts the capacity of cancer cells to hide from the immune system, while stimulating the immune system to boost its attack or help it select the right target.

Thus, immunotherapy is much more specific than, say, chemotherapy, which attacks all cells that divide a lot – even those that do so quite naturally, such as the cells that form our hair. Another major benefit of immunotherapy is that it can be used against cancer that has already spread. You see, the fact is that the primary malignant tumour virtually never kills.

In the case of a single tumour, it can be removed by surgery, following which the area can be treated with radiation therapy. The real problem arises if individual cancer cells leave the primary tumour and travel into the body, establishing new tumours. They are called metastases, and when there are many metastases, treatment becomes impossible.

At least that used to be the case. Now, incredible stories have begun to emerge, in which various forms of immunotherapy, which have still not been fully tested, miraculously cure patients who had been given just a matter of weeks or months to live. Several of these patients suffered from cancer that had spread so violently that conventional methods would never have been able to fight off their disease. One of the most prominent examples is former US President Jimmy Carter. Carter had contracted melanoma, and the cancer had already spread to his brain. So, it seemed to be one of the cases in which chemotherapy could not accomplish much. Instead, Carter was given the immunotherapy, pembrolizumab (Keytruda), which blocks access to the brain's brake pedal, so the cancer cannot misuse it and hide from the immune cells. And it worked. Today, Carter's cancer is virtually gone.

One of the most promising immunotherapies in the pipeline is called CAR T. We are already hearing stories of patients who had been written off by doctors, but who still got rid of cancer thanks to CAR T. This therapy removes about a billion so-called T cells from the cancer patient. T cells play a major role in the immune system's decision about what to attack. The cells are then reprocessed outside the body, for example, using CRISPR/Cas9, so they subsequently express a receptor that can specifically recognise a patient's cancer cells. Thereafter, the cells are allowed to grow in favourable conditions, where they can divide substantially, before being returned finally to the patient. And then something else happens. When the T cells recognise the cancer cells, the attack starts. Every single T cell can kill thousands of cancer cells. It is not particularly pleasant for the patients who experience the attack. In fact, it is like the worst imaginable bout of influenza, with pain and an extremely high temperature. And that is also the other side of the coin. Several patients have died of the treatment, because it is so toxic for the body. But if it succeeds, most patients become cancer free. Even those who had been on the verge of death.

Another interesting area of cancer research relates to a protein called p53, which is generated from a gene called *TP53*. Given its capacity to prevent cancer, p53 is often called 'the guardian of the genome'. Like with almost all genes, we inherit a version of the gene from each of our parents. In rare cases where one of these two is defective (Li-Fraumeni syndrome), cancer almost certainly breaks out. Now, cancer always starts from a single cell that has a critical combination of mutations and then spreads. So, all things being equal, you should expect that the longer average lifespan an animal has, and the more cells it has in its body, the bigger the risk of cancer. But this is not the case. This puzzle is known as 'Peto's Paradox'. For instance, bowhead whales have maximum lifespans of over 200 years and can weigh up to 100 tons – which should mean several thousand times more risk of cancer than in humans. And yet, to date, no one has ever found cancer in such an animal. In fact, overall, whales and elephants are far less prone to cancer than humans. The reason seems to be that they create many more variants of p53 than humans. The genome of elephants, for instance, contains 40 variants of p53 (and still two versions of each of them – one from mum and one from dad). So, in the future, can we add elephant variants of *TP53* to human genes in order to create almost totally cancer-resistant humans? Time will tell, but the area is certainly interesting.

New, improved treatment of both cancer and a variety of other diseases, together with greater understanding of healthy living, makes it inevitable that average life expectancy will continue to increase. Exactly how much is hard to predict at this time, but a conservative guess suggests that it may reach 120 years in the foreseeable future. Some scientists, though, are even more optimistic. The gerontologist Aubrey de Grey believes that the first person who will live to an age of 1000 is already living. De Grey's main point is that we do not need to develop the technology to live 1000 years in the near future. Instead, we just need to be able to prolong people's life expectancy quickly enough to keep them alive until the time when new technology can help them grow older. In other words, technological development must be able to add years of life faster than, or virtually as fast as, chronological time snatches them away.

New cells for old lives

The aforementioned examples of biochemical and genetic health work are the expression of an overall phenomenon. In health care we frequently replace (1) physical solutions with (2) chemical ones and then (3) biochemical ones. And that creates progress.

Inevitably, when we live longer, we are more prone to illness – at least initially. In the distant future, there is no doubt that many diseases will be prevented in the first place. But soon, it is certain that more people will have survived a life-threatening disease and that more people will therefore live long enough to experience more wear and tear. So, would it not make sense if we could simply get spare parts like an old car?

Yes, and that is precisely one of the visions of stem cell research. Research into stem cells really started to gain momentum around the turn of the millennium, and it looks as if we will be seeing the first treatments within the next 5–10 years. Before we delve into the new treatments, it is important to understand just what stem cells are.

One type is the embryonic stem cell. When an egg cell is fertilised by a sperm, a structure called a zygote is formed. It immediately begins to divide and later turns into a structure called a blastocyst, which is made up of 200–300 cells. From this, scientists harvest embryonic stem cells. These cells still possess the ability to turn into all kinds of cells in an adult individual. During the development of the foetus, over time the cells differentiate into increasingly specialised cell types. It is a bit like climbing a tree. First you have the trunk. From there you have a choice of routes for climbing to the top. But the more branches we encounter on the tree, the fewer our options. In the vast majority of cases, the same is true of the development of cells. That brings me to the smart thing about stem cells. We know many of the developmental processes the cells undergo as they evolve into various cell types. That means we can also imitate the process *outside* the body. Thus, scientists can get stem cells to develop into fully developed specialised tissue outside the body and then insert the tissue where it needs to be used. So, there you have it: spare parts!

There may be both ethical and technical problems when it comes to working with embryonic stem cells, but fortunately they are no longer the only option. In 2006, the Japanese scientist Shinya Yamanaka discovered that adult cells, which (using the same image as before) have in reality crawled up into the crown of our hypothetical tree, can be reprogrammed to resemble embryonic stem cells again. And what is more, it is relatively simple to get them to do it. As a result, Yamanaka was awarded a Nobel Prize in 2012.

Thus, in the future, both the reprogrammed cells, known as induced pluripotent stem cells (iPSCs), and embryonic stem cells can be used to grow tissue, which can replace missing or damaged tissue in patients, such as diabetic patients. In the case of type 1 diabetes, the body's own immune system mistakenly attacks the insulin-producing cells in the pancreas, which are known as beta cells. When beta cells die, diabetics lose their ability to regulate their blood sugar. Consequently, the disease used to be fatal.

Today, diabetics have devices to monitor their blood sugar and inject insulin when they need it. However, this is a very primitive form of treatment, which impairs quality of life. But one day this will be a thing of the past. Several groups of scientists – for example, at Harvard University and the University of Copenhagen – have already been able to create insulin-producing beta cells from embryonic stem cells. This treatment has succeeded in curing mice of diabetes. Once the treatment has proven safe in clinical trials, diabetics can have the beta cells implanted in a protective capsule and can then live and function normally with no subsequent treatments.

Artificial tissue can thus solve problems elegantly and permanently. And it will not only be used to treat patients directly. Even now, artificial tissue is in the process of creating a revolution in biomedical research, where it can be used to test medicine. This can save tonnes of time and money, because it is far quicker to identify medicines with side effects, and medicines that simply do not have the effect scientists believed they had, on the basis of cell cultures. One of the leaders in the field is the American company Organovo. They can make 3D-printed liver tissue, which is already being sold to pharmaceutical companies. Interestingly, Organovo also cooperates with L'Oréal, who aim to use 3D-printed skin to optimise their beauty products, test safety, and discover new ingredients.

Incidentally, recent IT technology also helps to reduce development costs in the pharmaceutical industry. Companies can use the technology to make computer simulations of what is happening in an entire cell. Using these simulations, they can test what effect different pharmaceutical products will have – before they even make them.

All in all, these digital technologies signify the prospect of many state-of-the-art treatments that can cure us of today's worst diseases. Of course, this does not change the fact that it is always beneficial to avoid treatment altogether, and specialist health centres are already looking into this. One example is Health Nucleus, which was started by the aforementioned Craig Venter. Health Nucleus offers consistent checkups, which include full decoding of a patient's DNA (for example, for the risk of hereditary diseases), an MRI scan (a 3D image of the entire body), cognitive tests (for possible dementia etc.), metabolic analyses (is the metabolism healthy?), and a microbiome analysis (of the body's natural bacterial and viral population). The last time I checked, the starting price for this examination was $25 000. So, it is not cheap. Nevertheless, the interest in being scanned for the incipient stages of various diseases at regular intervals is huge.

By the way, just a few years back very few health workers would consider microbiome analysis relevant to a normal health check. But it obviously is relevant. For instance, new research has provided strong indication that autism is largely caused – or at least amplified – by a lack of some bacterial strains in the gut.

In any case, all of these tests provide a completely unique overview of each patient and facilitate intervention before a disease sets in. It also makes treatment processes much simpler – especially for cancer, which in the very early stages is significantly easier to combat. As the concept spreads, prices will fall and, in the long term, such holistic tests may become quite common.

Wearables, self-diagnoses, biohacking, and lifestyle medicine

The prevention and diagnosis of disease will also be significantly improved in other contexts – again with digital technology playing a major role. Automated diagnosis comes from the increase in the number of so-called wearables: bracelets, jewellery, etc., which you wear. The collective name for this movement, incidentally, is 'quantified self'.

One example is the jewellery company Bellabeat, which our venture fund Nordic Eye funded in 2018. The company has managed to progress from a start-up company with an idea but no product to a turnover of just under $100 million – in just five years! Wearables such as Bellabeat's send continuous information about your health to a computer, which reacts if the figures look questionable. Some wearables can also be used to dispense medication, so people do not forget to take it and constantly get the correct dose – another example of the fact that digital economy is precision economy. And Apple watch with EPG can detect heart diseases.

In addition to being used purely for medical purposes, self-diagnoses will also be invaluable for so-called biohackers. The goal of biohackers is to optimise their own health, to 'hack' their bodies, and they use data they themselves have collected for the purpose. A company by the name of The Odin sells a do-it-yourself biohacking system for $159, and the company's founder, our aforementioned Josiah Zayner, demonstrated its use by boldly injecting himself with a CRISPR-based compound intended to eradicate the gene myostatin, which inhibits muscle growth. This took place at a conference in San Francisco in 2017 (and, incidentally, led to some legal trouble for practising medicine without authorisation).

As data collection gets significantly easier and better, we will experience a growth in all sorts of self-experiments conducted by amateurs and professionals in the field of biohacking. In combination with the biohackers' environment, which is greatly inspired by similar movements in the field of software, this development could be revolutionary, even though my own entrepreneurial experience tells me that much of it will go wrong. But overall, biohackers will contribute significant, new knowledge when they are able to conduct their experiments more quickly, more cheaply, and more easily: partly because they ignore most of the cautious laws that apply to the development of commercial pharmaceutical products. What you do with your own body is not easy for the state to control.

For all the reasons mentioned, in my opinion, the future of the health sector looks extremely positive, and it is possible that we are on the brink of a golden age of medicine, when we will eliminate a large number of diseases that afflict us today. And, as already mentioned, this will not only mean that our life expectancy will continue to increase greatly, but also that we will have the opportunity to remain hale and hearty for a lot longer than before. Long live innovation!

Along the way, we will also see an increasing use of lifestyle medication. A current example, which is particularly prevalent in elite communities in California, is injections of 'young blood'. It sounds pretty vampirical to me, but it is about the cell-free blood plasma that can be left over from the use of blood cells. Tests on both animals and humans have shown that it has a significantly rejuvenating effect. However, each time it is done, it also entails a small risk of disease transmission. But, given that it seems quite effective, it will undoubtedly trigger research aimed at developing safe, derived products. The procedure also has a parallel in so-called blood doping, in which athletes inject themselves with their own red blood cells before major sporting events. My guess is that blood doping with synthetic young blood plasma may become quite common in the future.

Another example of lifestyle medication is so-called nootropic or cognitive performance-enhancing drugs, which can improve our power of concentration and memory. They have become widespread among university students and in highly competitive business environments. We have all heard of doping with anabolic steroids, used by the likes of bodybuilders and certain top athletes, but a professional chess player can dope his or her brain in a similar way. There is also a myriad of other substances that can boost the immune system and raise our stress threshold etc. Could it be that one day we will see genetically modified plants that will produce lifestyle medication to sprinkle on our yoghurt every morning? If so, it will be classified as a so-called functional food: in other words, a food that is consumed for its specific effects on our health.

The intelligent healthcare of the future

Let me round off by saying that the future of healthcare will be significantly different and probably more holistic and far more effective. Health centres and wearables will provide us with access to a wealth of information about ourselves and will help us spot the smallest signs of incipient disease. Doctors will regularly resort to omniscient AI (more on that in Chapter 4). Hospitals will be streamlined with new types of sensors, big data, and robots (I cover that as well in Chapter 4), while doctors and specialists will use remote-controlled robots to provide emergency services and perform operations on people to whom they do not have physical access.

And there is much more. Emergency medicine and emergency equipment will be flown in with drones. Research will be enhanced by the Internet of DNA; pharmaceutical companies will be able to test medication on computer-simulated cells and on human organs made from stem cells. Smart prevention, and genetic and (in the broader sense) microbiological methods of treatment will gain increasing ground.

Overall, we are looking at a period in which we will begin to cure lifestyle diseases and physiological problems fully rather than simply treating their symptoms. And when people get ill anyway, we will tackle it with an amazing precision and elegance. It will be a revolution for human civilisation.

4.
COMPUTERS, SOFTWARE, AND ELECTRONIC NETWORKS

The first time I wrote a book (or a 'compendium' as it was called) was for my lectures as an external lecturer at the Danish Royal Veterinary and Agricultural University in 1982. I wrote it by hand, after which a secretary typed up the text on a typewriter. I think she hated me.

I wrote my second book on a typewriter myself in 1984.

The following year – 1985 – I bought a PC for one-and-a-half months' post-tax salary and wrote my next book on it. I thought that was really cool. I found most of the information for that book by spending endless hours in a variety of libraries. Later, I began to search for information for my books on the Internet, and the process of searching became even easier when Google and Wikipedia came on the scene. But what will writing books be like in the future? Here is one possibility.

Let us suppose that in 20 years' time we have a software program called 'SpeedWriter'. SpeedWriter is programmed to be a data-driven fox that continuously scans the Internet and other intelligent sources such as scientific study databases. And because it is based on artificial intelligence (AI), it can also understand the *meaning* of everything. Further, unlike many people, it has an impressive ability to distinguish idiocy from brilliance, and it knows that scientific studies are better than conspiracy theories, just as a scientific meta study is more valuable than a single study.

Imagine that on this day, 20 years from now, I have to write a textbook on economic growth theory. So, one morning I ask SpeedWriter to list the most quoted thinkers in the field. A few seconds later, the computer gives me a list of the 25 leading authors in the subject – assessed according to how often they have been quoted by other leading scientists.

Next, I ask it to visually show me where these writers live or lived and when they published their most important works. SpeedWriter shows me this in a chart. I now ask it to classify the authors according to schools of thought. The program sorts that out in seven seconds. Having studied that, my thoughts turn to the structure of the book. And then I dictate the following: 'Write a 150-page book on theories of economic growth. Main structure: chronological. Secondary structure: theoretical schools. Style: academic. Technical illustrations: 20–40. Photos of authors: 5–10. Flesch-Kincaid readability index: 25–30.'

The computer delivers a manuscript after a couple of minutes, after which I sit down on my couch with my tablet and browse through it. It seems academically strong, but also somewhat dry, so now I ask Speed-Writer to find all the anecdotes that involve at least two of the quoted authors at once and insert them in the right places in the book's timeline. I also request it to change the style to popular science and the readability index to 50. The results appear shortly after, and it is much better. 'Add 10–15 summary boxes,' I say, and it does so immediately.

'Now we're getting there,' I think. But then I get an idea. I dictate: 'Make 10 30–120-second film clips featuring the leading thinkers explaining their most important contributions. Include one in which two of the authors, who were active in the field at the same time, discuss a topic.' SpeedWriter now uses images of the two most important thinkers to create computer animated films, in which they have a discussion. It actually spends a whole minute on this, but the result looks extremely lifelike.

'OK,' I think. 'Now we're almost there.' All that's missing is an interactive test for the reader. So, I say, 'Add a multiple-choice test on the subject. And a tutorial.' It does so immediately, after which I upload the result to my digital e-reader and go into the garden to study it. One hour has passed, but I want to try and get a sense of whether the book is more or less ready. It is, so I can still fit in a game of tennis before lunch.

Welcome to the book world of tomorrow as I believe parts of it might be.

From exceptional to magical

The enormous changes in life as a writer, which we have already witnessed and will witness much more of in the future, are of course due to the development of the computer. Computer capacity is sometimes calculated in MIPS or millions of instructions per second. In 1972, when I was a schoolboy, IBM launched a computer with a revolutionary 1 MIPS capacity. A robot with that capacity could, for example, follow a white line or magnetic line. In fact, a few years later I saw a presentation of this at a Tetra Pak factory in Sweden, which I thought was amazing. But the development progressed, and with 10 000 MIPS a robot has 3D vision and can detect and grab objects.

We reached that stage in 2005, and in 2017 AMD launched a chip with 305 000 MIPS. MIPS are increasingly being replaced by other measuring units, but it is worth mentioning that when manufacturers reach a capacity of 100 000 000 MIPS, that will probably be the equivalent of the human brain. In other words, it will take about 3000 of AMD's 2017 chips to provide the capacity of a human brain.

Another way to calculate it is by so-called floating operations per second or FLOPS, and here there the scientific consensus is that the brain performs approximately 10^{17}. The Sunway TaihuLight computer from 2016, which cost $300 million, has reached the same capacity. However, it will hardly take anywhere near this capacity to compete with the brain, and in 1998 the robotic expert Hans Moravec estimated that it could be done with 10^{13} FLOPS, since much of the human brain is idle at any time. 10^{13} FLOPS was a huge number back then, but by 2015 you could buy a computer with this capacity for $1000. Even though the numbers I just mentioned diverge somewhat, I want to say that we are approaching a stage where computers will be on a par with human brains and where totally amazing human-like things can happen. In fact, totally amazing human-like things *are* already happening.

Unrivalled acceleration

In a classic text about exponential development from 2001, *The Law of Accelerating Returns*, the serial entrepreneur, author, and Google researcher Ray Kurzweil shows that Moore's Law actually dates all the way back to the 1880s. Bearing that in mind, it may not be over-optimistic to assume that the development will continue – even though Moore's Law, as originally conceived, is at the end of its road. By the way, Moore's Law is not the only law to effectively describe the exponential development of information technology. There is also the following, for instance, which is named after a professor at Stanford University, Jonathan Koomey:

16. **The energy requirement needed for a given amount of data processing is halved every 18 months (Koomey's Law).**

Allow me to immediately list more of the same kind:

17. **The total bandwidth of communication systems triples every 12 months (Gilder's Law).**

18. **Network speeds for advanced private users are increasing at a rate of 50% per year, the equivalent of doubling every 21st month (Nielsen's Law).**

19. **Performance per price content for a hard drive increases by 40% per year (Kryder's Law).**

It is intense, and that is one of the reasons traffic on the Internet increases just as significantly. In 1992, traffic amounted to 100 gigabytes a day.

10 years later – in 2002 – the number was the same – only it was per second. In 2016, the figure had grown further from 100 to 26 600 gigabytes per second, and Cisco expects that by 2021 the figure will be more than 100 000 gigabytes per second. Curiously, this is happening as we pass peak telephony, which has already taken place in the developed world, where people increasingly prefer to book the likes of Uber, restaurants, etc. online rather than calling a company, and where they also substitute speech with text in professional and private dialogues. In parallel with these phenomena, the number of radio channels has exploded on account of the following law:

20. **The number of radio frequency calls that can be conducted simultaneously in a given area doubles every 30 months (Cooper's Law).**

In fact, this law is particularly interesting in that it has been in operation since the time of Marconi's first transmissions in 1895. Moreover, we are now witnessing a revolution in the available bandwidth through 5G mobile telephony.

Whereas the transition from 3G to 4G did not feel that radical, the leap from 4G to 5G will be like the change from copper telephone wires to optical fibres. 5G will be approximately 100 times faster than 4G, and 10 times faster than the broadband connection that many modern homes have today. Imagine downloading a film in two seconds and not having to worry about whether Netflix now loads fast enough when you wish to stream your favourite series.

5G will also be at the very heart of the development of the Internet of Things (IoT), since it will facilitate the connection of approximately 1000 times more sensors than 4G for a single transmitting station. Furthermore, it will enable autonomous cars to communicate intensely with each other, and we will also be able to control drones all over the globe with no collisions, because they will also communicate.

One weakness of 5G is that it is not so efficient when it comes to penetrating barriers. On the other hand, though, it can radically streamline communication within buildings. As a result, it can be used to create 3D Global Positioning System (GPS) inside buildings: for example, it can guide an airline passenger directly to his or her flight. Or you to your car, if you have forgotten on which floor of the multi-storey car park you parked. With 5G, we can also capture altitude position, which is hugely important, given that soon we will connect billions of sensors to the Internet in the context of developing smart towns and cities. In other words, 5G is Gilder's, Nielsen's, Kryder's, and Cooper's laws on steroids!

A similar – albeit slower – law applies to batteries:

21. **The performance of batteries doubles every 9–14 years.**

More precisely, the growth rate of performance per unit weight has fluctuated between 5% and 8% annually. That makes battery-driven electronic gadgets ever more useful, but it also means that, in principle, we have been able to predict when electric cars would make their commercial breakthrough, and Elon Musk wasted no time in benefiting from the consequences. But let's just pop in another rule:

22. **The price of computer memory drops at a rate of 20–30% per year.**

Bell's Law of new computer classes

Having said all this, IT development is about far more than the exponential curves in performance and falling prices. Compare, for example, Koomey's, Gilder's, Nielsen's, Cooper's, and Kryder's aforementioned laws. It is also about regular paradigm shifts: cf. Bell's Law of computer classes: 'On average, a basic new computing concept appears every 10 years.' Each new basic concept leads not only to new applications, but also to new opportunities for cross-combining technologies in co-evolution. As a consequence, they kindle cascades of new services and products. Personally, here is how I would classify the previous main paradigms:

- Integrated circuits – which replaced the much slower, more expensive, and more unreliable vacuum tubes (in the late 1960s).

- Master-slave computing – central mainframe computers, which can only be operated by highly specialised experts (also in the 1960s).

- Client-server computing – large central servers collaborate with decentralised minicomputers that are pretty easy to use (in the 1970s).

- Personal computing combined with Local Area Networking (the 1980s).

- Networked computing – millions (later billions) of computers collaborate via the Internet (the 1990s).

In this context one can say that Bell's Law of paradigm shifts did prove correct every 10 years. However, then the computer classes picked up speed:

- Ubiquitous and edge computing – computers are everywhere in the environment, often embedded and invisible, or mobile and handheld – for example, via smartphones and tablets (in the 2000s and particularly following the launch of the iPhone in 2007).

- Cloud computing – computers store data and perform data processing in the cloud. This results in virtual computing via networks of computers that work in swarms: in other words, where the demanding part of the calculation is done collectively on computers located in the cloud, far away from the user. That also gives rise to computing as a service. Initially, this was driven mainly by Amazon Web Services (2006) and Microsoft Azure (2012).

- AI – computers can operate autonomously by solving tasks such as knowledge development, reasoning, problem solving, perception, learning, etc. Consequently, they start to resemble human brains.

- IoT – has developed exponentially through the 00s and also encompasses edge computing, in which billions of simple objects, discreetly built into our environment, create small computer routines and, in the case of IoT, are connected to on the Internet.

- Big data – has also evolved throughout the 00s, combining, for example, data from IoT with data processing via AI.

- Smart robots – robots that not only repeat fixed instructions, but can also learn from experiences and exchange them.

- Smart remote controls – smartphones and smart watches are becoming kinds of magic wands that control everything around us that has built-in intelligence.

So, there were 7–8 new paradigms in 20 years, which puts paid to Bell's Law. It seems overwhelmingly likely to me that further paradigm shifts will happen even faster in the future. Some, for which I already foresee major breakthroughs in the future, include:

- Quantum computers – a new type of computer that can perform certain kinds of computing tasks up to billions of times faster than traditional supercomputers.

- Virtual reality (VR) – presentation of an imaginary reality that comes across as considerably real and convincing.

- Augmented reality (AR) – presenting reality with an extra layer added by computers.

- Ambient user experience – digital experiences without being disturbed by the transition from network to network or computer to computer, in which data processing, online networks, and monitors are increasingly being seamlessly and elegantly integrated into our environment.

What follows is a short description of the latest paradigms in this list, kicking off with cloud computing.

Cloud computing and the as-a-service movement

Who wants to buy a house if you only need to be somewhere for a limited period of time, and when your space requirements vacillate between just you, more, or many people? No one. That is why we have hotels. Cloud computing comprises 'computer hotels', in which a computer user purchases neither an entire data centre nor 17 computers, but instead pays for time-limited online access to a certain amount of computing power, storage capacity, or use of software. The amount can vary from very little to huge, and the time span can range from one second, from time to time, to years. The benefits are generally great: from greater security, capacity, and flexibility to lower costs and faster deployment. One effect of cloud computing is that users increasingly refrain from purchasing software and hardware, instead preferring the right to use software in the cloud. Not only is this model more flexible, it also allows you to purchase the right to use software – one module at a time.

Accordingly, as the market matures, the business model is often changing from selling products to leasing services. The result is countless new as-a-service provisions, including not only IT-related ones such as Software as a Service (SaaS), but also in other industries such as Energy Storage as a Service (ESaaS) and Mobility as a Service (MaaS). The possibilities are virtually infinite. For example, there are people who provide sock subscriptions – in other words, Socks as a Service.

A related phenomenon is the introduction of greater granularity. In software coding, this is known as Object-Oriented Programming (OOP): the division of complex software into a number of clearly separated modules. A similar division is made when product sales pass from all-or-nothing to the option of purchasing parts at a time, just as when we progressed from having to buy an entire CD to being able to download or stream individual songs from it. This leads me to the following rule of thumb:

23. **As technologies, products, and services mature, resources are often divided into smaller components, which are marketed flexibly and separately by** *as-a-service* **providers.**

AI – the career cul-de-sac that suddenly got hot

The so-called 'Turing test', formulated by the English mathematician Alan Turing in 1950, is a way of determining whether a machine displays human-level intelligence. It states that you have created AI if you can make a computer act in such a way that people actually believe it is a human being.

The concept of AI emerged in the mid-1950s, and in the following decades people's attitude to AI often ranged from enormous scepticism to great optimism.

For many years, the pessimists on the whole were right. Many promising careers crumbled because skilled people firmly believed that now – just around the corner – there would be a major breakthrough in AI. But no. Instead, time after time, an 'AI winter' set in: development came to a standstill, sources of funding dried up, and political interest waned, because it did not really work.

Right now, however, we are in an AI spring, because now it *does* work. In fact, big time. The reasons lie in a number of technological breakthroughs, including the introduction of some software systems called Deep Learning. This means that a machine learns in layers. The first layer only provides a very rough representation, but each subsequent layer refines the representation by using the information from the preceding layer. It is a process, incidentally, that resembles that of the brain, the function of which is excellently portrayed in such books as *On Intelligence* (2005) by Jeff Hawkins and *How the Mind Works* (1997) by Steven Pinker.

In addition, we discovered that we could run the process 20–50 times faster by switching from traditional Central Processing Unit chips (CPU) to using Graphics Processing Units (GPU), which were actually designed for creating 3D experiences in computer games. What is more, Google for one has developed other process units called Tensor Processing Units (TPU), specifically for the purpose, and in general lots of so-called neuromorphic AI chips are now being developed.

In the context of AI, computers typically learn by being fed huge amounts of data and by practising again and again with information from the real world. For example, before IBM's supercomputer Watson famously beat two champions at Jeopardy in 2011, it had been fed the whole of Wikipedia, 200 million pages from books and 180 000 tips from previous Jeopardy contests. Chomp, chomp, chomp. Even the smartest and most knowledgeable people in the United States were no match for it. But if they bear a grudge at having lost to Watson, they should be delighted that soon after, the Watson of 2011 would have received a real hiding from its later big brother – who also happened to be much smaller physically.

Earlier on, when IBM's Deep Blue computer beat the chess champion Kasparov in 1997, some people thought it only won due to the raw power of being able to memorise an infinite number of chess games and simulate endless combinations of moves. Because of this assumption, critics claimed that, when it came to the popular game of Go, a computer would never have a chance. And why not? Because in a game of Go with 19×19 fields, there are $208\,168\,199\,382 \times 10^{170}$ possible outcomes. That is 90 times more than the number of atoms in the universe ('only' 10^{80} atoms).

So, a computer could not tackle this challenge with pure computing power – no way. But in 2015 Google came up with their AlphaGo program, which ran on 1202 CPUs and 176 GPUs and defeated the European Go champion Fan Hui five times in a row. It then played five games against the South Korean professional Go player Lee Sedol, who was considered number 4 in the world. AlphaGo won four out of the five games (Netflix has a great documentary about this called *AlphaGo*).

So, I repeat: it works, and AI today is incredibly strong and extremely widespread, even though it is often completely invisible to us and not something to which we give a second thought. For example, much of what you use your smartphone for is only possible with AI, such as when your phone suggests the word you are trying to type in a text message or when it helps with translations or with finding the fastest route from A to B.

Every time you search on Google, the company uses AI to find the best answers. Actually, you could call Google a huge AI company that is constantly being trained by all of us who use the machine. When you shop in a supermarket, it is also AI that makes sure that the most sought-after products are on the shelves at all times. Supermarket chains use it to analyse vast amounts of data about consumer preferences – and yes, computers are rapidly getting better at it, and can factor in everything from the first day of school to the weather forecast and sporting events in their sales expectations. Hot weather tomorrow? Buy more ice cream. Soccer match on Saturday? Beer! What is more, Amazon has recently replaced many of its purchasing managers with AI, as it proved to be better than human buyers at calculating optimum purchasing volumes and prices of items. AI is also part of our lives in lots of other ways. When you switch on Netflix, what the streaming service suggests for you is a product of AI, as are Amazon's recommendations.

In other words, AI is a big deal, and maybe it is useful to consider the following: (1) Electric power supply began to spread and be used commercially in the 1880s, revolutionising virtually every industry and creating a whole host of brand-new ones. It was a huge deal. (2) The Internet made its breakthrough in the 1990s and had a similar effect, it changed everything. And (3) AI broke through in the 00s and will also change everything.

That's how I see it, anyway. We will probably witness a continuous convergence of human and AI, where the AI will increasingly resemble human intelligence. You can compare it to a farmer driving the crown of a tree through a large gate into his barn. When did the crown pass the threshold? The issue is a bit contentious. First a few twigs cross it, then more branches and twigs, and then even more. In other words, in the process, part of the crown of the tree will be outside, part just on the threshold, and another part firmly inside. Similarly, AI is gradually surpassing us in one discipline after another.

Not until it beats us at *everything* – when the metaphorical crown of the tree has passed right through the gate – can we talk about artificial general intelligence (AGI). That also includes artificial emotional intelligence or affective computing, where computers appear to show emotions.

Why is AI so interesting now?

To see what the spread of AI will be like, we just have to take a look at some of the areas in which people were so sure that humans would be superior to machines far into the future. Today, it is difficult to spot exactly when an activity or task is too creative for a computer to tackle it. Some observers stress that what the computer cannot deliver is interaction with another person. However, in an increasing number of areas (for example, personal care and digital entertainment), machines are fast becoming more skilled – for example, more skilled in a way that is difficult to describe other than by saying that they seem more human. The development of artificial emotional intelligence, which is clearly in the pipeline, will mean that it will be far easier for us to form powerful emotional bonds with machines. Today we are seeing the creation of journalism, painting, and chamber music, which experts cannot tell came from a computer. In a number of limited areas, machines have already passed the Turing test. And it seems likely that in the long term we may achieve some sort of emotional attachment to AI computers – just as, bizarrely enough, we can be really moved by a computer-animated film. In this context, one of the newer techniques used is so-called deep structured learning (DSL), which attempts to create learning in a way that resembles that of the brain.

A few years ago, Nicklas Boström, a Swedish professor at the University of Oxford, who is deeply concerned about the development of super-intelligent computers, carried out a meta-survey on when the most-quoted experts believed that a computer's intelligence would overtake human intelligence. The average was 2050. However, as I have already suggested, I think that such a one-dimensional question is somewhat meaningless, since even now AI surpasses humans in several areas, while in others it is lagging far behind. But in any case, the fact is that if, say, in 2050, computers act like a human being with an IQ of 100, by 2052 they may have an IQ of 200, and by 2054 an IQ of 400. After all, the performance of cars did not stop at one horsepower – the fastest cars today have more than 1000. We already see a parallel to this today with computers doing arithmetic thousands, if not millions of times faster than humans, and beating the best chess and Go players in the world. Our imaginary farmer has clearly driven quite a bit of his tree crown across the threshold of his barn already.

Examples of what AI can do

It is hardly worth writing a list of industries or fields in which AI is gaining ground. It would be far too long. It would be like listing industries in the past that would benefit from electricity or the Internet.

As often before, however, there is a big difference in how *fast* things go in different companies and different industries, but the trend is clear-cut and inevitable. Just to mention one example, I am sure anyone would love a really talented butler who knew us inside out and could predict our desires and needs almost before they even enter our mind. I certainly would. God knows, I could use one! My electronic dream computer, which, by the way, is extremely friendly and polite, makes bookings and orders for me and generally takes care of trips, shopping, and a large number of other practical things in my life, which I would much rather be free of and happen to be really bad at (according to personality tests, I am a geek). At the same time, my digital butler can be proactive and suggest different things or remind me of enquiries and questions I have not answered, and suggest options I will find interesting. Wouldn't that be lovely?

Yes, it would, and therefore we will soon get there – we already have quite a few precursors.

Another fascinating application is automatic hypothesis generation. AI has proved to be phenomenally fast at reading through thousands of scientific research reports and looking for useful ideas. In some cases, and in next to no time, a computer can achieve what would take a team of scientists decades to achieve. Yet another example of how parts of the farmer's tree crown are well beyond the threshold of the barn. Accordingly, in 2014, Watson was given the task of reading abstracts of 186 000 scientific papers from before 2003 to come up with a proposal for how to activate our previously described protein p53 that curbs the spread of cancer. Watson came up with proposals for nine different processes, seven of which turned out to work. In this case we have a combination of extreme speed-reading and a kind of intuition that really kicks ass.

Here is another example. AI computers have turned out to be fairer than humans when marking exams. In many situations they are also far better than doctors at diagnosing diseases, because diagnosis is largely based on how many similar or related cases have been encountered. In some cases, computers can also outperform people as advisers: for example, in the context of helping with homework (a kind of EdTech – educational technology) or automating legal procedures (RegTech – regulatory technology). They are also very adept in many financial procedures, such as trading on stock exchanges. This is part of FinTech – financial technology. Use of AI in RegTech and especially FinTech is already considerably widespread.

So, AI will continue to gain ground in all sorts of areas and, if you believe that you will not be specifically affected, you may have to think again. I did anyway. When we founded Nordic Eye, my view was that there was no way the work of venture capitalists could be a relevant area for AI. No. There was no darned computer that could do our job! But I was at least partly wrong. In fact, AI *can* tackle some of it. It turned out that AI is incredibly efficient at selecting the start-up companies that will go on to achieve most growth and become most valuable. Thus, as I write, we are working on implementing AI as a supplement to our own work.

Intelligence amplification

At Nordic Eye, when we collaborate with AI computers, you might call us centaurs – those legendary creatures from Greek mythology that are half-human and half-horse. Skilled riders are familiar with the sensation of horse and rider becoming one, just as a musician becomes one with his or her orchestra, and a racing driver with his or her car. When that same fusion can take place with AI computers, we will achieve what is referred to as IA – intelligence amplification. The point is that precisely because human intelligence and AI are very different, by combining the two we can achieve an overall intelligence that is stronger than either the human or the AI alone. The combination of human intelligence and AI is powerful.

In the future, many of us will probably be assisted in every possible way by intelligent machines that will help us when we are in trouble: when a doctor makes a wrong diagnosis; when a lawyer overlooks a precedent from a relevant court case; when a scientist disregards some studies; or when a stock trader is on the point of making a dumb deal. Or the twit who falls asleep in the fast lane.

IoT – nerve fibres for the mechanical world

Founded in 1900, Carnegie Mellon University in Pennsylvania is an acclaimed research university. In 1982, David Nichols was sitting in the university's computer science department, longing for a cold cola. But the cola vending machine was far away and frequently empty – and even if it was not empty, the cans of cola were often lukewarm. In Nichols' opinion, there was no need for such a situation. So, he enlisted a couple of friends to help him create a program that could monitor the lights on the machine, which indicated whether there were any cans of cola in it and – via some sophisticated shortcuts – whether the cans of cola had been in the machine long enough to get cold. They then gave everyone with access to ARPANET (the forerunner of the Internet, to which 300 computers were connected at the time) access to information about the cans of cola in the machine. Consequently, without Nichols and his friends being aware of it, the cola vending machine was probably the first thing in the IoT.

In 2017, there were 8.5 billion things associated with the IoT, and at the time of writing there are probably approximately 30 billion. After the cola vending machine, a long period of time passed, during which there was increasing discussion about the possibilities of creating a network of things that could communicate with each other without human intervention, but the technology did not exist, and maybe we did not fully foresee the potential. For a long time, it was mostly just talk, partly also because the sensors that were required were too large, expensive, and unreliable. Added to this was the fact that the Internet's fourth protocol, Ipv4, only had about 4.3 billion Internet addresses, which was not even enough for one connected thing, such as a computer or phone, per capita in the world.

However, when the demand for smartphones and later applet computers exploded, the sensors quickly became much cheaper and much better. So did quite small specialised chips that facilitated edge computing: in other words, small calculation algorithms at the end of the digital nerve fibres. It can make the systems faster and more dependable. For example, it would be both risky and slow if a car's automatic distance control or wake-up system for sleeping twits were to be run on computers on the other side of the globe.

At the same time, the introduction of the sixth version of the Internet protocol – Ipv6 – in summer 2017 means that now there are plenty of unique addresses on the way for all the things we would like to see connected to one another. In fact, this protocol has enough Internet addresses to connect approximately (wait for it!) 600 000 000 000 000 000 000 000 different things to the Internet. And that is not the total number. That is for every single square millimetre of the Earth's surface.

That's huge. Moreover, that means that every human being on Earth could now, in principle, own billions of objects that were connected to the Internet. In practice, we are on the way to achieving a trillion (1 000 000 000 000) digital sensors in the world. In terms of connecting some of these, International Data Corporation, a market intelligence company, estimated that worldwide technology spending on the IoT would have a compound annual growth rate of 13.6% over the 2017–2022 period. However, since unit prices of the connected devices fall rapidly, most estimates put IoT unit growth rate at approximately 15–20% per year.

24. **The annual growth rate in the number of Internet-connected (IoT) devices is 15–20%.**

To put it in a different way, we are on the point of supplying the mechanical world with billions of new nerve fibres.

Billions of IoT in operation globally, 2015–2025 (estimate)

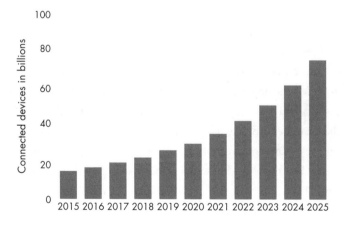

But what 'things'?

IoT is spreading everywhere. For example, today we already use chips for labelling domestic animals. In addition, today there are about 200 sensors in new cars, and 60–100 in the slightly older ones, and given that there are just over one billion cars on the streets, the number of sensors in this context reaches the 100+ billion mark. To the extent that cars and their data streams get connected to the Internet, the IoT universe will expand substantially. For example, the sensors can exchange information on how drivers drive for the purpose of training autopilot systems. Sensors can also inform the workshop and the manufacturer about the technical condition of the cars and, in the event of an accident, send a message to the emergency despatch centre, informing them how serious it is. Insurance companies can offer cheaper insurance policies if you agree to have your driving tracked (and maybe if you accept zero coverage if you drive too fast).

IoT will also play a major role in so-called life tracking, in which we utilise sensors to follow our own lifestyle and state of health. Furthermore, it can be used for predictive maintenance, so machines get serviced when they need it – neither before nor after. Many experts expect that this alone will make a significant contribution to the streamlining of our industry.

An even larger IoT market in our world is retail, where the products on the shelves are equipped with RFID chips or some such, partly to create a real-time overview of flow of goods, and partly to facilitate the unstaffed operation of shops. An RFID is a non-battery chip that automatically sends an echo back with a code if you direct an electronic signal at it. In 2018, Nordic Eye invested in such a company. The idea is that the customer installs an app that can disable the chip on a given product when the customer pays for it with his or her smartphone. Once the item is paid for, the customer can take it out of the shop without triggering an alarm. The future of retailing probably also means much greater use of vending machines, like those we know from the world of cold beverages – just smarter. This will save on both space and labour costs, and it will reduce the risk of theft. When robots also have the task of filling the shelves, the design of shops will change and turn into something like a huge vending machine: a gigantic physical sales robot.

IoT can also be incorporated into intelligent homes or smart homes. Light, heating, air conditioning, security, and media/entertainment can interact and report to enhance user-friendliness and convenience, and to act in a more environmentally friendly way. One example is Google's Latitude doorbell, which rings with a different sound, depending on which person is approaching the front door. For some reason it makes me think of the song 'One Way Out' by one of my favourite groups, The Allman Brothers Band. 'Ain't but one way out baby, and Lord I just can't go out the door. Cause there's a man down there, might be your man, I don't know.' Latitude would have given the nervous man a clear answer.

Within the health sector, the potential of IoT is also extremely great: for example, to measure how patients are or where exactly the relevant medicine for a specific patient is located in the organisation etc. And there will be a rapidly increasing market for the likes of jewellery and toothbrushes that will check your lifestyle and health indicators, and display them on your smartphone, which will then compare them with statistics and tips from the Internet – cf. our investment in the smart jewellery company, Bellabeat.

The agricultural sector has wasted no time, and today uses IoT in the context of monitoring drought, crop growth, spread of diseases among plants, nutrient content in the soil, and much more besides. Overall, the technology facilitates more precise fertilisation, less waste, increased crop yield, etc. In particular, IoT is an essential ingredient in precision farming, in which via detailed optimisation the yield per soil unit is massively increased.

Incidentally, one interesting aspect of IoT is the fact that because there are sensors in the things, they will be easy to lease and share in the new sharing economy, which we will look at later in this book.

Big data = big deal

Data is sometimes referred to as 'the oil of our time'. It will play at least as crucial a role in the global development of the decades to come as oil did following the invention of the combustion engine. People with oil often made money. Going forward, increasingly it will be people with data that get rich. From the 1940s to the 1970s we had the Seven Sisters – seven huge oil companies, which together controlled most of the oil trade. Now we have seven companies that control a massive amount of electronic data. I am talking about Facebook, Apple, Amazon, Google, Baidu, Alibaba, and Tencent. And on the stock exchange, the seven data sisters have now clearly overtaken the seven oil sisters.

But what does the term mean? Putting it simply, big data differs from more traditional data concepts in the following ways:

- It is often based on so-called data exhaust: data that was not primarily created with the intention of analysing it – but which is now analysed anyway.
- It uses continuous, rather than periodical, analysis.
- It follows all relevant data instead of selected representative sample data.
- It includes not only text but also speech, sound, image, movement, temperature, direction, location, speed, etc. – often collected via IoT.
- It is capable of pattern recognition, so can extrapolate where data is missing and simulate projections of even very complex processes – often via AI.

Please note that this description of big data refers to both AI and IoT. You see, these three technologies constitute a trinity – let us call it the IoT, big data, and AI 'power triangle'. This trinity is hugely powerful and, in addition, self-stimulating. This is so because, together with IoT, big data is crucial for the development of AI, precisely because intelligent machines learn mainly by reviewing as much data as possible. The algorithms can learn things by themselves, in the sense that they can extract things from datasets and use the patterns they find to further refine the work. Even when there are patterns that no human has discovered.

The IoT, big data, and AI trinity

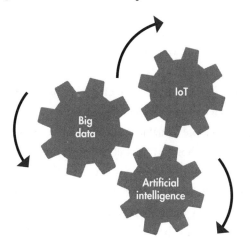

The amount of online data is growing exponentially, and as I write this, adding up all the numbers I see, the impression I get is that the annual trend growth for digital data creation is approximately 40%, for storing it is 10%, and for analysing it is around 20%. So, let's derive at least one basic rule from this:

25. **The amount of digital data in the world doubles** every **two years.**

At the same time, the most expert companies and researchers develop tools that make it far easier and faster to retrieve valuable information from these very large datasets. This means that the value of the same data increases even faster than its volume, and that is a crucial argument when explaining not only why the new seven data sisters are worth thousands of billions of dollars, but also why the appraisals of some companies in the sector look extraordinary, given that they are mainly based on renting apartments and a taxi service.

Let me give you one of an infinite number of examples of the value of big data. If you have a business, you want to let people know when it is open. People need to be able to see it on Google. So, you can fill out an online form on Google My Business with the information. But, if you do not do so, and simply write it on your website, Google can easily find the information and run it anyway. But – and this is where it gets really out to lunch – Google can also run information about how busy that business is at different times of the day. It collects this information by looking at the GPS to find out where people's Android smartphones are and when.

Google, Facebook, and other companies with many users and large data streams have an obvious networking effect in the sense that the more other users there are, the more valuable it becomes for each user. In the case of Facebook that goes without saying, but Google learns from people's search activity etc. and therefore the more it is used, the better it becomes as a product. For example, when Google offers to translate what you are reading, it can only do so by means of very large amounts of data. The fact that they often run the first and best answer to your search at the top is because that was what other people ended up perusing in the same search. The same goes for the ability to decode your psychological profile by trawling through all the text you produce. More than 100 billion monthly searches via Google provide a tremendous amount of information.

Big data has countless other applications. An extreme example is finding out the state of the global economy – today! I mean, right here and now. For example, did China's economy grow *today*? We will come closer to that kind of overview as we can combine a variety of real-time statistics such as power consumption, e-commerce orders, credit flows, etc. Another example is the way retailers follow real-time consumer trends and, for instance, predict how they may be locally affected by weather forecasts, sports events, and so forth. All this is yet another reason why the value of data is increasing. So, it is not surprising that in recent years, a company like McKinsey, whose employees are not known for their lack of skill, has invested heavily in acquiring rights to data streams.

In reality, what we now replicate with the IoT, big data, AI trinity is biological life and ecosystems. We create artificial brains via AI, sensors via IoT, nervous systems via the Internet, and prerequisites for pattern recognition via big data. Is it not a fascinating thought and a privilege that we who are alive now are getting an opportunity to be part of this? I think so anyway. What is equally exciting is the fact that this development of artificial brains, sensory organs, and nerve cells is taking place as we develop a completely new ecosystem of artificial species. I mean robots.

Smart robots – the new ecosystem

Imagine you are throwing a party at the weekend. You visit Amazon and purchase the basic robot you need, including the necessary extra features. You then visit Amazon's app store and download bartender and waiter apps for your new member of staff. Enjoy the party. But wait! Wouldn't it be fun if it had an arm with a corkscrew at the end? So how do you get hold of that for tonight? Oh yes, you download the 3D description and get it printed in metal in the 3D printshop around the corner. The robot you just bought is versatile and can service your guests: one that can be assembled like Lego bricks and to which you can add software apps like a smartphone.

Sure, it is not on the market yet, but it will not take long. And the multitude of functionalities that robots already have, and the multitude of tasks they can carry out, are quite overwhelming. For example, even today, robots take care of about 80% of the manual work involved in manufacturing cars, which explains the huge robot cluster around Munich. But there are also robot clusters in the likes of Bristol, Delft, Hamburg, Massachusetts, and Odense, as well as in various locations in Japan, South Korea, and India.

Altogether, thousands of technicians in such places are working to create a huge mechanical ecosystem, which I cannot help but think of as a counterpart to the world of insects. But with two major differences. Firstly, manmade insects can be much bigger than biological ones. Secondly, ultimately, they can become cleverer than humans. By the way, in 2018 Nordic Eye invested in the third-largest robot company in Denmark: Blue Ocean Robotics.

What controls the robots?

It goes without saying that robots must have instructions or have the capacity to train themselves. The first method – giving them instructions – consists of a rule-defined language written in codes, and is quite a common control system on digital devices. This is what the typical robot in a car factory, a robot arm riveted to the floor, uses.

An important technology in the industry is LiDAR sensors, which are not only used in robots, but also in autonomous cars. LiDAR stands for Light Detection And Ranging, and it emits lasers at all angles to create a virtual 3D map of the surroundings around a given LiDAR system to ensure its efficient, safe navigation.

Over the past decades, automated guided vehicles (AGVs) have been used increasingly to move things around in warehouses and factories. Their more sophisticated big brothers are AMRs or autonomous mobile robots. The principal difference is that AGVs follow fixed routes, which are usually indicated by wires or magnets embedded in the floor or ground. Think of them as trains. Conversely, think of AMRs as autonomous cars: in other words, they navigate intelligently in surroundings that are complex and varied. They do this with the use of sensors and smart user interface, and software for robot operating systems.

The other method for controlling robots is AI. Here we teach them to teach themselves the process in question, or we give them a pre-specified set of rules as a basis for further learning. The really cool thing about this type of digital learning, which is stored in the robot's 'brain', is the fact that what the robot acquires via a single transfer can then be learned by thousands of other robots in minutes via the transfer of the code, which the robot has automatically generated during the learning process. Imagine that your Swedish friend learns to juggle eight balls while speaking French, and that in no time at all these skills can be transferred to you and 1000 other people. We cannot do this. But robots can.

Finally, we can simply show the robot visually or physically how to perform a given job, after which it can repeat the process. In fact, you can already programme your own robotic process automation (RPA) by using applications such as Workflow and IFTTT.com, which stands for 'If-This-Then-That'.

Cobots and multiplicity

Whereas, for instance, the robot cluster in Munich concentrates mainly on fully automated robots, most of the robot companies in Odense focus on robots that cooperate flexibly with people, often implemented via personal service of the robot or reinforcement learning.

Cobots are robots that can interact with humans. They can be robots in factories that help with selected tasks, or robots that help us with household tasks: for example, cleaning, laying the table, etc. In this context we can use supervised learning. For example, a tradesman gets hold of a robot arm and lets it carry out a process, so it can acquire the tradesman's tacit knowledge – the unwritten skills.

Telepresence and teleoperation

Telepresence means sitting somewhere in the world and controlling a robot somewhere else, and using its microphone, camera, and speakers to communicate with others. Or, to put it another way, it is a mobile machine that can see and hear, and make video conferences.

Human teleoperation is a situation in which a person remotely controls a robot. The most familiar example is a remotely controlled robot that treats, or even operates on, a sick person – for example, because the person is a long way from a good hospital. But you can also have teleoperation without telepresence. One example is the doctor who performs an operation on a patient right in front of him using a robot to gear down hand movements, thereby minimising the effects of shaking. The laparoscopy robot Vecloc developed by Blue Ocean Robotics is one such robot. Robots are much better than humans at laser operations on eyes, for example, for long or near sightedness. If I have to have to have something done to my eyes, I'll take a robot, thank you very much.

And then of course there are drones, which most of us probably perceive of as remote-controlled or programmed driverless aircraft or helicopters. But drones can also be ships or submarines. However, so far, in practice they are mainly flying machines. Until recently, approximately 90% of drone turnover has been military. But, with drones becoming much more user-friendly and affordable, the situation is changing. The latest quadcopters are cheap, they can stabilise themselves in moderate wind, they can find their own way home, fly around obstacles, and are easy to control. In the world of business, demand is increasing, particularly in the fields of construction, agriculture, insurance, and infrastructure inspection. There are even drones that can lift fire hoses to the top of high-rise buildings.

One of the reasons for the major breakthrough in terms of drones for the private market is the same we witnessed vis-à-vis IoT: the fact that the price of sensors has dropped rapidly and the sensors are better quality – thanks to the huge sales of smartphones, which contain these sensors. Another reason is that, in 2005, groups of scientists discovered that a drone with four vertical rotors can navigate incredibly efficiently simply by adjusting the speed of the various rotors, so you do not need the likes of moving wing flaps etc. And a third reason was the availability of microprocessors, making it possible to create a computer the size of a packet of cigarettes.

Two of the major development areas in drone technology are autonomy and swarming. Autonomy allows you to send a drone on a mission, which it then tackles without a human being having to observe or control it. For example, drones are used to make express deliveries of drugs and tissue samples etc. to hospitals in Switzerland.

Swarming gets a group of drones to work as a team. Possible applications include entertainment: in other words, drone shows, which we can already see in Cirque du Soleil. Another application is military operations –a combination that in the future a low-tech adversary will find it almost impossible to outwit. Armed military drones with significant firepower cost less than one hundredth of a manned fighter and no pilot's life needs to be put in danger. Modern robot-based guns can almost instantly shoot back in response to a surprise attack thanks to extremely fast sense–think–act configurations.

Another example is personal drones, which, for instance, automatically follow and film their owner or friends when they are up to something fun. This is already pretty common. I myself have a DJI Mavic drone, which I have used to film the likes of water skiing. It can fly right next to the water-skier and film in amazing quality. Farmers can have drones that automatically take off each morning to take photos of the condition of their crops. And of course, there are countless applications in industry, construction, border control, etc.

For a long time, the development of robots suffered from Moravec's Paradox. This took its name from the robotics researcher Hans Moravec and is all about the fact that it turned out to be relatively (OK – very relatively) easy to make robots that were good at chess and other cognitively challenging activities, but it was very difficult to invest them with even fair motor skills. They could not walk down stairs or move in hilly terrain. In general, they tottered around like children who had just embarked on the difficult process of learning to walk. However, this is no longer the case, because now robots can move smoothly, quickly, and with great agility. Atlas, Boston Dynamics' latest robot, uses LiDAR sensors to capture objects in the environment and obstructions en route, and it can move about on any type of surface, even in snow and sleet where it is slippery. Reinforcement learning has facilitated the development of a sense of balance in Atlas, which is being increasingly refined.

This means that, in the years to come, we will see an overwhelming diversity of robots, with many different specialist skills, including versatile robots that can easily be programmed to tackle a huge variety of tasks.

Smart remote control – the magic wands of reality

Who wouldn't like a magic wand like those in the Harry Potter stories? The future will not exactly be like that, but in some respects it will not be far off. Why? Because there is a huge demand – both latent and acknowledged – for making things happen remotely, simply by pressing a virtual button on the likes of your smartphone.

For example, hotels have started to introduce a service where you can download an electronic key to your hotel room on your smartphone or smartwatch, so you do not even have to check in. Similarly, smartphones can be used to make payments and control everything from television to light, sound, and heating in your home, garage doors, and a myriad of other things, such as releasing security tags in self-service shops while the item gets paid for online. Personally, I actually think that any remote control in your life that is not controlled by your smartphone is basically one remote control too much (with car keys as a possible exception). In other words, it ought to be possible to operate pretty much everything with your smartphone. And that is the direction in which things are heading. Our smartphones are becoming a kind of counterpart to magic wands, whereby we avoid countless other remote controls, keys, and credit cards.

Quantum computers – billions of times faster

Since the 1980s, scientists have been working on building quantum computers, or quantum computing, which, as the name suggests, calculates by utilising certain phenomena from quantum physics. And now they are becoming a reality, though still barely commercial quality and not yet on a large scale. When that happens, they will revolutionise many industries.

And that day is not far off. IBM engineers have proposed measuring the efficiency of quantum computers in so-called quantum volume, which measures what is actually produced by the notoriously unstable quantum bits in these new computers. In 2017, IBM achieved a quantum volume of 4. In 2018 it was 8. And in 2019, their new Q System One had achieved 16. Accordingly, they believe that there will be a Moore's Law for quantum computers, in which the quantum volume will double every year, which is now called Rose's Law. However, this view has been challenged by Google, which is also developing quantum computers. In December 2018, scientists at Google ran quantum calculations, which they could simulate on a standard laptop. Then, a month later, they did a new quantum calculation with an improved version. Now they needed a more powerful desktop computer to simulate it. But a third quantum calculation done yet another month later was so powerful that standard computers in their building couldn't simulate it; they had to request time on Google's giant server network mobilising millions of processors to do it. This has led to the term 'Neven's Law', which says that the progress in quantum computing is 'doubly exponential' – meaning that the exponent is also growing exponentially, along the lines of 2, 4, 64, 16 777 216, etc. (the next number in the example has 36 digits and the following has 216). This leads to the following tentative law:

26. The number of possible qubits in scalable quantum computer architecture may double every year according to Rose's Law, but it might also be double exponential according to Neven's Law.

As I write this, it's too early to say whether Rose or Neven will be closest to the truth. However, in September 2019, a Google quantum computer spent 200 seconds doing a calculation would have taken the most t advanced classical computer approximately 10 000 years. The explanation for the strength of quantum computers is chiefly based on the technical difference between bits and qubits. Traditional computers like your PC, Linux, or MacBook use bits. Bits have two states, namely 0 and 1, and the number of states grows exponentially with the number of bits: 1 bit has 2 values, 4 bits have 16 values, 8 bits have 256 values, and so on. For example, a 32-bit computer has 2 147 483 647 values.

In the 1980s we all listened to what we called chiptune music, which had 8 bits and therefore only 256 different sounds (2^8). Today, instead, we usually listen to 16-bit music, which due to the explosive increase in value has 65 536 different sounds (2^{16}). So, a huge difference has emerged in terms of both quality and options. Of course, the explosive increase in value becomes much more extreme when the number of bits increases.

For 64-bit applications like iTunes, Excel, and Spotify, which you have probably installed on your computer, the number of different values is no less than 9 223 372 036 854 775 807. Mind-blowing. But compared to quantum computers, it is still like comparing a mole hill to Mount Everest. You see, Q qubits, which is what quantum computers use, are not binary, but can exist as 0 or 1 or both at the same time. That is why quantum computers can store much more information and, for some types of tasks, count much faster than traditional computers will ever be able to.

An example. We need to find the two numbers that have to be multiplied to arrive at the number 15. A traditional computer can answer that question in a matter of nanoseconds. But what if it has to find the two numbers that need to be multiplied to arrive at a number with 617 digits? This would take the biggest traditional computers in the world up to a billion years to answer. Conversely, a quantum computer will be able to do this in up to 100 seconds: in other words, 315 360 000 000 000 (315 billion) times faster.

This has big implications. For example, quantum computers may render much modern encryption useless, since a quantum computer may quickly solve all the computer science codes that currently make Internet banking secure. The same may apply to blockchains in their current form. One large-scale quantum computer might be able to mine cryptocurrencies with great ease. This is due to the fact that both blockchains and online security systems are based on making an astronomical number of calculations in order to break their code. With their limited power, traditional computers have to try every single combination one by one, which can take ages. That is the task that has to be solved, but the idea counts for nothing if you have a computer that can carry out the astronomical number of calculations in seconds.

Quantum computers are therefore extremely powerful but can only utilise their enormous capacity for beating traditional computers in certain areas. If you want to browse the Internet or watch a film on Netflix, quantum computers will probably not be better than traditional computers. However, if you want to calculate how very complex protein molecules may fold in 3D space – one of the most demanding computing tasks today – quantum computers may make a huge difference to the benefit of biochemical science, healthcare, and more.

The mammoth technology giants and military institutions etc. will probably be the first users of large-scale quantum computers: for example, in the fields of electronic warfare, AI, and medical research.

IBM, Google, Microsoft, Intel, and some small-scale players are probably at the forefront and, even though the technical difficulties are still huge, progress in recent years indicates that commercially useful quantum computers are no longer a distant dream. Even today, via the Internet, you can access the likes of IBM's 20 quantum-bit quantum computer. As I write this, Google's latest quantum computer has 72 quantum bits, while IBM's very latest has 50. Microsoft's does not have as many, but, on the other hand, seems to be more stable. A target of 200 quantum bits is probably not unattainable in the coming years, and with 200 quantum bits you can evaluate more states than there are atoms in the universe.

The private sector is optimistic that we will see quantum computers on a large scale somewhere between 2025 and 2040. The US National Institute of Standards and Technology (NSIT) estimates that useful quantum computers will become a reality by 2030, though with a price of (wait for it!) $1 billion each. Conversely, some people believe that we will never be able to develop and maintain large-scale quantum computers. But in my opinion, like so many other things that humankind would 'never' be able to develop, quantum computers seem to be a widespread practical reality in the foreseeable future.

VR – dream worlds for real

Some of the clearest examples of computer technology's magic will stem from VR, the most familiar and widespread examples so far being computer games. But many more are on the way. We will not all get to visit Mars, take part in the Olympic Games, or watch the FIFA World Cup Final from the ecstatic grandstands, but VR can get us pretty close. For example, in the entertainment category there are great options in the fields of games, concert experiences, films, museums, and tourism. And VR can also be used for things that have a major influence on society. For instance, it can help mechanics and engineers to locate problems in complex machines, and in the military VR facilitates training for situations that would be extremely expensive, dangerous, and complex to simulate. It has already been used for a long time in pilot training.

The technology can save lives, save huge sums of money by reducing machine downtime, and enhance soldiers' opportunities for successful action and survival. In building projects, VR can be used to verify hypotheses about the safety of a building and to reduce the contractor's costs in the event of building defects. It can also be used by estate agents for showings.

AR – Pokémon GO on steroids

AR is strongly correlated with VR. The obvious difference, though, is that AR extends reality, while VR creates a new or simulated reality. Here is an example of the difference. VR means you can visit a furniture shop in your home and see its range, as if you were actually in the shop. AR enables you to see what the various furniture from the shop would look like in your own living room.

In other words, AR is a combination of actual reality and computer-generated data. For that reason, AR is also referred to as 'enhanced' or 'expanded' reality, since the technology combines the real world with virtual graphics and audio.

Another example could be a sports star who, thanks to AR, seems to be physically taking part in an interview on the biggest TV channel in his or her home country, while the star in question is in fact sitting in a changing room on the other side of the world. A Belgian TV channel actually managed to do this during the 2018 World Cup in Russia. But the most famous example of AR to date is probably Pokémon Go, which took the world by storm in the summer of 2016. In the future, we can imagine AR games that will be even more outlandish.

AR can also revolutionise industries. In the retail sector it may be used for better presentation, for example, of custom-made products such as motorcycles and cars, which appear as full-size graphics before the customer's very eyes with a variety of colours, wheel trims, and interiors. An exclusively online retailer will be able to create a 3D shop, in which the customer can move around and even try on a new shirt. This will result in more sales and fewer returns. Another example might involve studying the product on your smartphone and getting in-depth informative labelling and some stories about the product. In other words, the product, as it were, speaks directly to the customer – a totally new form of branding.

AR can also be used in tourism. Imagine exploring a city, where you can see the buildings as they looked 500 years ago. Or walking around wearing a pair of specs that display speech bubbles with translated text when someone speaks to you in a foreign language. AR can also enable people to feel their immediate environment. One example is systems that allow a fighter pilot to feel the overload of a wing by physical pressure on his arm. In the future, fighter pilots will probably be replaced by drones, but AR will only increase.

It is difficult to say whether VR or AR will end up being the most important of the two technologies. So far, VR has attracted the most headlines, but AR is moving fast. AR also offers great opportunities for upskilling, enhancing people's professional skills through training that can, for example, improve safety and reduce error rate.

Ambient user experience – the frictionless total experiences

As bandwidth grows and computers become increasingly powerful, our IT products will also provide us with better user experiences. However, although, for instance, Apple and Microsoft have come a long way, we have not yet succeeded in making the transitions between various devices entirely smooth and almost imperceptible. When you leave your computer on your desk and continue working on your phone on your way home or at a meeting, it still often feels a bit like starting from scratch.

Ambient user experience is the term for a state in which this is no longer the case. A state in which you hardly notice that you are changing from one device to another, because the experience is designed to feel the same and is constantly optimised. It is immaterial whether you are working on your computer, your tablet, your phone, your smartwatch, or any other wearable device, such as a piece of jewellery that checks your pulse or spectacles with a built-in camera. Clearly, the likes of Apple have come a long way in this regard, but there is still room for improvement, and Gartner Group, a leading research and consultancy company, has heralded ambient user experience as one of the strongest technology trends for the coming years. It is something users are obviously demanding.

It requires a strong device mesh for all the potentially relevant devices to interrelate. In addition to the items already mentioned, it also applies to domestic electronics: for example, white goods, household appliances, cars, and a variety of other devices. It also means that their various cordless connections must be efficient – a task where 5G can play a part.

Another aspect of ambient user experience is the option of incorporating screens and speakers into everyday objects, thereby providing us with 'living' wallpapers and house façades and all sorts of other features. That way it will not only be dedicated technology gizmos that can provide us with digital experiences, but also our surroundings in general.

Finally, let me add that, just as there is a strong IoT, big data, and AI trinity, I also foresee a trinity composed of VR, AR, and ambient user experience.

The perceptual trinity

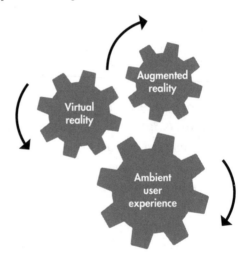

Cyberattack – crime-as-a-service and lots more besides

The intense technological development that leads to so many benefits also entails a host of new problems, including screen dependency, which turns some people, especially young men, into total screen zombies. While for many others it creates a kind of separation anxiety in relation to their smartphones.

Another problem is the new forms of serious cybercrime that accompany technological development. This is partly to do with all the information that is available, because today our digital activities are already so much part of our lives. The story of Robin Sage, a young, attractive woman who worked as an analyst specialising in cybercrime in the US Navy, serves as a good illustration.

Soon after her appointment, Robin Sage began sending friend requests to other people working in the same and/or related sectors from her profiles on LinkedIn, Facebook, and Twitter. She quickly made many contacts: for example, the Supreme Military Chief of the US Army (Chairman of the Joint Chiefs of Staff) and the then National Security Agency Information Manager, and leading figures from the largest military weapon suppliers. Soon, she also began to receive job offers and invitations to give lectures, and she was even sent confidential material to review and comment on. All in all, things were really going well for Robin Sage and her career.

The only snag about all this was that she did not actually exist. Sage was invented by a security consultant, Thomas Ryan, to investigate how easy it was to access confidential information through social media. According to Ryan, it was not a difficult task, and he had not been trying that hard. Robin Sage's photo was that of a lesser-known porn actress. Ryan had given her the same address as the security firm Blackwater. And Robin Sage is even the name of a major annual military exercise in North Carolina. Nevertheless, no one was suspicious. On the contrary. Everyone gladly shared important, even confidential, work-related information with Robin and, what is more, it was people who worked in the field of security on a daily basis. The story of Robin appears in the book *Future Crimes* (2016) by Marc Goodman, who has devoted his career to the field of digitally funded crime. Goodman is worried, and the book makes a convincing argument for the fact that, cognitively speaking, we are lagging far behind when it comes to understanding the seriousness of digital threats.

The new stalker economy

Our own openness and naivety are one problem. Another is the inconceivable amount of data about us that digital platforms collect. (If we were even to hazard an estimate, we could say that now, every 10 minutes generate as much information as the first 10 000 generations of people.) The reality is that we have ended up in a stalker economy where we believe, say, that the agreement is that we get free apps in return for living with some targeted ads – ads for apps.

In a way, information sharing is good and an expression of a huge win–win situation. Given that ads are still necessary to fund the services that are free for users, they might just as well be relevant to users. Personally, I definitely think so, but problems can arise when, in return for the free apps, we provide information about where we are, our search history, our contacts, our calendar, and a lot of other personal information – and it ends up in the wrong hands.

Of course, the platforms themselves benefit from the huge quantities of information, but they also sell that information to other companies with other agendas, and, ultimately, they do not always manage to take care of it. Google and Facebook and countless others have been hacked (in 2011, Facebook explained that on a daily basis they had 600 000 compromised logins). So, the data, which we have already allowed companies to use themselves and sell, sometimes ends up in the hands of criminals. Therefore, some observers stress that the issue of the right to privacy is the central problem in the context of cyber security. In the current situation, this right is increasingly and constantly being undermined by technology: in some cases with our consent, but in many more cases without us being aware of it.

Another issue is sheer complication. Each of us frequently click 'OK' to digital agreements that we have not read. And for good reason. A study from some years ago (and the problem has only increased) showed that it would take Americans 76 working days a year to read the agreements, which on average they enter into without knowing their content. So, the simple reason we have not read them is that it is practically impossible.

That brings us to the concept of surveillance society – a situation in which all our movements are closely monitored, and the state knows how everyone uses their electronic money, where they are, etc. This is surveillance capitalism, if not a surveillance society – also based on Ziman's Law.

Digital robberies

As Marc Goodman points out in *Future Crimes,* it is no longer worth robbing a bank if you are adept at programming. It is far more effective for people with this ability to sit at home and hack you – or hack lots of other people.

Identity theft and financial crime, and stalking as well as harassment and related crimes, are also growing at an intense rate. And children are far more vulnerable to being victims of identity theft than adults. The crimes can vary in terms of seriousness, but often victims of the most vicious crimes do not only lose large sums of money, but also the social consequences can be disastrous, and many are traumatised for years or life.

Digitally competent criminals have great opportunities, and they utilise them. Even at the most serious end of the scale. A large number of terrorist attacks in the past 10 years have thus been funded partly by hacking and digital credit card fraud: for example, in the form of phishing. We have already witnessed hacker attacks, in which more than a million people simultaneously had their personal information stolen. Then there is the other worry. The fact that, unlike physical bombs, digital weapons in the form of viruses and other malware can be used over and over again and do not disappear once they have been triggered.

According to research conducted in 2018 by the security company Bromium, illicit and illegal online markets generated $860 billion a year globally, theft of trade secrets generated $500 billion, data trading $160 billion, crimeware-as-a-service $1.6 billion, and ransomware $1 trillion. That added up to $3.6 trillion, or some 4.5% of the global economy, although with double counting the overall result might be lower.

However, the previous year (2017), a report by Cybersecurity Ventures set the figure at $3 trillion, while estimating that it would grow to $6 trillion by 2021, because they factored in more effects. For example, one should not just count the fraudsters' earnings, but also what it costs to protect yourself against them and the wasted time once you have been attacked. It also includes the fact that, according to some estimates, we are approaching 8% of global GDP – far more than we spend globally on education, which is almost 5%. It might be that bad.

Several experts, including Ondrej Vlcek, Chief Operations Officer at Avast, one of the largest IT security companies in the world, points out that we are witnessing a war between machines. The good as well as the evil will mobilise their strongest resources within the field of AI – and one day quantum computers – and the attacks will be autonomous, independently carried out by machines that will make decisions themselves along the way. Humans will simply supervise the processes while computers battle against each other.

The consequence of all this is that while cybercrime is big business, so is cyber security. In 2017 it took an average of 203 days before a digital security breach was detected. Greg Edwards, Chief Executive Officer of the cyber security company WatchPoint, points out that before long it will often take a mere matter of seconds for companies that embrace the opportunities that lie in cooperation between humans and AI. And some new defence software is indeed based on AI, which learns from its real-time experiences and shares that learning with users. For example, the Israeli company Deep Instinct, in which I happen to be a shareholder, has produced software which the company trained by introducing it to millions of files, some of which contained viruses and other dangerous software, and some of which did not. Accordingly, the software was able to identify viruses even before the first damage had occurred – so-called zero-day detection.

5.
THE PATH
TO INFINITE
ENERGY

People have often lacked energy sources – for heating, cooking, and all sorts of other things. Actually, when you think about it, that is pretty weird, given that the vast quantity of radioactivity in the subsoil of the earth – chiefly in the form of uranium, thorium, and potassium – contributes substantially to the fact that 99% of the soil is hotter than 1000ºC and only 0.1% – the thin crust on which we live – cooler than 100ºC. Added to that is the fact that global energy from solar radiation is about 7000 times greater than our current global consumption of energy.

Nevertheless, throughout the history of humankind, the struggle to obtain the necessary energy to sustain life has often been one of the hardest. However, this was generally due to lack of *innovation*, as when our ancestors would sometimes die of cold, lying on twigs and branches that they could have turned into a big, warming bonfire – if they had just known how to light it. In other words, there was no lack of resources; merely lack of the technology for using them. Once again, this illustrates that the ultimate resource is always innovation.

Together with the use of animals for transport and the like, burning wood and twigs (not forgetting manure) was people's main source of energy in the Stone, Bronze, and Iron Ages. Approximately 3000 years ago, however, the Chinese began to use coal to extract iron, and directed natural emissions of natural gas through bamboo pipes so they could use it for boiling seawater and extracting salt. And, nearly 2000 years ago, in Dacia in present-day Romania, the Romans extracted oil. However, the large-scale commercialisation of oil extraction only kicked off in the mid-nineteenth century in the United States. Following that, the use of fossil fuels – both coal and gas – rose steadily throughout the world.

Fossil fuels – the culmination is approaching

Given the fact that this has been so important to our civilisation, it is interesting that some analysts believe that the use of fossil fuels will come to an end pretty soon. The following graph from the University of Utah provides an (uncertain) estimate of development in the world's total energy supply.

According to this particular estimate, we are now only around 15 years from 'peak fossil', which incidentally includes peak oil and peak gas – unfortunately followed by 'peak coal' just a few years later. However, I have to add that there is considerable disagreement among analysts about these forecasts. That said, this forecast's revolutionary development can be ascribed chiefly to three factors: (1) the fact that global population growth is slowing down; (2) we are developing new forms of energy; and (3) we are getting better at utilising the energy we consume. Just look at the graph here, which shows the development in US GDP in relation to the development in Americans' energy consumption.

Forecast for the development of the global energy supply, 2017–2050

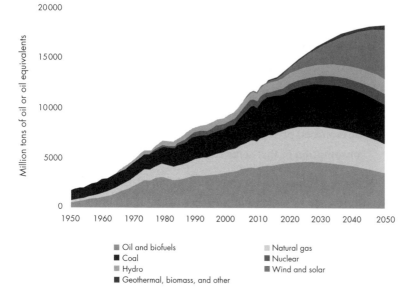

US energy consumption per unit of GDP

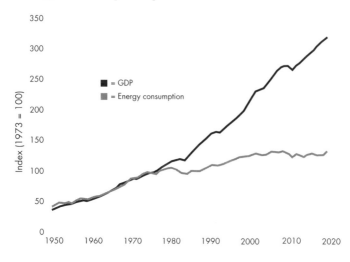

The population is growing, and wealth is increasing, while energy consumption per GDP unit is falling – and this development is expected to continue. It is not some pie-in-the-sky fantasy. The development is already well underway.

However, we should not expect that this will also lead to a drop in *global* energy consumption in the foreseeable future. This is partly due to the following rule:

27. When technological advancements result in more efficient use of resources, prices can fall, which can then lead to increased consumption of that same resource (Jevon's Paradox).

Almost anywhere in our current energy infrastructure, efficiency may continue to improve significantly. An example: our use of traditional light bulbs resulted in the loss of 99% of the original energy. However, as we change to LED, the efficiency improves approximately six-fold, and it continues to improve since networks and LEDs get ever more efficient.

The efficiency of solar panels has also been substantially streamlined and has followed Swanson's Law, which states that the price of solar modules tends to drop 20% for each doubling of cumulative shipped volume. In recent years, this has halved the cost per unit approximately every 10 years. However, neither solar cells nor LED are IT and, within the foreseeable future, they will encounter some physical limitations.

Vast, constantly growing reserves

When a peak in the global consumption of fossil fuel comes, will it be created by lack of supply or by lack of demand? For many years, as previously mentioned, people believed that the adventure would come to an end on account of lack of *supply*. Now we actually seem to be quite close to this peak fossil energy, but the reason is not that the supply will fail, but that the *demand* will, just as the Stone Age did not come to an end because we ran out of stone.

This is remarkable. But what makes the story even more amusing is that the end of the oil era is likely to happen while the reserves are almost at their highest level ever – and while the real prices are rarely low.

Let's take a look at the reserves first. This graph shows the developments in oil and gas reserves since 1980, when panic about a future depletion of oil was rife.

Proved oil and gas reserves

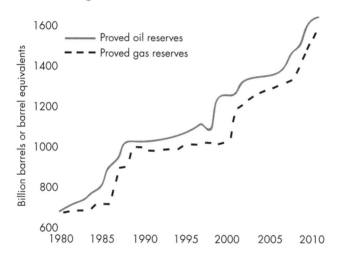

As can be seen, these reserves have increased steadily, even though we have also burned huge amounts of oil and gas.

If, as expected, production peaks in a limited number of years, my guess is that, during the subsequent period of scaling down, we will consume more or less the same as we did on the way up. If so, that means that our consumption of coal, oil, and gas will gradually de-escalate over perhaps 100 years or so, after which we will leave the vast majority of our fossil deposits in the subsoil, and never use them as fuel.

And that brings us to the issue of prices, because leaders in Saudi Arabia, Russia, the United States, and other oil-producing countries are quite clear about what is happening. They now have to live with a feeling that can be compared, say, to 10 restaurants, each of which has baked 100 beefsteaks – in other words, a total of 1000 beefsteaks – for that evening's guests, only to discover that just 500 guests are coming. As I write this, Saudi Arabia has shown an interest to list (and thereby partly sell off) their national oil company (which, by the way, was the most profitable company in the world in 2018), and the Americans are fracking oil at an unbelievable rate – they are actually expected to become net self-sufficient in oil around 2022 and then to start exporting more oil than they import. Sell, sell, sell! And the production costs of fracking are dropping.

So, the current reserves of coal, oil, and gas are vast, and larger than we will probably ever use. But, on top of that, we have methane hydrate, a combustible hydrocarbon, believed to be 2–10 times more widespread than natural gas, which means it could potentially stretch to centuries or millennia of further consumption. The Japanese, for instance, are actually experimenting with it. But it seems unlikely to me ever to become big business – we have plenty of coal, oil, and gas, for which we already have a well-developed extraction and distribution structure.

To understand what will happen as the fossil era gradually winds down, it is not a bad idea to be aware of this rule, which I have taken the liberty of formulating on the basis of research by the physicist Cesare Marchetti:

28. **The world's energy supply is undergoing an exponential shift from carbon to hydrogen, which, if it continues, will be completed by around 2150 (Marchetti's Law).**

This shift started around 1860 and, if the rule continues to hold true, it will be just about completed by about 2150.

The global shift from coal to hydrogen

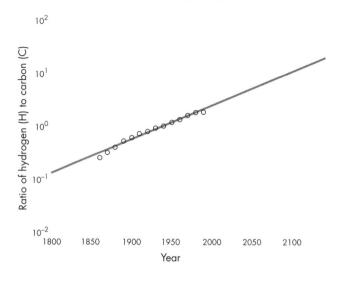

In other words, over an approximately 200-year period, humankind will implement an exponential shift from carbon to hydrogen. But do not misunderstand me. It does not necessarily mean that we will be driving around in hydrogen cars with fuel cells. What it does mean is that, unlike hydrogen, the carbon atom is not an energy source, but more akin to the branch on which the useful grapes grow. Carbon in itself does not provide the desired energy gain; during the burning process, it merely lets go of the valuable hydrogen. Carbon then reacts with oxygen to form carbon dioxide, whereas vast amounts of energy is released as hydrogen reacts with oxygen to create water. The reason for Marchetti's Law is that, while there is an immense amount of carbon per hydrogen unit (and energy unit) in wood, there is less in coal, even less in oil, and very little in natural gas. The ratio goes from 0.1 hydrogen atom per carbon atom in wood (i.e. 0.1:1) to 0.5:1 in coal and 2:1 in oil to 4:1 in natural gas. In other words, gas is approximately 40 times less carbon-intensive than wood, and eight times less carbon-intensive than coal.

Human carbon dioxide emissions since 1850

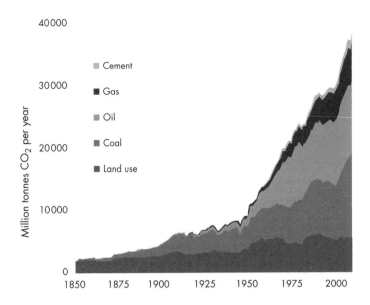

As the illustration shows, our carbon dioxide emissions have increased fairly linearly since World War II due to Jevon's Paradox more than offsetting Marchetti's Law. We reached the halfway mark through the shift from a mainly carbon economy to a mainly hydrogen economy back in 1935. And, if this trend continues, we will have a 90% hydrogen economy by 2100, when our total energy consumption will also be much greater than today, but when our consumption of fossil fuels will probably be lower than now.

According to the International Energy Agency (IEA), an energy research institute created by the 30 OECD countries, as we head towards 2040, natural gas and renewable forms of energy (mainly solar and wind) will be the fastest-growing forms of energy (in absolute figures), but energy-saving technologies will also play an important role. However, there are certain limits to how much wind energy can and, in my opinion, *should* be scaled. In 2009, the serial entrepreneur Saul Griffith estimated that if, over a period of 25 years, we were to convert 80% of global energy production (which was 16 TW) to new forms of energy, the consequences would be highly significant. So, transferred to more recent figures and something we can relate to, the following applies:

- If 2 out of 11.5 TW is to be covered by photovoltaic solar power (which generates electricity), in 25 years we need to install 80 000 km^2 of solar panels to generate electricity. That is the equivalent of 1.8 times more than the total land area of Denmark. If a further 2 out of 11.5 TW is to be covered by solar thermal panels (which heats up fluids), in 25 years we need to make just under 40 000 km^2, which amounts to just under the area of Denmark. If we put the two types of solar cells together (photovoltaic and thermal), so that solar cells constitute 4 out of 11.5 TW, or 25% of a global energy consumption of 16 TW, we will need to build just under 120 000 km^2 over 25 years. That means covering the whole of Denmark, the Netherlands, Switzerland, and North Korea entirely with solar panels.

- If a further 2 out of 11.5 TW is to be replaced by wind turbines (3 MW turbines), we will need to erect 2.6 million of them over 25 years, or alternatively 800 000 giant wind turbines such as the V-164, which can produce up to 9.5 MW. Given that the average service life of a wind turbine is approximately 25 years, we will then perpetually have to scrap and replace approximately 100 000 regular wind turbines or 25 000 giant wind turbines annually.

- If we were ultimately to convert 2 TW to nuclear power, and if each of them was about 1000–1600 MW, we would have to build between 2000 and 1250 reactors. Given that there are normally two to four reactors per nuclear power plant, this would correspond to about 700 or 800 plants.

Of course, all these figures will change in tandem with technological development, but it is interesting to see that a single nuclear power plant supplies roughly the same amount of energy as just under 3000 wind turbines, 1000 giant wind turbines, or 160 km² of solar panels – and this is without accounting for the complicating fact that sometimes the wind does not blow and the sun does not shine. In this context, however, it must be said that 160 km² of solar panels do not necessarily have to take up space and replace forests and meadows. As we will see later, it is possible to make building-integrated solar panels, such as solar-utilising roof tiles, flat roofs, walls, and even windows, so that a building actually becomes a virtual solar panel without it being immediately visible or taking up more space for that reason. Especially in the wide belt around the equator and a long way above it, and in certain places within the temperate zone, this is already starting to make economic sense.

Nuclear power – a renaissance on the way?

When it comes to nuclear power, as I write this book, there are approximately 450 nuclear reactors in the world, providing about 7% of all energy, including around 17% of all electrical power. Nuclear power is shrouded in an exceptionally apocalyptic aura, making it difficult for people to relate objectively to the technology. This is a result of a number of extremely effective campaigns – complemented by dramatic Hollywood films – at times when safety was significantly inferior to now and the issue of waste unresolved. And there have also been accidents. However, even though these accidents have led to relatively few or no fatalities, and often very minor long-term effects, they have always entailed a significant setback for nuclear power. This is unfair, because, based on the experience of more than half a century, nuclear power – even in its first, primitive versions – has proved to be the safest form of energy in the world by far. This is even though most existing nuclear power plants are based on technology that has long been superseded by something far safer.

A comprehensive study conducted by Markandya and Wilkinson showed all the fatalities – both direct and indirect – per TWh, produced by different forms of energy. Here it is:

- lignite (brown coal): 32.75 fatalities
- coal: 24.62 fatalities

- oil: 18.43 fatalities

- biomass: 4.63 fatalities

- natural gas: 2.82 fatalities

- nuclear power: 0.07 fatalities.

It is striking that the global death rate for a coal-based energy unit has been approximately 400 times greater than that for nuclear power, which was hampered by the 'safety risk'. According to some estimates, the activism against nuclear has led to something like 10 million extra fatalities.

I would also like to add that the tremendous fear of radioactive radiation in itself is unjustified. Yes, of course you can die from an overdose of radioactivity, just as you can die from falling off a ladder when attempting to install a solar panel – or from lung cancer caused by the smoke from a coal-fired power plant. But then, scientists have been struck by studies which showed that people who lived in an environment with an unusually high daily dose of radioactivity had *less* cancer than the rest of the population. This led to two interesting meta studies: reviews of the overall research on the effects of radioactivity on health. Both reports concluded that a certain daily dose of radioactivity is actually healthy and prevents cancer, and that the optimum dose was 20–100 times more than we receive on average. It sounds totally off the wall, but is probably due to the fact that radioactivity stimulates chemical error correction in DNA – although it can also *cause* errors.

Incidentally, this observation is part of a broader phenomenon called 'hormesis', in which small doses of otherwise hazardous substances or conditions can be healthy. For example, it has been discovered that small doses of pesticides can be healthy because they stimulate or train our chemical defence mechanisms. Similarly, moderate exposure to bacteria is healthy because it stimulates the immune system and prevents autoimmune diseases such as allergy. One modern recommendation, therefore, is to eat 3.5 kg of dirt per year. When I was a boy, many of my friends were instructed to wash their hands before they ate. But my parents did not tell me to, nor did I do so with my own children. Everyone needs a bit of dirt!

Moderate exposure to stress can also make us more mentally robust, just as moderate exposure to physical hardships makes us physically stronger. Yes, of course we can sustain harm or die from too *much* radioactivity, toxins, infections, stress, and physical exhaustion, but, on the other hand, we should not have too *little* of them all.

Unfortunately, our old friends the fact-resistant hedgehogs have played a significant role in the nuclear power debate. But so far, the most important *rational* arguments against nuclear power have been related to the waste issue and to the fact that it has been very expensive to build nuclear power plants, since too few were built to make it cheap.

Now, however, we are developing smaller, far safer, and much cheaper nuclear reactors, which make it likely that nuclear power will have a well-deserved renaissance – especially in Asia. For example, the old reactor designs from Chernobyl and Fukushima Daiichi have been replaced by new ones, including Toshiba's 4S (Super Safe, Small, and Simple) or Lawrence Livermore Lab's SSTAR (Small, Sealed, Transportable, Autonomous Reactor), which are also referred to as 'atomic batteries'. In addition, in the future we are likely to be able to transmute the waste into something harmless.

At the same time, much is happening on the actual fuel front. Deploying already-known technologies, we will have uranium for the following thousands of years of consumption, and if we also start extracting it from the sea, we will have enough for hundreds of thousands of years.

Thorium: enough for 100000 years of consumption

Long before then, however, we may switch to thorium. Just 1 kg of thorium contains approximately four million times more potential energy than 1 kg of coal. More or less the same applies to uranium but conventional uranium-based reactors only utilise approximately 0.5% of this energy. Sure enough, there are more recent reactor designs for uranium which can reach almost full utilisation, but it is easier with thorium, which is used in this context as part of a molten salt. The waste problem is also much less with thorium.

Imagine that the energy consumption for your entire life was produced on a machine that only left behind a quantity of waste less than the size of a golf ball. I am talking about *all* the energy you use throughout your *entire* life: for heating, air conditioning, refrigerators and freezers, car trips, train transport and air travel, energy for building homes, at work, and all the products you consume. Power and hot water. Maybe even a bit of luxury from time to time like relaxing in a sauna or swimming in a heated swimming pool. And ski lifts. *The lot.*

This would be possible if it were based solely on a golf ball of thorium, leaving an amount of waste approximately a third of that size, which means equal to, say, a walnut. This waste would turn harmless within some 300 years. In my view, if we had thorium energy today, it would be by far the safest and cleanest form of energy. Currently, Thor Energy in Norway are working on creating thorium solutions for conventional reactors. India is working on an advanced thorium reactor, which is smarter than the existing reactors, yet has many of the same problems as conventional reactors. The Danish company Seaborg Technologies is making a new type of reactor – a molten salt reactor or MSR – which will be capable of burning thorium, conventionally enriched uranium, and old nuclear waste. China is also making an MSR, and they claim they are working with thorium. But it is a military programme, so we cannot know whether they will actually use uranium instead, given that its resultant waste, unlike the waste from thorium, is suitable for nuclear weapons.

Incidentally, thorium is everywhere, and the known reserves, which can currently be mined for less than $50 per kg, are enough for 200 years. If we extract it from seawater (expected to cost approximately $200 per kg), we will have enough for 100 000 years, which we can compare with the great fossil period that, according to the likes of Marchetti's Law, started in 1850 and will probably last until about 2150 – in other words, roughly 300 years. So, there are so many arguments for a nuclear renaissance that I believe it will come about. By the way, I should also add that, if we actually do extract reactor fuel from seawater, it is a renewable form of energy, since it constantly seeps out of rocks on the ocean floor.

Nuclear fusion – the ultimate energy solution

However, the ultimate technology is nuclear fusion, and governments and private companies are now competing to get there first. In this case, the fuel is hydrogen. Hydrogen, it should be said, is element number 1, in the top left-hand corner of the periodic table, and it is also the most prevalent atom in the universe. It comes in three variants or isotopes:

- 99.98% of it consists of the stable protium (^{1}H) with one proton and one electron;

- 0.02% consists of the equally stable deuterium (^{2}H) with one proton and one electron, but also with one neutron – this is also referred to as heavy hydrogen, because the addition of the neutron adds to its weight;

- there are quite minimal amounts of tritium (^{3}H), which, as well as one proton and one electron, has two neutrons – this is why it is also called super-heavy hydrogen.

Tritium develops spontaneously in the atmosphere when hydrogen is hit by neutrons whizzing from the universe in the form of so-called cosmic radiation. The reason why it is still extremely rare in nature is that it is unstable and, with an average half-life of just about 12 years, it is transformed to helium, which is number 2 in the periodic table and the second-most prevalent atom in the world.

Today, large amounts of tritium are produced in traditional heavy water reactors. Otherwise, it can be created by bombarding lithium with neutrons. Lithium, it has to be said, has three protons, three electrons, and usually four (sometimes three) neutrons. As is obvious from its name, it is used in lithium batteries: for example, in electric cars or notebook computers like the one I am writing on. If one day we all drive electric cars, we will drown in used lithium batteries, unless we change to another type.

Now comes the interesting part. If you combine deuterium and tritium in a process of so-called nuclear fusion, the result is helium. Helium has two protons, two neutrons, and two electrons, which means that there is one neutron too many in the process, and it is ejected at tremendous speed. Together, the resultant helium and the ejected neutron weigh a mere 99.3% of what the deuterium and tritium, which it was created out of, weighed. The remaining 0.7% mass is converted into energy: cf. Einstein's famous equation $E = mc^2$. In fact, a *lot* of energy!

In other words, here we have a process that involves the most and the second-most prevalent atoms in the universe, which, incidentally, are responsible for well-nigh 100% of all energy generation in the universe: the energy of all the stars.

There is something really ultimate about it. It is, as it were, the mother lode of energy – the energy form above all others. And it is even four times more compact than thorium itself. The energy content of the fuel for nuclear fusion is approximately 10 million times greater per unit weight than coal. In addition, the waste from nuclear fusion will be our harmless helium. It happens to be what we use for blowing up balloons for children's birthday parties, which gives some indication of just how harmless it actually is.

Your bathtub can probably hold about 300 l of water, and the hydrogen in that water probably contains all the deuterium you will need for your entire life's personal energy consumption, if supplied with nuclear fusion. In addition, we must then obtain an equivalent amount of tritium, which can be made from the amount of lithium found in two small batteries from a normal notebook computer. These amounts are so small that scientists estimate we can provide enough of it to supply the world with clean energy for somewhere between 30 million and countless billions of years – solely through nuclear fusion. In this context, note that the lowest estimate – 30 million years – is about 100 000 times longer than the 300 or so years the fossil period is likely to last. Also note the extra twist to this story. If we actually introduce nuclear fusion later this century, it will be the solution that will propel Marchetti's Law towards a pure hydrogen economy.

But how will we accomplish this? The major technological challenge is to achieve a so-called triple product, which is critical density multiplied by temperature multiplied by time. We have this within stars, including the sun, where the pressure is 100 billion atmospheres, the temperature 15 million degrees, and the process fortunately permanent. Since the 1960s, work has been done to raise the triple product, which has actually doubled on average every 1.8 years:

29. **Since the 1960s, nuclear fusion experiments have doubled triple product – the combination of density, temperature, and confinement time – every 1.8 years.**

That means it has increased approximately 100 000 times since the start of experiments and, at the time of writing, we are only missing a factor of five before we reach the level required for the major engineering breakthrough in the form of a functioning reactor. In other words, we are almost – but not quite – there. That's the good news. The bad news is that it has been a struggle to achieve the necessary density.

Now there are about 20 fusion reactors up and running and a dozen in the pipeline or under construction. The majority fall into two categories: magnetic fusion and inertial fusion. The former uses a circular or twisted-circular fusion chamber, into which the deuterium and tritium are blown. They are held around the centre with a huge magnetic field while being heated to a point at which the fusion process (hopefully) occurs. Here it is primarily the input of heat, rather than pressure, that is needed to trigger the process.

The leading project of this kind in the world has arguably been the Joint European Torus (JET) project in the United Kingdom, which has set the 'world triple product record'. However, if it has not already been surpassed by the Chinese or others, it probably will be by ITER in France, which is funded by the European Union, China, India, Japan, Korea, Russia, and the United States. ITER is expected to start in 2025, and there are reports that the process should work by around 2027 – give or take a few years, I assume. However, neutral nuclear power experts I have spoken to are extremely sceptical vis-à-vis magnetic fusion technology and think it may very well be a dead end.

The major alternative is inertial fusion, in which the experts I have talked to have greater faith. Here pressure rather than heat is the key element that triggers the process. One principle involves shooting 'cartridges' of deuterium and tritium into a combustion chamber and then hitting them in the air with a number of extremely powerful laser beams, which then ignite them. It is a bit like automatic clay pigeon shooting. The pioneer in this field is the National Ignition Facility (NIF) in the United States, which has already achieved short-term partial ignitions, and in France they are in the process of creating a *laser mégajoule* (LMJ), which should be capable of achieving the same.

In addition to such public experimental reactors, there are a number of others, many of which are private. In this context, one of the alternative concepts is to shoot fuel components into each other with particle accelerators. Another, which is being developed by General Fusion in Canada, uses a circular space, in which molten lead and lithium rotates. This eddy current creates a vortex, into which one pumps deuterium and tritium. This is then ignited by targeting the container with rhythmic piston strokes from the outside. Another intriguing project is Sparc, which is a collaboration between Massachusetts Institute of Technology (MIT) and Commonwealth Fusion Systems. They expect to have a commercially usable reactor up and running by around 2030.

In addition to getting triple product up to the point where they have stable nuclear fusion, the goal is to increase the amount of energy that comes out in relation to what needs to be brought in. In the industry, this ratio is referred to as 'Q', and a Q below 1 obviously makes no commercial sense. Most experiments are now aiming at a Q of at least 10.

So, when will we have sustainable nuclear fusion with a meaningful Q? Let us just peruse some published timelines for the six nuclear fusion projects:

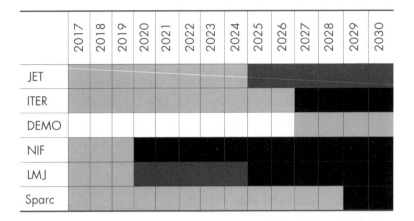

Here, the light grey indicates that the projects are under development, the dark grey indicates attempts to raise Q to above 1, while the black indicates attempts to raise Q to above 10, at which point it becomes commercially interesting. In other words, by 2030, according to their own published plans, ITER, NIF, and LMJ should be well underway with projects with $Q \geq 10$, added to which breakthroughs may occur in various private projects.

It is totally unclear whether these six timelines will turn out to be viable, nor do we know whether other projects will be the ones that first reach the goal. But what we do know is that from the moment a test reactor delivers stable $Q \geq 10$, it will take some time before a plant can run profitably and stably. One challenge relates to the thick walls of the fusion chambers of some of the designs. They are dimensioned to absorb the constant bombardment with neutrons from the fusion chamber, which cannot be held by a magnetic field, since they lack electromagnetic charge. This bombardment will be so powerful that the walls with their current materials will only last one to two years. Then the reactor will have to be switched off, and the wall – which in some designs is big, very heavy, and slightly radioactive – replaced. With regard to the radioactivity of the walls, this will be phased out over about 10 years, but, as a professor from MIT once explained, the problem could easily be fixed by immersion in a water basin for 10 years, following which you could probably stand next to it.

Another challenge lies in making the plants smaller and cheaper. ITER, for instance, takes up an area equivalent to 60 football pitches and costs €20 billion. All the private initiatives are aimed at making something more compact and cheaper. For example, the company General Fusion's reactor is located in what they humorously refer to as a (large) garage, and Sparc is 1/65 the size of ITER: partly because they use super-magnetic adhesive tape to create the magnetic field, which is extremely compact. In addition, Sparc seeks to reduce the problem of the core wall by making it much thinner, so that a large number of the neutrons pass through. So, behind this, liquid salt containing lithium will then circulate, turning, as a result of the neutron bombardment, into tritium. That's pretty damned smart! Similarly, as already mentioned, since General Fusion will also mix lithium into their rotating molten metal, they can extract tritium from that. Again, brilliant!

So, what are we to think about all this? I think it doesn't sound impossible that by 2025–2030 we will have at least one project that demonstrates continuous nuclear fusion which has a Q above 10. And it will probably be based on inertial fusion. It is no coincidence that Helion Energy, the NIF, General Fusion, and a number of other serious operators in the field are pursuing various varieties of inertial fusion. But I cannot be more certain than that. No matter which projects eventually reach a high enough Q to make it interesting, the people behind them will be aware when many of their approaches have already become obsolete. Then I guess the activity in the field of fusion, which is currently worth only about $4 billion a year, or around 0.005% of global GDP, will explode into a kind of other-worldly gold rush.

Regarding what is happening with different energy technologies, it is also important to point out that, contrary to how it is often portrayed in the media, the world is not up and running in terms of an impending complete conversion to solar and wind. According to the IEA's 2018 World New Policies Scenario – which is very different from the one from the University of Utah that I described earlier – by 2040, these energy forms will account for just 4.1% of the world's energy supply. And that is IEA's *most* optimistic scenario, which assumes that every nation's targets for renewable energy will be reached. The same statement assumes that the rest of the world's heavily increasing energy needs will be met with increasing consumption of fossil fuels. In this context, we should remember that solar and wind are not digital technologies, and there is no way they will experience sustained exponential increase in efficiency.

Yes, this illustrates that there are big differences in forecasts, but historically speaking, time and time again, it has taken humankind 60–70 years to make a significant shift in terms of the dominant type of energy, and if we are to repeat that in this context, it is going to require a technological 'black swan' – the introduction of one or more radical new technologies. Thorium is one idea and nuclear fusion an even better one – if it works. And other ideas may come up.

Maybe things will work out as follows. In or around 2040, maybe (*maybe!*) the first commercial nuclear fusion plants will be connected to the power network. Around 2060–2070, nuclear fusion will be one of mankind's dominant forms of energy. And by 2100 it will have become the biggest and actually predominant – maybe with solar energy as number two, followed by wind and natural gas. Of course, I'm only guessing. There are so many uncertainties.

I would also like to add that, ultimately, it may not be deuterium-tritium fusion that ends up taking the lead in fusion. Instead, it may turn out to be fusion between proton and proton or between deuterium and lithium, neither of which produce excess neutrons. Either would be jolly good, in my opinion.

6.
THE IMPOR-TANCE OF INNOVATION FOR RESOURCES AND ENVIRONMENT

Throughout my childhood and youth, I was bombarded by newspapers and books etc. (we did not have television at home) with forecasts of an impending acute lack of resources, global famine, and air pollution. One book claimed that air pollution was getting so grave that everyone in big cities would soon have to wear gas masks. One of the prophets was the aforementioned Paul Ehrlich, who was expecting total collapse within a matter of a few years. I have to admit it all got me a bit flustered, and it did not get any better when I was 9 years old and William and Paul Paddock published their bestseller, Famine, 1975! *(1968), which described the global famine that would occur in 1975 – in other words, when I was 18 years old. Terrible! Meanwhile, my parents' bookshelves contained* The Limits to Growth *(1974) by Dennis L. Meadows, Donella H. Meadows, William W. Behrens III, and Jørgen Randers, which predicted that humanity would soon run out of a number of essential raw materials. Here are the book's most important forecasts in terms of when we would run out of things:*

	Pessimistic scenario	Optimistic scenario
Aluminium	2005	2029
Zinc	1992	2024
Copper	1995	2022
Gold	1983	2004
Silver	1987	2016
Natural gas	1996	2023
Oil	1994	2024
Mercury	1987	2015

So, according to the book's pessimistic scenario, by now – in fact, a long time ago – we would have run out of aluminium, zinc, copper, gold, silver, natural gas, oil, and mercury and, according to its optimistic scenario, we would have run out of gold, silver, and mercury by now and the other resources in just a few years' time. In fact, by 2025, there would only be some aluminium left, and by 2030, that would be gone too.

But none of this either happened or is anywhere near happening. In fact, the total opposite happened.

The reason is innovation. In the mid-1990s, the American economist William Nordhaus, who incidentally has now been awarded the Nobel Prize for Economics, conducted a number of experiments involving various sources of light. First, he lit a bonfire, then a Roman oil lamp, then a light made of animal fat, and then a light of whale oil, while constantly measuring how many lumens – the units we use for measuring light – each source of light produced. Nordhaus wanted to clarify how much cheaper a light unit had become. The result was overwhelming. Imagine the work a Stone Age man had to invest in making a bonfire to produce light of reasonable quality for 54 minutes, when today modern man can produce light of the same intensity – for 52 years! This means that the so-called time-price – how much time you need to work in order to achieve a given material good – has dropped 500 000 times for light since the Stone Age!

And it is still falling rapidly. For example, there is now a global shift to LED, to which the following rule applies:

30. **For every decade, the price per lumen (light unit) generated by LED decreases by a factor of 10, while the amount of light an LED unit can generate increases by a factor of 20 for a given wavelength (colour) of light (Haitz's Law).**

So, we have a Moore's Law for light. But there is also one for heat. The Stone Age people's sole man-made heat source consisted of the controlled burning of wood or cowpats. Coal, oil, and natural gas were not a source of heat for them and thus not resources in their view. Nor were metals resources for mankind before the Iron Age. And nor was sand available for making glass or grain for making bread. And that brings me to what I consider the most important – or at least the most underrated– rule in this book:

31. **Innovation is humanity's most important resource. Only through innovation can we obtain new resources and, given that our innovation is exponential, our access to resources will also be. That is why innovative societies do not run out of resources.**

Please read it one more time. Innovation is humanity's most important resource. This is the central point in the major work by the economist Julian Simon: *The Ultimate Resource* (1981). Simon partly used the development of commodity prices to conclude that, generally speaking, scarcity of Earth's resources will not be a major problem in the future. In fact, he claimed that it would become an increasingly *minor* problem, as was the case for a long time in the past.

Simon actually thought (unfortunately he died in 1998) that, as a result of our ability to innovate and come up with new solutions, we would not run out of the raw materials that are the prerequisite for maintaining and further developing human civilisation, even in the very long term. Other authors have expounded a similar view, including the eminent quantum physicist David Deutsch (whose books include *The Beginning of Infinity* (2011)) and Matt Ridley, the former science editor of *The Economist* (author of such books as *The Rational Optimist* (2010)). If you want to follow the progress of Simon's prophecies, I recommend taking a look at the so-called Simon Abundance Index, which calculates prices and availability for 50 commonly used raw materials. From 1980 to 2017, i.e. 37+ years, it showed the following:

- Inflation-adjusted prices had fallen by 36%.
- The time-price (average time people had to work in order to buy raw materials) had fallen by 65%.
- For every 1% growth in the world's population, the time people had to work in order to buy commodities fell by 0.93%.

Innovation, dear friends. Innovation!

For some reason or other, many people find it extremely difficult to understand how important innovation was in the past and, therefore, will also be so (actually even more so) in the future. Chapter 5 featured examples of the extreme energy technologies that are being developed. It also showed the dramatic declines in real prices for heat and light. Here is another example – the following graph shows the astoundingly stable drop in prices for industrial raw materials, which, as mentioned, were not a resource for the people of the Stone Age.

Real prices for industrial raw materials

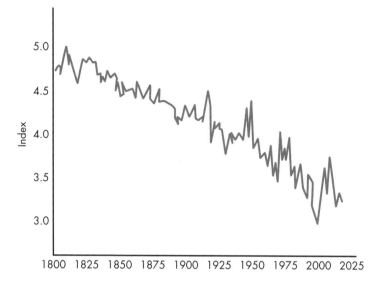

And here follows the long-term development in real prices of wheat, which was not a resource in the Stone Age either.

Real prices for wheat

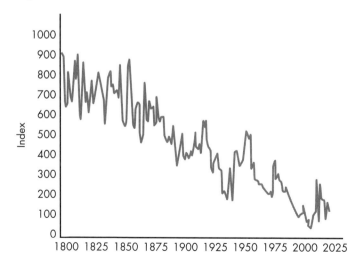

As can be seen, from 1800 until the present day, the price has fallen intensely and almost constantly. This is principally due to the fact that from 1800 onwards we developed crops and cultivation methods that made the production of wheat grow even faster than the massive population growth and better nutritional condition required, while also reducing the waste involved in distribution.

In other words, our innovative power has succeeded in ensuring that we do not have large proportions of the global population starving anymore. Far from it. In fact, today, for the first time, there are more people on the planet who are categorised as *over*weight than *under*weight.

Absolute poverty is also abating globally to such an extent that this development should be regarded as one of the most important triumphs in human history. Apart from the poverty caused by highly deluded political systems, such as in North Korea or Venezuela today (and previously in the likes of Mao's China and Communism in the Soviet Union), we have been on a constant journey towards eliminating famine and absolute poverty.

This is wonderful. But far too many people are simply not aware of this positive development that is actually taking place. And this lack of understanding of the consequence of innovation is a problem that not only frustrated the aforementioned Hans Rosling, but also Julian Simon, who in a 1995 CATO Institute report thus expressed his vision of the future:

> *This is my long-run forecast in brief: The material conditions of life will continue to get better for most people, in most countries, most of the time, indefinitely. Within a century or two, all nations and most of humanity will be at or above today's Western living standards. I also speculate, however, that many people will continue to think and say that the conditions of life are getting worse.*

Today, you cannot exactly call the whole world creative in the scientific and technological sense of the word. But the West and large parts of Southeast Asia in particular are highly creative, and it is that creativity that ensures that the entire planet is spared resource shortages. Even though we are consuming more and more, there is increasingly *less* scarcity of commodities and increasingly *lower* (inflation-adjusted) commodity prices, and this has been the case for several centuries. This is because we produce more efficiently, recycle more, substitute more, and synthesise more, and because of the sharing economy that has recently mushroomed.

You could say, in fact some people actually *do* say, that human civilisation ceased to be sustainable in a static sense at around the time when the global population seriously began to grow. In other words, we kissed goodbye to sustainability in its stable form at least 500, if not 1000 or 10 000, years ago. Why? Because since then we have based our lifestyle on one totally unsustainable solution after another. For example, as we have seen, the people of the Stone Age wiped out an abundance of megafauna and chopped down vast areas of forest when agriculture was rolled out across the continent. If we had continued along the same lines, not a single tree would have remained today. So, there was no way that was sustainable.

But people did *not* continue, and a scientific article in *Nature* from 2018 presented satellite measurements that showed that global forest cover had grown by 7% over the 34 years of the study. This does not overlook the fact that, even today, the highly objectional destruction of forests is still occurring in tropical areas. But it does indicate that human civilisation can now grow without forest as such becoming a scarce resource. At the same time, since 1990, the world's agricultural areas have stopped growing. Instead, for approximately 30 years they have remained virtually unchanged, despite huge increases in production. According to the environmental researcher Jesse Ausubel of Rockefeller University, they are likely to decrease over the coming decades, as population growth declines and productivity per unit area continues to rise significantly.

Let me say some more on the subject of sustainability. In 1894, a gloomy projection in London claimed that 50 years later there would be 3 m high piles of horse excrement on the streets if the use of the horse as a means of transport continued to grow. Was it sustainable? No. But did it continue? No. Because we invented the car, and the horse excrement vanished.

For the period 1881–1885, a statement showed that the people in London had only one-sixth of the hours of sunshine compared to in English villages because of the city's pollution, and if that situation continued to develop, London would end up in a state of permanent darkness. But today, London's air is far cleaner than back then – thanks to innovation.

In 1895, a few years after the dreadful measurement of London's lack of sunlight, in a letter to *The Times* the famous physicist Michael Faraday described what he had observed during a boat trip on the Thames: 'The whole of the river was an opaque pale brown fluid . . . the river which flows for so many miles through London ought not to be allowed to become a fermenting sewer.' However, today the water in the Thames is much cleaner than it was then, and species of fish, which had at the time disappeared, have now returned – because England converted to new technologies.

The point is, of course, that a creative society continuously replaces bad or unsustainable technologies with some that are better, and that this often happens exponentially. And that is why prosperous, creative communities are sustainable in the long term. You see, they have at their disposal a particular resource that is both exponential and endless: innovation.

32. **Creative societies are not always sustainable, in the event that innovation disappears. But they are if, as is usual, it continues.**

Ideas – the ultimate resource

Nevertheless, many people talk about the unsustainability of our current societal model, as if our innovation were about to stop right here. Others see a cessation of innovation and the restoration of older forms of work as sustainable, but it is those retro technologies and fear of technology that would actually lead to disasters in terms of the environment and resources.

Moreover, the principle of dynamic sustainability can be illustrated by the lack of tenability implicit in the constantly-growing use of the word 'sustainable'. As suggested in a famous cartoon (xkcd.com), if the exponential growth in the use of the word continues sustainably, very soon all the words in writing and speech will be 'sustainable', making every single conversation an endless and unsustainable repetition of that word. And that will not happen.

Why the use of the word sustainable is unsustainable

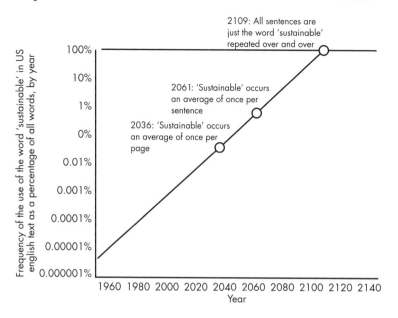

Now, part of the sustainability discussion is often based on an underestimation of the amount of resources available on the planet. For example, the aforementioned global bestseller, *The Limits to Growth*, is in my point of view a really odd book, since it massively underestimated the impact of human innovation, as do countless people today too. But it also underestimated the amount of resources we have, and perhaps the authors should have thought about what the economist Wilfred Beckerman (1996) of Oxford University said about metals:

> *In fact, given the natural concentrations of the key metals in the earth's crust, as indicated by a large number of random samples, the total natural occurrence of most metals in the top mile of the earth's crust has been estimated to be about a million times as great as present known reserves. Since the latter amount to about 100 years' supplies, this means that we have enough to last about one hundred million years.*

One hundred million years of consumption is quite a lot – for example, around 300 times as long as humanity has existed. And to put this into another perspective, there is enough aluminium in the Earth's crust to cover all the land masses on the planet in a layer several kilometres in height. And yes, I am talking about that very aluminium that, according to the pessimistic scenario in *The Limits to Growth,* was supposed to have run out by 2005, or by 2029 in the optimistic scenario.

By the way, here is a funny fact. In 1920, US authorities estimated that the world's oil reserves amounted to 60 billion barrels – sufficient for 10 years with the annual consumption at the time. In the years that followed, up until 2014, annual consumption increased steadily, and aggregate consumption reached close to 1000 billion barrels. But in 2014, even though approximately 1000 billion barrels had gone up in smoke, US authorities estimated that there were now more than 1600 billion barrels left in reserves.

Even funnier... for years, many people have been pretty paranoid about the fact that the Chinese were sitting on 97% of the world's production of so-called rare earths, which include the elements neodymium, lanthanum, samarium, lutetium, europium, scandium, terbium, erbium, and yttrium – substances that were crucial for certain high-tech products. Anxiety increased in 2010, when due to a disagreement with Japan regarding fishing rights, China tried to block sales of those rare earths to Japan. However, in 2018, Japanese scientists announced that they had found mudflats off the island of Minami-Torishima, which, in their estimate, contained enough yttrium to supply the whole world (on the basis of current consumption) for 780 years, and there was sufficient europium for 620 years, enough terbium for 420 years, and enough dysprosium for 730 years.

Synthetisation

So how exactly are we managing to avoid running out of things? In addition, for example, to finding mud banks with tons of rare earths, we can start with synthetisation. As already described, there is a switch from (1) extracting resources from the environment to (2) cultivating them and then (3) synthesising them.

The treatment of diabetes is a good case in point. Initially, (1) we extracted insulin from the stomachs of cows. Then (2) we used genetically-modified microorganisms to synthesise it. And soon we will be able to (3) genetically modify human tissue in diabetics, so the need for medicine will entirely disappear.

Or take nitrogen fertiliser. Initially, (1) it came from guano – accumulated bird droppings. Then (2) we discovered how we could use chemical processes to extract it from nitrogen in the atmosphere. The next step (3) will be the genetic modification of plants so they can do it themselves.

Or food. (1) First, as hunter-gatherers, we hunted and fished for our food in nature. Then (2) we turned to cultivating it through agriculture and fish farms. And now, (3) synthetisation and genetic modification are in full swing.

Was there a limit to the resources of guano, cow stomachs, fauna, and flora in nature that could be hunted or collected? Yes. But genetic or chemical synthetisation is not limited from any practical perspective. What these transitions mean is that production becomes digitised, programmable, intelligent, accurate, and more compact. In early civilisation, we used biological life as rough, analogue resources. But now we use it as a computer platform, as mentioned in the first of our 50 basic rules in this book.

One example. We want medicine, so we program yeast or bacteria to produce it for us. Or we want food, so we program cells to grow and divide in steel tanks and turn into meat for our burgers. I will come back to that.

Compression

As mentioned, synthetisation often leads to very compact technologies. However, such compression can also be done in many other ways. A good example is mobile phones, which initially weighed 25 kg, but today weigh more like 100 g, even though they now have computer power that far surpasses a mainframe computer from the 1970s that weighed several tons. By way of another example, studies have shown that the capacity of the existing road network to move cars will increase by 30–300% if they are all autonomous and electronically connected via

V2X – a technology that allows cars to communicate with each other, while at the same time they use GPS and online traffic information. The improved efficiency will be due to the fact that the cars will be much closer to each other, even at high speeds, and will automatically find their way around overloaded road areas. In addition, with the new technologies, we will have far fewer crashes, while autonomous lorries will drive at night, causing no inconvenience to other traffic. Autonomous cars will also be able to serve as Uber cars instead of taking up room in garages for the 95% of the time that their owners are not using them. In other words, we will gain considerably greater road capacity without having to expand the roads.

Another phenomenon that makes production compact is the fact that robots and IT often make people in workplaces redundant. The fewer people involved in production, the less space it normally requires. A factory with a given capacity per hour can be made more compact and, at the same time, thanks to robots run 24 hours a day, including weekends and holidays.

Compression is also taking place in farming, where, since the 1980s, the amount of farmland per capita has been cut to around half, which has led to a peak in global farmland. This is likely to be followed by a long-term decline over the coming decades. This 'peak farmland', as it is often called, is due to more efficient farming technology, including what is called precision farming – a set of technologies that continue to emerge quickly and be rolled out globally. If all farms in the world were as efficient as the most sophisticated farms in, say, the United States and Northern Europe, we would be able to reduce global farmland by some 85%. And furthermore, there are even now successful experiments with so-called vertical farming, which is the practice of producing food and medicine in vertically stacked layers, which is becoming economically feasible due to the rapid decline in the cost of LED light combined with the fact that it works in all seasons. This technique can lower the amount of land needed per unit of food produced by a factor of 4 to 30 depending on the crop.

Of course, the production of cultured meat can also compress food production. And oddly, a Finish company called Solar Foods have developed a method to create so-called 'Solein' out of just carbon dioxide, water, and electricity. Solein looks and tastes like flour and contains some 50% protein, 5–10% fat, and 20–25% carbohydrate. But it has never seen a plant, an animal, or a living cell. And the production is very compact indeed.

Virtualisation

Today we take communication via satellites, mobile masts, and wi-fi for granted, but it is relatively new. Previously, electronic communication was mostly via heavy, expensive, and resource-intensive copper lines. Thus, communication has been extensively dematerialised.

If we return to the smartphone, it also represents a huge degree of virtualisation, given that today it serves as a supercomputer, calendar, notebook, camera, videorecorder, alarm clock, photo album, stereo, DVD collection, record collection, translator, clock, tape recorder, directory, and hundreds of other products, which together would fill a farmyard and cost the same as a chateau. In fact, approximately $30 million in today's money; mainly because of the supercomputer part. So, most of these objects have disappeared from the lives of millions of people. But they still have the functions – they have just become cheaper, more compact, and, yes, far better.

Another method for making compact technology is 3D printing. It started as a smart tool for rapid prototyping (which my daughter's company Invisiboble also uses extensively to develop new hair and beauty products), when companies needed to quickly assess whether a particular design would work as intended in its physical form. Today, it plays an important role in many industries – from hair bands to aircraft engines. The technology is smart, because you save a lot of material when you do not have to cut in order to customise.

3D printing has been shrouded in a lot of hype for a number of years, and people have come up with some pretty dramatic suggestions about how the technology might transform the world as we know it. Much of the hype has not yet come to fruition and, at the risk of sounding like a lot of silly technology pessimists from the past, personally I am not so sure that many people will want a 3D printer in their home unless it can print amazing culinary experiences (Ups, did I really say that?).

But in other contexts, it makes a lot of sense. For example, based on scans, dentists can print braces to straighten teeth, implants, and crowns. Both the scanning and the printing are done at the clinic.

You can 3D print with an increasing variety of materials, including plastic, nylon, glass-filled polyamide, epoxy resin, gold, silver, titanium, steel, wax, ceramics, photopolymers – you name it. You can also print templates or matrices to grow living cells in desired structures.

The combination of 3D printing and nanotechnology has sparked many new hopes in the world of medical science.

Recycling

As societies become richer, much of their recycling approaches 100%. Organic waste is used, for example, to produce natural gas, heat, and humus; metals are recirculated; paper is recycled; etc.

Waste technologies are also continuously improving. An extreme technology such as plasma gasification enables us very simply to convert mixed waste from rubbish dumps into a combination of lava, liquid metal, and natural gas. Increasingly, society's still-usable objects are also being resold by the likes of Autoscout24 (car market), Chrono24 (clock market), or eBay (global flea market), making it significantly easier for buyers and sellers of cars, watches, and anything else to get in touch with each other. The overall term for this is 'circular economy', and it is growing rapidly.

Sharing economy

A variation of the circular economy is the sharing economy, in which numerous people or companies shift to using the same asset via, for example, Uber, Airbnb, or server farms in the cloud. One interesting element of this type of sharing economy is the fact that it largely relates to so-called latent goods: in other words, goods that would not be used without this model. A future example could be autonomous cars, which automatically make money for us when we are not using them ourselves. When otherwise empty offices, homes, cars, or boats are shared in this way, it seems as if there are more of them – which again illustrates how innovation creates resources. In addition, there is the fact that the way you do it is especially beneficial to the middle classes by providing them with services or income they would not otherwise have got.

Substitution

The aforementioned example of wireless telecommunications is not merely an expression of virtualisation, but also of substitution: in other words, an example of replacing the use of one commodity with another that is better, cheaper, and perhaps virtual, or which can be endlessly synthesised.

Even wireless communication is becoming less resource-intensive. Mobile communication accounts for a large and increasing part of our total Internet traffic. Due to the distance, it requires a lot of energy for a smartphone to communicate with a mobile mast, but at the moment mobile networks account for only about 5% of this Internet traffic, while most of the rest is done via wi-fi, which took off internationally around year 2000, and which is usually connected to optical fibres. This innovation saves huge amounts of energy.

Let us take a few more examples: Internet shopping and video conferencing reduce the need for personal transport, and email and social media replace physical letters. Another example is the use of carbon fibres instead of metal, because carbon fibre is lighter, stronger, and stainless.

One more good example of substitution is aquaculture. The global fish catch in lakes and seas peaked in the mid-1990s and has since been fairly stable. On the other hand, aquaculture production (fish farms) is booming, and in 2012 it overtook traditional fish catches. Aquaculture is actually the fastest-growing food production and has a significantly lower carbon footprint per unit produced than meat from terrestrial creatures. You see, unlike warm-blooded animals, fish do not have to generate thermal energy to keep their bodies warm, so a larger part of the fish's food is converted into body mass.

For many years, fish farming has been big in the freshwater sector, but only recently has it been realised with saltwater species such as salmon. In 2007, Akvaforsk, a Norwegian research group, published a report that showed that three decades of Norwegian salmon farming had made them grow twice as fast as those in nature. Efforts are concurrently being made to develop genetically modified variants, which, for example, have better resistance to serious diseases.

An important part of fish farming is also what food you give to the fish, and in this context they are looking at whether one can give fish plant food, which does not put pressure on the production of fish food from other resources. And from this and the previous techniques discussed, we can deduce a general rule about resources in creative societies:

33. **A creative society becomes ever better at meeting demands without running into fundamental resource shortages. This is due to continuous – and often exponential – progress in (1) synthetisation, (2) compression, (3) virtualisation, (4) recycling, (5) sharing, (6) substitution, and (7) digitalisation.**

Digitalisation

An all-encompassing theme behind the six mentioned drivers of resource creation is the previously mentioned transition from analogue to digital.

All sectors of modern economies are being subject to extensive digitalisation. Basically, what this means is that, by finding, manipulating, or creating digital codes, we can get increasingly larger parts of the world to solve tasks for us spontaneously. In a way, we give it life, and program it to work for us. Given that productivity development in IT is often substantially faster than in analogue technologies, it means that one area after another of our economy is being abruptly raised from slow, predictable development to a revolutionary restructuring.

The driving forces behind creative society's increasing resource efficiency

Innovation makes a huge contribution. Deepika Kurup, an American with Indian roots and currently studying at Harvard, was only 17 when she invented an easy, inexpensive way to clean water using sunbeams, zinc, and titanium. We have also seen the invention of drinking bottles with built-in pumps that direct the water through a nano filter and clean it, so you can use the water that is in the area, although it is initially infected. This is smart, because it is often expensive to transport large quantities of water over long distances.

However, one of the most important technologies for solving the problem of water shortage is desalination, which is already being implemented on a large scale. For example, half of the water in Israel comes from desalination plants, which are undergoing a classic development, for which the price is dropping continuously. Sorek, the largest of four plants in Israel, can produce over 600 000 m³ of fresh drinking water a day. The price of desalinated water used to be the major challenge, but in 2018 Sorek sold water to the Israeli authorities for just under $0.60 per 1000 l. Several of the Gulf states are now also using large-scale desalination, and California is also moving in that direction. It is worth noting that the new plants in the pipeline in California are primarily intended to desalinate saltwater from rivers and underground pockets, which are significantly less saline than seawater, and therefore cheaper to clean.

Meat produced without animals

One of the great international growth areas today is what one can call an 'anti-meat' movement in the rich parts of the world. More and more restaurants are meat-free, and others often feature a number of meat-free starters and main courses on the menu. Consumers' motivation for preferring a meat-free diet can relate to their own health, animals, or the environment. But, at the same time, most people actually like the taste of meat, so now there are plant-based meat substitutes.

But something else is also going on. In 1931, Winston Churchill predicted that, in 50 years' time, we would have learned to make meat without animals. However, only now is his vision becoming a reality. Because now researchers and entrepreneurs have grown muscle fibres and animal fat in closed tanks. Memphis Meats, a Californian company, whose investors include Bill Gates and Richard Branson, have developed and refined the methods, creating both chicken and beef using stem cells and tanks. In the future, it will probably be quite normal to eat a burger or chicken salad, without a single cow or chicken having to be slaughtered for the purpose.

Today, when you 'grow' a cow, the energy from the feed that you give it is not only growing its meat, but also its organs and bones, as well as being used for moving the cow around, keeping it warm, etc. That is why companies like Memphis Meats will concentrate on growing the meat without the cow.

The method of making cultured meat, or *clean* meat, which manufacturers optimistically call it, is often triggered by taking a sample from an animal's muscle. From here, muscle stem cells are isolated and then manipulated to divide quite rapidly and continue to become muscle cells. Of course, they will be chosen from cattle (or other animals) that are known for having particularly good flavour. In addition, for example, the Israeli company Future Meat Technologies has begun to grow fat cells to mix into the meat, so there is the perfect balance of fat and meat, and optimum flavour. One can even genetically modify such fat to make it healthy rather than unhealthy. The cells used, which start off as connective tissue cells and then can be modified to either fat or muscle cells, are grown in tanks where they are supplemented with nutrients and stimulated to divide. Once the process has started, in principle it will be possible to produce endless meat from the same original cells. It will also be possible to expand the principle to all sorts of meat which we cannot farm properly today. It will thus allow us to expand our repertoire from the usual handful of types of meat and include meat from more exotic species. Anyone fancy a zebra steak? Or artificial tuna, for example, produced using cells from fish or via genetically modified plants? I have to say, what I personally would like to see is cheap truffles!

It should also be mentioned that many start-ups are experimenting with making meat substitutes from the likes of plants and even methane. For example, Impossible Foods produces burgers based on plant ingredients that taste like meat.

Currently, a number of milestones have already been achieved in the field of cultured meat. The first cultured steak was made by Dr Mark Post of Maastricht University in 2013 and eaten at a product demonstration in London. Professional tasters gave the taste a positive rating. But it cost $300 000 to make the steak, and it took two years. Fortunately, the price has since dropped significantly. Memphis Meats report that a similar steak in 2018 cost $600, and the declared goal is approximately $2.2 for a 200-g steak, which, if they can continue this productivity growth, should be achieved by about 2023. However, in the spring of 2018, the head of Future

Meat Technologies stated that they expected cultured meat to reach a price of $2.3–4.5 per US lb by 2020: the equivalent of about $5–10 per kg. It is still more expensive than traditional meat but, as the saying goes, the trend is your friend.

One of the benefits is the conversion rate from feed to meat. It is approximately 15% for cows, 30% for pigs, and 60% for chickens, but is approximately 90% for cultured meat. Another advantage is that animal grazing areas are huge and have led to deforestation in countries like Brazil. Cultured meat products are, in other words, extremely compact and use on average about 99% less soil, not to mention far less water, and in the majority of cases considerably less energy than farm-produced meat. And since it doesn't require farmland, you can do it anywhere.

Who will do it? Future Meat Technologies intend to collaborate with breweries or pharmaceutical companies to exploit their capabilities and knowledge of bioreactors, as the tanks are called. It is estimated that a bioreactor of 20 000 l can implement the production from cell to meat including cleaning, sterilisation of the reactor, and preparation for the next production in 10–18 days. Incidentally, Future Meat has an interesting business model. While some cultured producers are committed to producing the meat themselves or, for example, in collaboration with pharmaceutical companies that are good at operating bioreactors, Future Meat has developed a kit for farmers. The farmers then have to buy everything they need to produce cultured meat, including both mechanical equipment and raw materials. Once the meat has been grown, it is delivered back to Future Meat Technologies for processing, so that they can achieve optimum taste and texture.

A continuation of this price development will pave the way for cultured meat to embark on various authorisation procedures within a few years and then find a market – ultimately a gigantic market, in my humble opinion. A restaurant has already opened in the Netherlands, Bistro In Vitro, which specialises in cultured meat. It is also pretty interesting that start-ups like Wild Earth and Bond Pet Foods have begun to make dog food from cultured meat cells or protein developed by fungi. In the

United States, where it started, dogs account for about one-third of total meat consumption.

With the transition to increasingly more cultured meat, it is easy to imagine an impact on other industries. For example, what will become of the leather industry? It will probably go the same way as meat production. The American company Modern Meadow are ready to launch Zoa: leather made in a laboratory. The method is not identical to that of cultured meat. Instead, they use yeast cells that have been genetically engineered to produce collagen, a protein normally found in cow hide (and quite a lot in other contexts). The collagen is then assembled into a fibrous material and treated in the same way as normal leather. The production process enables Modern Meadow to experiment with the material and make it stronger and lighter than traditional leather. Therefore, future artificial leather will often probably end up being different from the present natural kind. One can thus expect a material that for some purposes will be better in terms of the qualities important to buyers, and which will also be more environmentally friendly to produce and devoid of ethical, animal welfare-related dilemmas – and still feels like real leather.

What about cultured milk? Well, several companies are working on that. One of these, Perfect Day, produces synthetic milk protein for production of cheese and other dairy products. By the way, its name was chosen after its founders read that scientists had discovered that cows yielded more milk if listening to music and that their favourite song was 'Perfect Day' by Lou Reed.

Cultured meat, milk, leather, and other substitution technologies are also interesting, because they can be a kind of lightning conductor in the growing conflict between vegans and carnivores, who at worst accuse each other of being fascists. But in another way too. Because once we get going with these cultured products, it will basically involve programming the DNA of cells in the way we program self-replicating robots. Thus, we can create from scratch the organic products we want without them necessarily having some relation to something that nature itself has managed to do. Just as we do not need physical instruments today in order to make music.

New materials

But there is one funny thing about all this. Neither synthetic meat, nor carbon fibre, thorium, deuterium, tritium, lithium, or protons were even mentioned in the book *The Limits to Growth,* which makes it one of the inanest books I have ever read.

Today, when we need to solve a problem, we have an almost endless arsenal of materials at our disposal. Materials with amazing properties that we can manipulate to suit our aims, which can withstand cold and heat, and whose surfaces keep something out and something else in, exactly as we want, and which are intelligent and almost alive. And the development will continue exponentially.

Take graphene, for example. This super semimetal, which we have known about as a theoretical option since the mid-twentieth century, is a very thin layer – or tube – of graphite like the one used in pencils. By very thin I mean one atom thick, which is a millionth as thick as a human hair. This is why it is sometimes described as the world's first virtually 2D material. It is also the strongest material we know: more than 100 times as strong as steel. For good measure, it is also transparent, flexible, suitable for conducting electricity, and can keep out certain gases and liquids if used as a filter.

Graphene was first produced in 2004. Two scientists from the University of Manchester, Andre Geim and Konstantin Novoselov, polished a lump of graphite with ordinary tape and discovered that very thin flakes of the graphite remained on the tape: graphene. The discovery – and the way it cropped up – was so bizarre, yet so banal, that initially it was hard for them to get other scientists to understand that they were serious and that it was interesting. In 2010, however, they were awarded the Nobel Prize for physics for their discovery.

Graphene is still expensive, but expensive technologies tend to get cheaper. And more and more potential applications emerge all the time: everything from flexible mobile phones and wearables to small machines that can easily travel around within our body and solve health problems. Graphene may even revolutionise the solar cell industry and replace the silicone cells that we use today. The same applies potentially to computer chips. Because water, but almost nothing else, can penetrate graphene, the material can also be used to purify infected water. Oh, by the way, as I write this, many engineers are raving about the basic concept of 2D materials, and the new kid on the block is borophene, which is made of a single layer of boron. It does a lot of what graphene does, and then some.

Graphene and borophene are examples of the new materials we are constantly discovering, and the creativity is almost inconceivable. For example, engineers make concrete with a magnetic mineral that absorbs shocks and vibrations, and which can be sprayed onto existing buildings. Others have developed ceramic bricks, which at the same time act as a cooling system for the building. Edible packaging in the food industry; organic chewing gum and underwear; and biodegradable building materials are being made out of desert sand. We are in the midst of a material revolution, the beneficial effects of which are huge.

Greater prosperity, better environment

Many people today are anti-materialists. It is not the first time we have witnessed this. Ancient Greece, for example, had a similar movement known as Cynicism. Just as in the Middle Ages, the Cynics (cynic comes from the Greek word *kynikos* = dog-like) had self-whipping flagellants. The 1960s saw the rise of a new type of anti-materialism; for example, among hippies, who actually maybe just wanted to smoke pot and watch the sunset. The modern form is sometimes called 'enoughism', which may be motivated by a desire to protect the environment by personally consuming less; a form of environmentalism that is sometimes referred to as 'light'.

The funny thing, however, is that the richest countries, the ones with the greatest consumption, are actually the cleanest. The most credible comparison of countries' environment is, in my opinion, the Environmental Performance Index (EPI), which compares 25 different environmental indicators for each of a wide range of countries. It is conducted in collaboration between two of the world's leading universities, Yale and Cornell, and researchers from the World Economic Forum and the European Commission. And the results, which anyone can Google, show quite clearly that the richest countries have the cleanest environments – and that poor countries often have appalling pollution. In the EPI's 2018 statement, for example, Switzerland was ranked as the cleanest country in the world, with France in second place and Denmark an impressive third. Conversely, the miserably poor countries, Haiti, Mali, and Somalia were at the bottom. As mentioned in one of the EPI's reports, the correlation is crystal clear: 'Not surprisingly, per capita GDP is correlated with higher performance on the EPI. In particular, overall EPI scores are higher in countries that have a per capita GDP of $10,000 or higher.'

In fact, statistics show that when GDP reaches approximately $4000 per capita, people usually begin to consider the environment and to rectify the first problems. Then, when it reaches $10 000+, the environment as a whole becomes cleaner. And this correlation continues up the wealth scale, in which Switzerland, for example, with a GDP per capita of more than $80 000 in 2018, thus had the cleanest environment in the world:

34. **When countries become richer, they become cleaner (the environmental Kuznets Curve).**

Because wealth improves the environment, there exists an alternative to light environmentalism, which is the 'bright' one. Bright environmentalism focuses on wealth and innovation as means of bettering the environment. I should mention that the terms light and bright environmentalism were coined in 2003 by American futurist Alex Geffen. Geffen also described 'dark environmentalism' as the third approach: one which recommended radical political overhaul to curb global consumption and create a sort of international rationing economy while also rejecting many new technologies.

Personally, I strongly favour bright environmentalism among the three and find dark environmentalism strongly counterproductive. Having said that, in what follows I would like to address some specific environmental problems that people are often concerned about.

Global warming in perspective

It is impossible to talk about the environment here without touching on the topic of global warming, which over the past few decades has been a really hot potato in the media and politics. Personally, over the past 15 years I have read heaps of books and reports on the subject. But it is a complicated area. So, in what follows I aim to summarise what science both *knows* and does *not* know. Let us start with a graph showing an estimate of temperatures and carbon dioxide over the last 600 million years:

Global temperatures and carbon dioxide concentrations over the past 600 million years

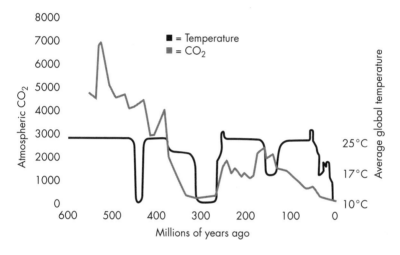

As we can see, the planet's average temperatures have fluctuated approximately 17 °C over this timespan. The range of carbon dioxide fluctuations, which are also illustrated in the graph, are more uncertain. However, despite the uncertainty and despite recent increases in carbon dioxide concentrations, we know that the current concentration is around the lowest in 600 million years.

Seen from the point of view of something we are familiar with, in the first 25 or so million years on this graph we had the so-called Cambrian explosion, which was an explosive growth in the number of species on Earth.

At that time, the average climate was probably approximately 10–14°C warmer than today, and the concentrations of carbon dioxide in the air 6–20 times as high as now (this is the interval of uncertainty the researchers indicate). The next thing I can add, for the fun of it, is the fact that the dinosaurs lived between approximately 245 and 66 million years ago, when the concentrations of carbon dioxide were between twice as high and 10 times as high as now (it fluctuated a lot over the period, and again there is some uncertainty on the part of researchers).

But why have temperatures fluctuated so much? There are a number of well-known reasons. We can start with the ones that are important in terms of the next tens of thousands or hundreds of thousands of years:

- Milanković Cycles – the Earth's orbit around the sun becomes more or less elliptical with a frequency of approximately 100 000 years, the slope of its axis changes slightly with a frequency of approximately 40 000 years, and finally, like a spinning top, with a frequency of 22–26 000 years, it flickers (precesses) slightly around its axis.

It is probably the sum of these Milanković cycles that is primarily responsible for the fact that in the last million years we frequently shifted between Ice Ages (during which, for example, Northern Europe may be situated under glaciers) and (like now) interglacial periods, during which the planet flourished and Northern Europe became habitable.

So, in other words, we are living on borrowed time between Ice Ages – in a temporary interglacial period. The most recent Ice Ages all lasted about 90 000 years, and the last four interglacial periods between them lasted 16 000, 20 000, 5000, and 14 000 years respectively or, on average, approximately 13 750 years. The current interim interglacial period is now 11 700 years old, so you would be entitled to ask climate scientists when they think it will end and the ice caps will return. But in this context, we are met with very different answers, ranging from, 'I don't know' to, 'In About 1500 years'. The latter answer perhaps refers to the fact that by emitting greenhouse gases, we have actually prevented the next Ice Age.

But let us proceed. As it happens, scientists have found a huge range of other factors, which make recurring impact within timescales of hundreds or thousands of years. The first five relate to the intensity of solar radiation and sunspots, where sunspots affect the magnetic field around the solar system, which in turn affects the weather – presumably a lot:

- Hallstatt Cycle – a cycle of solar activity with a frequency of 2200–2400 years.
- De Vries/Suess Cycle – a solar cycle with approximately 200 years' frequency.
- Gleissberg Cycle – a solar cycle with approximately 88 years' frequency.
- Hale Cycle or double sunspot cycle – a solar cycle with approximately 22 years' frequency.
- Schwabe Cycle or sunspot cycle – approximately 11 years' frequency.

Then we have five periodic shifts in ocean currents, alternately bringing warmer and colder water to the surface:

- Atlantic Multidecadal Oscillation – approximately 50–70 years.
- Pacific Decadal Oscillation – 20–30 years.
- Interdecadal Pacific Oscillation – 15–30 years.
- North Atlantic Oscillation – 3–8 years.
- El Niño–Southern Oscillation, La Niña – 2–7 years.

Unlike, for example, the Milanković Cycles, these solar, and especially sea, cycles are not particularly predictable. Their frequencies vary a lot and cannot be modelled securely in mathematical terms.

In any case, what we have just seen is that there are major impacts on the climate from three Milanković Cycles, five solar cycles, and five sea cycles. Furthermore, the climate is affected by random events such as eruptions of huge volcanoes on land and underwater, meteor strikes, and unpredictably vast emissions of the greenhouse gas methane, which is a violent greenhouse gas but which on average decomposes in the atmosphere in just 12 years. Then there are the changes in the topology of the landscape.

So, it was these and perhaps other forces of nature that were responsible for the huge climate fluctuations of the past. In addition, there are the recent decades of greenhouse gas emissions caused by humans (which was quite insignificant prior to World War II). Bearing all this in mind, let us now look at how the global climate has evolved in the last 450 000 years according to ice drillings in Antarctica:

Temperatures in Antarctica over the past 450 000 years

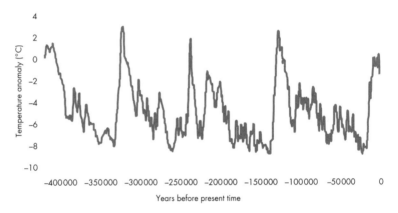

In other words, during this period we have had repeated and relatively cyclical natural temperature variations of approximately 13 °C. Incidentally, the current interglacial period is approximately 2 °C colder than the previous ones, even though now there is more carbon dioxide. The reason for this is unclear.

But let us then zoom in on what has happened in the current interglacial period – the last 11 700 years, which constitute the top at the far right of the last graph, and which, moreover, have led to a natural rise in sea level of – wait for it – approximately 130 m. It is during this period that human civilisation emerged. We can start with the following time range, which is based on ice core drilling in Greenland:

Temperatures on the Greenland ice sheet in the current global interglacial period

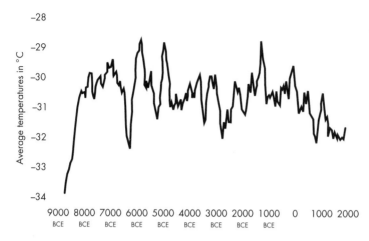

Note here the last cooling, which is referred to as the Little Ice Age. At least for Europe, it was an unpleasant chill, which contributed to famine.

However, there were also warm periods, which we know from many other sources. For instance, we know that the Vikings (the Norsemen) farmed in Greenland 1000 years ago, which you can't do today, and that the Normans in their *Domesday Book* (1086) actually counted a number of vineyards in England. We also know that in Roman times there was a period of significantly warmer weather in the Alps than now, as a result of which some of our current glaciers, such as the Schnidejoch in Switzerland, melted completely. Likewise, we know that, at the start of the period on the graph, North Africa was savannah rather than desert as it is today. This was due to warmer climate and more precipitation than today. But where is the so frequently mentioned global warming on this graph? It is missing because the ice drillings for the graph only give us reliable data until 1850.

Let me now present a graph that shows the course of the warming after the end of the Little Ice Age, this time not measured in Greenland, but as a global average:

Global temperatures 1850–2019

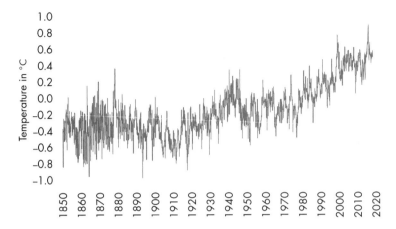

It shows roughly unchanged temperatures from 1850 to around 1920, after which came a warming of approximately 0.75 °C over the following 100 years. The warming also came in two roughly equal waves. The first, which lasted from approximately 1920 to 1945, can largely be attributed to natural causes, since the extensive man-made greenhouse gas emissions had not yet started. On the other hand, virtually all scientists ascribe joint responsibility to our greenhouse gas emissions for the second wave.

The fact that greenhouse gases warm the climate is, in my view, quite indisputable. The physics behind the phenomenon is simple. And the fact that its effect also has a certain duration is trivial knowledge. As mentioned, methane remains in the atmosphere for an average of 12 years, but carbon dioxide disappears more slowly. Between 65% and 80% dissolves in the ocean over 20–200 years, while the rest remains in the atmosphere for a slightly longer period (there is great uncertainty about these figures!). Apart from some scientific uncertainty, the broad interval cited here is due to that the fact that the natural reduction in carbon dioxide in the atmosphere depends on the initial concentration. Consensus today seems to be that if we stopped all carbon dioxide emissions in 2020, the concentrations in the atmosphere would drop from current levels of 405 ppm to approximately 340 ppm over the next 200 years and then more slowly towards a pre-industrial level of around 280 ppm.

Such calculations, moreover, relate to a statistical concentration, because along the way a single molecule can easily switch between the air and the sea several times. In fact, more than 95% of our planet's carbon dioxide has accumulated in the oceans rather than in the air. When climate warming occurs, or more specifically when ocean surface heats up, carbon dioxide is released from the seawater, thereby increasing its presence in the air, which is why climate graphs can show fluctuations in carbon dioxide that follow fluctuations in the climate – but delayed.

Incidentally, it must be said that when measuring direct effects only, it takes an exponential increase in carbon dioxide to create a linear increase in temperature – and we do not have that, because the increase of carbon dioxide is linear, not exponential. In cases where climate simulation models show stronger effects of greenhouses gas emissions, it is due to the expectation of self-reinforcing indirect effects.

The conclusion?

Allow me to conclude my review with a graph that pieces together the results of the ice core drilling in Greenland with later direct measurements of Greenland temperature (dotted line). Here we see that current global warming is the eighth of its kind within the last 11 700 years of the interglacial period, and it

Current warming in perspective

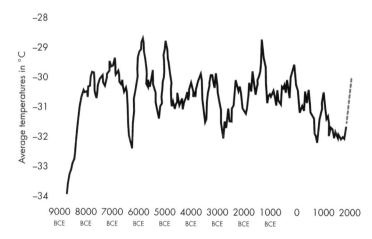

is the ninth, if we take into account the rise on the basis of the last Ice Age – a natural increase of 9 °C, which, as mentioned, raised the sea level by 130 m.

But what conclusions should we come to? In this context, people's opinions are all over the place. The attitude supported by the UN Intergovernmental Panel on Climate Change (IPCC) and most governments is that greenhouse gas emissions are a serious or even severely threatening problem, and therefore major intervention is called for. Regarding the nature of such intervention, people are divided along the lines of light, bright, and dark environmentalism.

Others, including (often retired) climate scientists, publicly state that the effect is moderate or minimal and does not require excessive measures. One argument some of these at times bring forward is that carbon dioxide only captures infrared light within very limited wavelengths where it is already largely blocked; more emissions won't change much.

There is also a group who believe that, since greenhouse gas emissions may delay or prevent the next Ice Age and that a greater carbon dioxide content in the air is undeniably stimulating faster plant growth, the greenhouse gas emissions do have some net advantages as long as they don't go on forever.

And finally, some scientists and engineers praise carbon dioxide as a resource for future direct air capture (DAC) technology. Just think about the Solein, which I mentioned previously: artificial flour created from carbon dioxide, water, and energy. This is a form of DAC technology. However, scientists are now pointing out that you also could use DAC to create fuel that can replace oil. This can be done in various ways, but the most promising so far is to transmit ambient air through a filter with an adsorbent. Various companies, such as Carbon Engineering, Global Thermostat, and Climeworks, are already doing this, and in 2018, National Academy of Sciences estimated that if the cost of extracting carbon dioxide went below $100–150 per ton of carbon, we could produce oil out of thin air at a lower cost than the traditional oil industry. To put that into perspective, Global Thermostat were in 2019 able to extract carbon dioxide at just $120 per ton and are expected to reach as little as $50 a ton within a few years. From such a perspective, airborne carbon dioxide becomes a valuable future commodity. Of course, it takes energy to extract the carbon dioxide, but this could come from solar or nuclear. The point of creating fuel becomes essentially to create a storage of energy – a liquid battery – which can be created anywhere on the globe and can utilise the current fuel-based infrastructure, from pipelines and gasoline tanks to internal combustion machines.

And there are countless more uses. For instance, the company CarbonCure has demonstrated that you can improve the quality of cement by injecting carbon into it. Another company, Carbon Upcycling UCLA, does something similar, which results in a concrete dubbed $CO_2NCRETE^{TM}$. So, there is this, but also plastics and many other materials made with carbon dioxide captured from the atmosphere.

In the face of such different views, I think it is up to every reader to come to his or her own conclusion about the truth. I personally know a number of incredibly bright, knowledgeable people who are divided vis-à-vis these opinions. So, instead of drawing a conclusion, I will concentrate on how I personally believe things are most likely to turn out in the future.

Firstly, neither the Kyoto nor the Paris Agreement on carbon dioxide reduction comes close in any meaningful way to solving the problem (if there even is a problem). For example, the Paris Agreement, if fully phased in, will cost about 1–2% of global GDP, but only contribute to reducing greenhouse gas emissions by approximately 1%. In other words, the agreements are extremely inefficient and expensive. Nor do I think that light environmentalism will have any meaningful impact, and dark environmentalism will, if anything, increase emissions over the long term.

What tends to happen – and will probably continue to happen – is that governments sign great treaties that will have little effect, pat each other on the back and drink toasts, and then most of them to some extent ignore them.

Ultimately, I think that energy conversion will take somewhere in the region of 60–70 years, or maybe even as long as 100 years – even if nuclear fusion works commercially in a few decades. Since the beginning of the major industrialisation of the world, the carbon dioxide in the atmosphere has increased from approximately 0.028% to 0.041%: in other words, an increase of 0.013%. If conversion takes 100 years, we may well see a further increase of the same magnitude: let us say to about 0.05%, which, viewed in a geological time perspective, will still be a very low level of carbon dioxide.

But what will drive the conversion? My guess is that it will be research and profit motive rather than international state agreements and 'enoughism' amongst consumers. Whether temperatures will continue to increase at the same, or more or less the same, rate as in the last century (0.75 °C per 100 years) or whether they will fall for natural reasons will probably depend largely on natural influences that we cannot predict with meaningful certainty.

The world is actually getting greener

Another important environmental issue is plant growth, because we are all keen on having a 'green' world. Some years ago, when I read Al Gore's book *An Inconvenient Truth* (2007) about climate change, I was quite stunned by a spread featuring a huge coloured image that presented a frightening scenario for a future, warmed planet, extensively covered by desert. It really amazed me, since one of the direct effects of carbon dioxide is the stimulation of plant growth. In fact, farmers often pump pure carbon dioxide into their greenhouses precisely for that reason.

On the occasions when the world has been warmer than now, there have been longer growing seasons, higher tree boundaries, and more rainfall: the latter because warmer seawater evaporates more. In practice, we are currently witnessing the fact that the world's green biomass is growing by almost 0.5% per year. Thus, a measurement from 1980 of the previous 30 years showed that the world's green biomass had increased by 14%, and later studies have shown that this is continuing. The reason cannot necessarily be ascribed only to concentrations of carbon dioxide, but also to more efficient agricultural technology, which leads to more biomass in fields and growth in the forest areas outside the tropics. In the wealthiest part of the world, this is actually resulting in the phenomenon now referred to as 'rewilding', whereby wild nature, including the likes of wolves, bears, and wild boar, is returning.

The sixth mass extinction?

Earlier, we looked at how our ancestors wiped out many large animal species. But what about now? There is a widely held belief that humankind is rapidly bringing about 'the sixth mass extinction' of species. Here are the previous five, to which they refer (figures for years and extinction vary from source to source):

- 450–440 million years ago: 60–70% of all species;
- 360–377 million years ago: 70% of all species;
- 252 million years ago: 90–96% of all species;
- 200 million years ago: 70–75% of all species;
- 65 million years ago: 75% of all species.

According to this account, each of the previous five mass extinctions affected 60–96% of all species. Moreover, the total, together with a regular change of species, is the reason why 99% of all species that have existed in the history of the planet are extinct. However, the number of species has almost never been higher than now, since new species have emerged all the time.

Today, all reports on endangered and suspected extinct species are recorded in the IUCN Red List, whose members include a number of governmental institutions and international organisations such as the Natural Resources Defence Council. In 2012, it appeared that, globally, between 1600 and 2012, around 900 known species had been wiped out. However, most scientific sources put the actual number of known species wiped out during these 400 or so years at just over 1000: c. 0.07% of known species.

The numbers correspond to an extinction of about 2.6 species per year: approximately 0.0001625% of all species. But what about species that die out without us ever discovering that they existed? If we estimate that about 150 unknown species have been further eradicated over the past 400 years, it would bring the total extinction to about 1200, or 3 species per year, which is equivalent to 0.034% of the world's species over 400 years, or 0.000085% per year. A frequent estimate of natural, balanced occurrence and extinction of species over the long term is one species going extinct and another developing per 400 years, so evidently, an extinction rate of three per year is approximately 1200 times the natural extinction rate.

So, is this the sixth mass extinction? I think it is a misrepresentation. If we are to come anywhere near the previous five mass extinctions, we will have to eradicate at least approximately 60% of the estimated 8.5 million species: the equivalent of about 5 million species. With three species a year, it will take 1.7 million years, which is around five times as long as humanity has existed. And this is without counting for the possibility that humans will start to create new species – and perhaps at rates that will soon exceed extinction rates.

It is, of course, sad and sometimes tragic that over the past few centuries more species have been eradicated than before. For sure, 1200 times the natural extinction rate is a very bad thing. But to assume that this extinction will continue unabated for the foreseeable future, let alone over a million years, seems to me extremely unlikely, given that the world's green biomass is increasing by approximately 2 billion tons a year, and that the size of global nature reserves has more than doubled over the past 50 years. In addition, international aquariums, zoos, and botanical gardens have set up breeding programmes, so together they will contain a considerable number of the world's known species, which will make it possible to release them into the wild again in the event of a crisis. Today there are also more than 1000 seed banks, where seeds from an increasing number of plant species are stored and regularly planted for renewal. Added to that, at exponential speed we are decoding DNA for the life of the planet and developing technologies to recreate extinct species. So, the future does not look as black as it is often depicted. But the main point is that the progress is mainly a result of the advice and technology we are acquiring to address the challenges. In other words, the advances are due to prosperity and innovation.

Let me round off my comments on environment and resources like this. For many leftists, the fall of the Berlin Wall entailed a massive loss of illusion when it came to a belief in the favourable influence of Marxism on the economy of the working class. That loss of illusion led to three ramifications: social democracy, ecofascism, and what we can call soft sustainability. One frequent component of this intricate web of points of view is dark environmentalism including, for instance, resistance to technologies such as nuclear power and genetic manipulation. These points of view have succeeded in creating a powerful narrative that claims that economic growth leads to resource shortages and environmental disasters. People often argue that the solution is a kind of command economy or rationing economy, and that the business community is the enemy of sustainability. This helps explain why environmental catastrophism is much more current among left-wingers than among right-wingers.

Considering how persistent this power struggle between 'panic-mongers' and 'deniers' (as they sometimes refer to one another) has been, I predict that there will be a continuing struggle between people who, on the basis of arguments about resource shortages and environmental threats, will choose dark environmentalism and move towards rationing societies, and others who, on the basis of arguments about growth, technology, and freedom, will lean towards bright environmentalism and thus seek to promote growth-oriented innovation societies. But also that, under this surface, there will be a political struggle related to inequality versus growth and, accordingly, collectivism versus liberalism.

7.
NEW NET-WORKS AND DECENTRALISED TECHNOLOGIES

'Creativity is just connecting things. When you ask creative people how they did something, they feel a little guilty because they didn't really do it, they just saw something.' These were the words of the co-founder of Apple, Steve Jobs, in an interview in Wired magazine in 1995. As far as I'm concerned, he was right. It is almost impossible to find any innovation that does not essentially combine elements that existed before. The same is also true of life, for example. There are only 118 different chemical elements, all of which are made of helium and hydrogen, but the atoms form the building blocks for our estimated 8.5 million living species (plus an astronomical number of different bacteria and viruses).

That is why the ability and the opportunity to combine things in new ways is crucial to the creation of innovation and thus prosperity. This is also evident in the fact that, historically speaking, prosperity was chiefly created where access to trade was easiest. Until the invention of roads, railways, and air transport, this generally meant in the vicinity of sea and rivers. Accordingly, empire upon empire (for example, the Venetian) evolved from people who had particularly good access to shipping. Probably the most advanced civilisation in Africa emerged on the banks of the only African river that was navigable throughout the year and ran into the sea: the Nile.

In other words, it is all about networking, and connecting people so they can combine their ideas, products, and services – not forgetting genes. And one of the greatest societal changes I have experienced in my own life is a huge increase in the possibilities of communicating with others, of course primarily through the Internet. However, now and in the future, there will be a number of processes related to the Internet that will create totally new dynamics and new opportunities. We're talking new forms of networking, new managerial structures, and new decentralised technologies. Let's take a look at them.

Geosocialisation. Who – and where! – you are

When I am stupid enough to drive to Zurich airport during the rush hour, my GPS sometimes sends me on a detour to avoid traffic jams. It combines knowledge about where I am and where I am going and traffic information, which means that I make my flight, despite traffic jams. But the knowledge of where you are can also be used for geosocialisation, or geosocial networking, in which people get together, according to where they are in purely physical terms here and now. For example, your smartphone might tell you which of your friends and acquaintances are in your immediate vicinity, whether you are near a shop that stocks a product you are after, or whether some of your friends have signed up for an event near your home. Professionally, one of the most interesting aspects of geosocialisation is the fact that it might enhance your understanding of who the people you are surrounded by at professional meetings, conferences, etc., really are and perhaps what they are looking for.

An early example of geosocialisation is the search engine Layar, which combines GPS, a smartphone, and a compass to identify where you are and what you are looking at. The information can immediately be used as a basis for our aforementioned augmented reality.

Synergy between geosocialisation and augmented reality

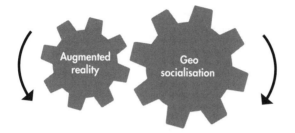

In order for geosocialisation to become useful rather than annoying or even dangerous, we must each be able to control whom and what we get information about. For example, only two people who *both* want to know whether the other is nearby, or *both* want to know about the other's interest in a specific area, should get the information.

The e-commerce revolution – far from over

One particular hallmark of recent years has been the struggle of physical shops to survive in the face of online shopping. Growth in the field of order-based, online shopping is huge. Dominated, particularly in the United States and substantially in other Western countries, by the giant Amazon, in 2018 it exceeded a market capitalisation level of more than $1000 billion.

Physical versus digital commerce in the United States

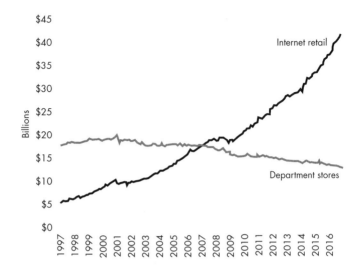

Online shopping saves time and makes it easier to find and compare the right products than in a physical shop. It also provides access to far more products. For example, Amazon sells more than 10 million different products, plus others from its 200 000 or so Amazon Marketplace dealers. However, e-commerce has a further advantage over physical commerce. In a department store, my shopping basket will reveal whether I have roughly the same lifestyle and taste as you. If I do, we could probably have a useful chat about products we have found and like. But that does not happen, because we do not chat to strangers in department stores, and we do not share our knowledge.

But something similar does, when we shop online via the electronically generated feature: 'Customers Who Bought This Item Also Bought…' In these networks you do not find out who the other people are, but you do learn from each other's experience. By the way, this is known as 'collaborative filtering'.

However, by leaps and bounds, Amazon is now entering the world of physical retail – a process that began when they acquired Whole Foods in 2017 for just under $14 billion. Obviously, Amazon's approach to physical retail will not simply be the same as that of its rivals, and that may mean moving towards a range of *hybrid* offers. For example, you order online but pick up your goods in physical shops. That is relevant if, say, you cannot get large packages delivered directly to your home.

One of Amazon's goals is also to create almost fully automated physical shops, where you can just take goods away, after which the money is automatically charged to your account electronically. This can be done via video surveillance and an ingenious combination of IoT, big data, and AI. Amazon has also patented a mirror, in which, via AR, you can see yourself wearing different clothes. The chain Sephora has done something similar. Via Modiface software, their customers can see simulations of themselves in different makeup.

Synergies in e-shopping

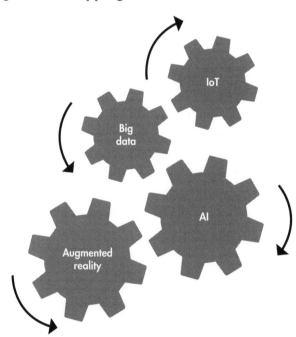

One consequence of this development is a new, interesting, and decentralised computer system that includes the so-called 'physical cookie'. The system takes its name from the online version of cookies, in which our digital footprints are used to target advertising at us. The physical version uses a chip with an isolated computer system, in which the user's behaviour in the shop is tracked. That facilitates the targeting of information for users.

Influencer marketing

Using influencers is a very old strategy in marketing: for example, via product placement in feature films (such as sponsoring James Bond's car) or using brand ambassadors such as Caroline Wozniaki, Tiger Woods, and Tom Cruise. Obviously that phenomenon will not disappear, but it will change. For example, using electronics you can control individually which product placements each user sees. You can also do it with virtual advertisements in live sports TV. However, a large growth area is influencer marketing: where, say, you get networks of popular bloggers to write about your product. It started by focusing on the biggest online stars, but in the future digital algorithms will increasingly be used to detect much broader networks of so-called micro influencers, who are normal people around you rather than online stars. This facilitates the promotion of products that appeal to even the most weird and geeky areas of interest. However, the really major effect is that micro influencers can be more effective, since we rely mostly on our friends and family. That is why companies are already using, and will increasingly use, what really are just average social media users.

The wild decentralised autonomous organisations

A concept that is really useful to know going forward is decentralised autonomous organisations, or DAOs. A DAO is a value-driven organisation that can run totally without management and, in principle, indefinitely, after the founders have left the helm. One version, by the way, is a decentralised autonomous corporation (DAC): in other words, a self-governing company.

An example of something quite like a DAO is Protestantism. Excuse me? No, really. Protestantism resembles a DAO in that, unlike, say, the Roman Catholic Church or Tibetan Buddhism, it has no Pope or Dalai Lama at the top. And yet, while Protestantism has no central top management, it organises and promotes itself relatively spontaneously. Similarly, and again spontaneously, it has often divided itself into subspecies such as Presbyterianism, Baptist, Quakers, and hundreds of other offshoots.

We can also describe the Internet as a partial DAO, although it requires some central control – particularly when it comes to the allocation of domains. But otherwise, the Internet spread globally and to all sectors with neither a plan nor control – almost like a virus. In addition, the Internet is partly a so-called network without infrastructure (NWI), given that it utilises all existing lines of communication. But it is not entirely a DAO and an NWI.

Natural life, however, is a mega-scale DAO. Perhaps with us an exception due to our consciousness of ourselves, life is controlled by the codes in DNA, which is the ultimate DAO, apart from when humans manipulate it. And each of the millions of species on Earth, like Protestantism, manages to organise and promote itself spontaneously, and to divide into new versions, creating spontaneous ecosystems with no top management.

Many recent 'super firms' such as YouTube, Uber, and AliBaba are in fact hybrids of traditional companies and DAOs, because a large part of these companies' assets are created in a decentralised, digital community, which is capable of continuing even if the companies' management take 12 months off.

We need to be aware that modern DAOs are predominantly digital and controlled by distributed software. These organisations can be very stable because they are not controlled from headquarters. Instead, they are distributed from people's computers around the world – and on each computer the entire company is often available. Malicious examples are computer viruses, which can often function completely without central control, and which also, like biological viruses, can be difficult to eradicate, once they are released. Another and more useful example is Orchid, which makes peer-to-peer Internet that bypasses all routers and thus allows free communication between people living in countries that have Internet censorship. And of course, I have to mention blockchain: the technological premise for the likes of cryptocurrencies. We'll come back to that. But overall, the following applies:

35. **As the world becomes more digitised, it creates increasing numbers of digital organisations and companies, which can be run and evolve without any form of classic/central management.**

The reason for this is, of course, that everything that is programmable can be programmed to perform automatic routines and, thereby, self-management. In principle, a DAO can also be programmed by AI, which would – or will – create spontaneous digital evolution.

Blockchain – the Internet of Value

Blockchain is an important technology for DAOs. It was invented and launched in 2009 by a person (or group) known by the supposed alias of Satoshi Nakamoto. His white paper on the idea relates to Bitcoin (written with a lower case 'b' when it refers to currency and an upper case 'B' when discussing the network), but the underlying technology is blockchain, which is also Satoshi's invention.

But what exactly is blockchain? It may be defined as a common register for recording a transaction history, which cannot be deleted or altered. Key components are:

- All parties must give their consensus before a new transaction is added to the network.

- A common register, which is impossible to manipulate. Once recorded, transactions cannot be changed.

- This eliminates or reduces paper processes, accelerates transaction times, and increases efficiency.

The first blockchain implementation was digital money, led by bitcoin, and overall its value rose from virtually $0 to $9 billion in May 2016 (which in itself was remarkable) and then to $420 billion at some point in 2018, which was gigantic and obviously dominated numerous front pages. In other words, there was no lack of interest.

It is no wonder that cryptocurrencies have evolved so rapidly. I mean, issuing your own money is a smart business model if it works. Who wouldn't want to own a central bank, ha ha?

Internet of Value

In simple terms, blockchain can also be described as a decentralised technology for recording and booking transfers of value or knowledge of them, without the data being hacked or altered. This can be used to create programmable money, securities, and contracts.

Cryptocurrencies have been criticised for the fact that they in particular have no value in themselves. But that is something of a misunderstanding, because the value lies in the network effect that follows Metcalfe's Law, which states that the effect of a telecommunications network is proportionate to the square of the number of registered users linked to the system.

Paper money works despite having zero intrinsic value, and the same can thus apply to blockchain. Today, blockchain technology can serve as a bookkeeping system, in which value such as money, music, bonds, gift vouchers, bonus points, and shares can be safeguarded. It means that people all over the world can perform peer-to-peer deals without an intermediary, without knowing each other, and without using any security other than that which the blockchain system provides by protecting information with cryptography, complex coding, and a decentralised register.

Decentralised applications and smart contracts

Together, this explains blockchain's ability to facilitate DAOs. The prospect can be explained as follows. It knows no bounds, in the same way that Airbnb allows everyone to rent directly to each other across borders, and it creates programmability in these values, just as your smartphone today has lots of apps – unlike the phone you had in 2005. In this context we refer to 'dapps', which stands for 'decentralised applications', which correspond to value units with programmed properties. Dapps can also be described as smart contracts, in which an algorithm can determine whether a given contract's content is being complied with, and then reward or sanction financially through blockchain technology, where the process will take place as a regular transaction.

The technology has a myriad of applications, such as a payment for shipping a container that is automatically triggered when a GPS sensor detects that it has arrived at a given location. It can also be used for so-called 'self-sovereign identity', whereby people can prove their personal rights without simultaneously revealing their other identity. Provisionally, the most prominent example of the use of blockchain technology is, as mentioned, cryptocurrencies, which can be programmed. A variation of this could be money that is only used in certain businesses, at certain times, or in certain circumstances – something occasionally referred to as 'coloured money'. It will also be possible to use perishable cryptocurrencies to counteract an economic downturn: for example, by issuing money that can only be used over the next six months, or when interest rates are negative so that the value will turn to dust in your hands unless you spend the money. You could even issue perishable coloured money in order to help a specific struggling sector of the economy during a specific time period. In other words, the technology has the potential to just about eliminate recessions. Imagine that everyone could have a crypto wallet on their smartphone. When a recession is about to start, the central bank would send them some easily perishable crypto money. That should certainly get the ball rolling.

Initial coin offerings

Blockchain is also the basis for so-called ICOs or initial coin offerings, sometimes also referred to as 'token sales'. It is a bit like stock market listings, but happens outside the usual institutions, and investors pay usually, but not always, with a cryptocurrency such as bitcoin. There are four types of ICO:

- Money: pure currency such as bitcoin or Ethereum.
- Gift voucher: a utility token/user token, which gives buyers access to a service.

- Stocks or shares: equity security, which gives buyers a share in an asset, such as a commodity or an operating company. This can be related to distribution of dividends.
- Bonds: debt allocation that gives access to returns.

In recent years, Nordic Eye and I have been bombarded with ICO offers. It is not something we have invested much time in, since we, and I personally, believe that an overwhelming majority of early ICOs will fail: some because they are simply fraudulent; and others because they are pretty frivolous. Also, partly because most start-ups simply fail. However, the most insightful observers of cryptocurrencies expect that, in most cases, these will just be teething problems for the sector, that the level of quality will rapidly improve, and that blockchain will spread to a variety of sectors. As I write, Facebook has announced its launch of a cryptocurrency which kind of sounds like a big deal for the sector. Wallmart too.

Blockchain can also help reduce poverty. Some 70% of landowners worldwide have only poorly publicly registered ownership of the land or property they actually have at their disposal. In virtually all countries, it is the state that registers land ownership, but in countries where the level of corruption is high, it often happens that property is stolen/redistributed without the actual owner being able to do anything about it.

Many experts believe that the lack of opportunity to register property is one of the major reasons that some nations do not extricate themselves from poverty: partly because people cannot provide security for loans to start a business or give their children a better education. This can be solved by using a separate blockchain system to archive all the information that states normally handle. That would prevent any public administration exploiting its citizens for its own gain.

Here is another example of social benefits. The largest capital outflow from the industrialised world to developing countries consists of private money transactions, estimated at approximately $600 billion per year. This is often people sending money to their families. As a rule, there is a fee of about 10%, and it can take up to six weeks before the money arrives. However, with the crypto-transfer app Abra, the same process can be completed in two minutes at a cost of 2%.

A third potential gain is in industries where individuals are underpaid for the digital content they produce. The music industry is a prime example. Today, songwriters and artistes are paid a mere fraction of the revenue that a hit single generates. The innovative music collective Mycelia is attempting to tackle this problem by linking musicians' songs to a blockchain, where you can only use the rights to the music if you own them in the block chain. If such projects succeed, it will be significantly more difficult to illegally distribute and share the pieces of music, films, and e-books that are covered: being able to enjoy the artistic content will require direct ownership. And this is an example of one of the most interesting potentials of blockchain: by eliminating middlemen – or at least reducing the need for them – it can spread rewards more efficiently to the people who create the actual value.

The rating economy – good for markets and culture

As is clear from what has been said here, in many of its applications blockchain is a kind of DAO, making, for example, tokens of value programmable, and solving a huge problem vis-à-vis trust between traders who do not know each other's identity. But what to do if they actually know the identity of the other person to some extent, but cannot necessarily expect to trade *again*?

That is an interesting problem. One of the important features of pre-industrial societies was the fact that you knew your suppliers and used them repeatedly, which meant that providing a good service was very much in suppliers' own interests, as pointed out eloquently by Adam Smith. What was the point of a blacksmith delivering a poor ploughshare for his neighbour across the lane, when it would be staring him in the face for the rest of his life?

However, as industrial production methods gained ground, and extreme specialisation and division of labour followed, anonymisation evolved, in which we ceased to know the people who made our things. This created bigger opportunities for fooling people.

The trademark or the brand became the solution.

Now, however, the situation has changed again. Thanks to social recommendations and collaborative filtering, we have access to precisely the products that are most likely to suits our needs, and we have access to an endless number of often very sincere assessments of a product's quality.

And that has its consequences. Indeed, with the growing spread of social recommendations and collaborative filtering, retailers are able to remove the trademark rights of some of the manufacturers – distributors instead introduce their own brands or 'brand-free' products, also known as white label, at lower prices for consumers and yet greater profit for the retailer. That is possible thanks to the new transparency. Yes, Louis Vuitton or Hermès will still have strong brands, but if you make toothpaste or nappies, it will be harder.

Ratings reflect a network (often anonymous) that streamlines our markets. And they come in many shapes and sizes. In the technology sector, headhunters sometimes use 'stack overflow ratings' to assess applicants. This stack overflow shows how often applicants' replies on technical social media have been upvoted to the best on the Internet. In other words, it is a kind of rating, the importance of which job applicants are probably not always aware of.

On average, the evaluations made by people, who broadly speaking have no motive to write false reviews, are very credible. The evaluations are also a crucial component of the sharing economy, not to mention a significant explanation for the fact that a service like Uber can function and provide better service than a traditional taxi company. Both parties in this transaction know that if the driver treats the passenger badly, he or she will get a bad rating and will therefore be deselected by other potential passengers or totally excluded from the network. Of course, it cuts both ways. The driver also rates the passenger.

The global village and its new cyber rock stars

The spread of the Internet means that a completely new, radical transparency is emerging, which is extremely meritocratic. If you live in a small village in eastern Angola and are really good at football, the whole world can spot your skills on social media – as long as you can film those skills and upload the film online. That was not possible before. Similarly, YouTubers quickly get a very large audience if what they offer is actually interesting and gets upvoted. The fact that the most talented and most dedicated people are discovered is a beautiful and just thought, and it certainly benefits society as a whole. A simple example of that benefit is that appalling restaurants seem to be getting fewer, because now they quickly get blacklisted on social media and lose their customers. And great ones gain fame quickly.

Thanks to rating technologies, over time it will be far more socioeconomically preferable for abilities and effort, rather than advertising budget, social status, personal network, origin, brand, or a particular surname, to determine how well you get on. And over time, it will more often be your customers' assessments rather than your formal education, family name, or trade union's demands that determine your personal income.

But it goes further than that. In itself, market economics, by experience, creates a more friendly culture, because people have to be good at attracting customers – and even more so if ratings are efficient. We can expect the rating economy to enhance this and to strengthen what is called social capital.

Another effect of this is that it counteracts traditional inflation in goods and services – simply because any buyer anywhere can easily find the cheapest supplier of anything, anywhere on the net. The result is that when central banks change money supply in order to change inflation rates, the effects are often more clearly felt in asset prices than in prices of normal products and services.

Share, care, and save (sharing economy) - hot, hot, hot

There is nothing new about sharing things, but because of IT, it can now be done to a much greater extent than before; and this is an area our venture fund Nordic Eye has invested heavily in by purchasing shares in sharing services for boats, bicycles, storage space, and motor scooters. The sharing economy has become one of the world's fastest growing segments, partly because it often reuses things that already exist. Its main purpose is to save money and resources, while increasing the supply of services by sharing things. There are three forms:

- As-a-service: flexible short-term rental of or subscription to objects or services that a central provider owns and looks after. Examples include server parks in the cloud or scooter rental in big cities. Then there are as-a-service subscriptions, for example, for socks, coffee, or beauty products, which can then normally be sold at reduced prices, because, following the initial sale, the manufacturer acquires a regular customer.

- Crowdsourcing: the same, but here the person in the street owns the leased objects or provides the relevant services. Uber and Airbnb are prime examples. What gets shared can be money, services, or, for example, cars, bicycles, scooters, and motor scooters.

- Peer-to-peer: the person in the street exchanges services without an intermediary: for example, over a DAO, which is not owned by anyone. In this context, ratings are usually required for things to run optimally. Cryptocurrencies, for example, are traded in peer-to-peer networks. But other examples include: Open Garden, where people are connected on the Internet via wi-fi and Bluetooth; Infin, which is a file-sharing application for digital artists; and WebTorrent, which is an anonymous streaming service.

Platforms such as Airbnb are sometimes referred to as peer-to-peer, but actually they are not really, because there is an intermediary involved. However, organised peer-to-peer networks, a kind of hybrid, are frequently the most efficient. Another rapidly growing example is 'cloud kitchens' or 'ghost restaurants', which solely serve online orders. In their ultimate crowdsourcing form, these can offer freelance chefs the use of the facilities to service online customers.

The synergies of the sharing economy

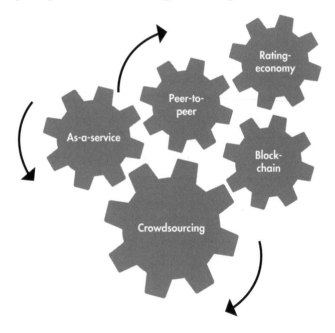

Amazingly, digital platforms facilitate sharing with the entire world. Previously, only your closest friends knew that you had empty seats in your car on Friday when driving from one city to another. Or that you wanted to share your lawnmower to get part of it paid for by others. Or that you were willing to remove people's garden rubbish on Thursday morning for a small fee. Or that you had a dog that needed walking. Or that you would like to share an evening meal with a family in Barcelona on Saturday. Or that you needed to collect a package at the post office and could take something else with you.

However, this is no longer the case; now you can share such desires – there are markets for them. In fact, you can now offer and request all the above-mentioned services and a huge range of others digitally, to/from a potentially global audience. It is both easy and user-friendly. It even relates to services that would not previously have been sold or shared.

The astonishing thing to many people is that overall you can totally rely on people. When you use Airbnb, eBay, Uber, BlaBlaCar, Lyft, La Ruche qui dit Oui, Munchery, Postmates, and many other of the countless digital platforms, you discover that, in general, people do stick to the agreements that have been made. In this sense, too, I believe that the sharing economy and its ratings improve culture:

36. **The sharing economy creates increasing trust among humans and thus increases the level of social capital.**

The absence of trust is an expensive barrier in all societies. Without trust, we are reluctant to enter into agreements with strangers, and if we do, we invest many, non-value-creating resources in trying to ensure that we do not get cheated.

Arun Sundararajan, an expert in the sharing economy and author of the book *The Sharing Economy* (2016), has pointed out that, historically speaking, there are some fascinating aspects to the sharing economy. One might immediately believe that the sharing economy yielded *less* growth, since fewer lawnmowers are needed if 20 people share each of them. Sundararajan, however, argues convincingly that the development will actually increase the economic growth rate. Historically, increased supply, increased variety, and better utilisation of existing resources actually lead to higher per capita productivity; and this higher productivity is a fundamental ingredient of economic growth, to which we can then add the positive effects of increased confidence. He says that this mechanism is stronger than the effect of not producing as many lawnmowers, because people are sharing them. And it is probably underestimated in statistical measurements by national economists, who will certainly detect how many lawnmowers get manufactured but not necessarily what benefit each of them generates. The GDP, which is interesting is the overall benefit or 'utility' that it reflects. The sharing economy can help with that. A lot, in fact.

Exponential organisations: big money!

I will round off this review of new forms of networking with a fascinating phenomenon common to many new networks: exponential organisations (ExOs) – a phenomenon which my venture capital colleagues and I love. I have already mentioned a number of examples, including various social networks and crowdsourcing organisations, but their common denominator is that they roll out their services across existing resources (such as the existing telephone network or the existing vehicle fleet) and activate people who are not officially affiliated with the organisation. Uber, Facebook, and Fiverr are examples of utilising existing, available capacity. ExOs often use automation and viral online marketing, and usually have enormous influence on the size of their organisation. Furthermore, they will frequently achieve network effects that can make them very robust, once they have a good foothold. By the way, a classic example is Tupperware, which was founded in 1942 and is a multi-level marketing organisation. Today they have – wait for it – 1.9 million sellers!

A phenomenon parallel to ExOs is replicators: things that can make copies and variations of themselves. Viruses and all living beings are replicators. But can people create replicators? Yes, absolutely. In addition to familiar shared-economy services, they include AI-based software that can write software by itself, robots that can build robots, and 3D printers that can print copies of themselves. We will also witness more of this in the future. The most important development will probably be the first: software that can write software by itself. Consequently, the combination of DAOs, ExOs, and 3D printers will be explosive.

The technology trio behind replicators

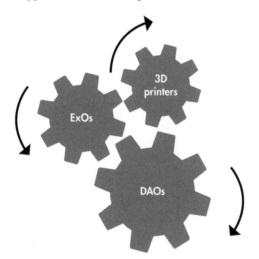

8.
THE TRANS-PORT, HOUSES, AND CITIES OF THE FUTURE

Housing, local environment, and transport play a major role in everyone's lives – in mine too. Even as a student at the Danish Royal Veterinary and Agricultural University and Copenhagen Business School, in my spare time I would often construct cardboard models of my dream houses and, to stop myself from falling asleep in my lectures, I frequently sat drawing houses. A number of years later, when I could finally afford something resembling what I had dreamed about, I spent a lot of time on interior design. Similarly, I have a great love of cars. So, I am equally interested in how these areas will develop in the future. What I think is especially interesting is that new modes of transport often help shape new structures in terms of housing and urbanisation. For example, cars created opportunities for detached houses in suburbs, and it is micromobility that now reduces the number of cars in metropolitan areas, freeing up space for pavement cafés, just as electric cars will reduce urban noise. Together, this will make cities more attractive as places to live and, as a result, people will move back to cities. Then funnily enough, when autonomous cars later make their breakthrough, they will once again lead to detached-house living, just as the first cars did. After all, there is certainly nothing wrong with snuggling up at night in a home close to nature.

The transport of the future – faster and more flexible

While we continue to travel more, there are some technical developments pulling in the opposite direction. First, the development of digital infrastructures has cut down on a lot of physical transport. Furthermore, the fast-growing robot revolution coupled with the spread of AI will provide 'backsourcing', which is the opposite of outsourcing. Outsourcing shifts production to countries where labour is cheaper, whereas backsourcing brings it back home again if automation is cheaper than cheap labour. Backsourcing will reduce the need for transport.

At the same time, however, we are increasingly trading across the globe, and this development will continue despite backsourcing, solely because we will increase in numbers and get richer. Our financial opportunities for travel are also improving, and our desire for it is increasing. When I was young, I had never heard of people flying off somewhere for a weekend. In fact, flights were so exotic and rare that when my father occasionally had to catch a plane, the whole family would accompany him to the airport to say goodbye, after which we waited there to watch the plane take off. That took half a day.

When I became a father myself, it was another world. In fact, it was often the case that my daughters, for example, would call and ask if I could pick them up from school in Zug or Zurich, but I would have to inform them that I was in London, but would be back in time for a late dinner. Likewise, people nowadays often fly off for a long weekend of skiing or a spot of Mediterranean sun. So overall, because technology is getting better and, most importantly, cheaper, transporting people and goods will only increase, increase, and increase again.

There are a few trends in the development that are worth dwelling on. Firstly, the former simple division of private and public transport is rapidly disappearing in the face of a division between three concepts:

- Private transport, such as private cars, bicycles, and, increasingly, quadcopters, etc.
- Shared transport, such as autonomous electric cars and shared bicycles, shared kick scooters, and shared motor scooters.
- Public transport, such as trains, buses, and planes.

In this context, shared transport is the big, exciting growth area within the larger phenomenon of the sharing economy, which I have already mentioned. This will spread further and acquire an extra dimension when we can share autonomous electric cars, including privately owned ones, like quasi-automatic Uber cars. For practical reasons, the sharing concept will be particularly prevalent in big cities. The same will probably apply to the distribution of goods via robots. In general, therefore, cities will have the best dynamics and transport options and also because traffic jam problems will be reduced as a result of the micromobility revolution.

Some people believe that in the future, due to the development of the sharing economy and the idea behind changing concept of ownership, there will be less demand for cars, just as the influx of people into big cities will mean that cars will increasingly be replaced by smaller-scale means of transport such as shared bicycles and motor scooters etc. In other words, fewer cars in the world.

I do not believe this will happen – at least not in the next few decades, and probably the remainder of this century. Firstly, the demand for cars in new markets will be far greater than the marginal decline that may come in big cities in the wealthiest countries on account of the sharing economy. And let us not forget that for many people the car is more than just a practical boon – otherwise there would not be so many car washes and car magazines! An incredible number of people (such as me) like, even love, cars. It is also practical, for example, to leave your children's seats in your own car, or leave something, which you bought yesterday and intend to deliver to your sister tomorrow, in the boot of your own car overnight.

Another trend is autonomous cars, or the phase that preceded them: assisted driving. The latter is already a reality and will further develop in the future. It will no longer be the car that monitors whether we are about to do something stupid, but vice versa – the car will drive itself, while we will just have to keep an eye on how it is going. In fact, that is already the way I drive on motorways.

We are probably a little further way from 100% autonomous, but they will come. Once we had lift operators to press the buttons in the lift, and we had petrol pump attendants to take care of petrol station, and sales assistants when we went shopping for daily commodities. But now the following is true:

37. Modern economies promote and enable self-service and automation of almost any kind.

This is often a three-step process moving from (1) human to (2) computer-assisted human (centaur) and on to (3) autonomous computer/robot. This trend will also affect the role of the driver. Of course, one exception will be that people will still be able to switch to manual drive, since many people, just like now, will enjoy driving. But the professional driver sector will probably end up going the same way as the lift operator sector.

I should also add that advances in micromobility and the prevalence of autonomous cars will increase mobility for children and the elderly. This will have positive social consequences, counteracting the stress of driver parents and the loneliness of physically-isolated elderly people.

Space travel

After decades when space travel has made no major progress, we now seem to be approaching a time that will offer several new excursions to the moon, and then to Mars. Two main drivers behind this are: (1) the fact that China, India, and other nations are reaching stages where they can afford such national programmes; and (2) that private companies such as SpaceX, Blue Origin, Virgin Galactic, and Boing are reducing the costs of space launches massively.

A particularly interesting aspect of this is the idea to use local 3D printing machines and robots to build accommodation on the moon and Mars instead of shipping it all up there. On Mars, where there is an atmosphere with carbon dioxide, one could even use DAC to create cement, food, and plastic out of the local atmosphere while powering this process with solar panels and/or small thorium reactors.

Long and medium-long distances

Traditionally, ultra-fast rockets were only used for, and associated with, space, but now supersonic aircraft are being developed that can cross the Atlantic in approximately three hours, and hypersonic aircraft that can do it in about one hour. One of the interesting technologies used in ultra-fast aircraft is the ramjet, and another version, the scramjet: jet engines with no moving parts that function optimally at approximately 3700 km an hour – some four times the normal cruising speed of commercial planes today. Ramjets and scramjets can only be started when the aircraft is already flying at high speed, but then they are extremely economical and reliable. So, an aircraft such as this requires two types of engine, which it combines. But, once the ramjet is in full swing, it kicks ass.

Another interesting combined-technology concept is hybrid aircraft. As I write this, hybrid projects for smaller aircraft for 50 passengers or less are ongoing. The idea is to take an aircraft that normally uses turboprops to produce two megawatts of power and replace it with turboprops of just one megawatt and batteries that can deliver another megawatt for the propellers during the 20 minutes needed for the steep climb to cruising altitude. Once the plane starts descent, these propellers work like a windmill, thus repowering the batteries.

For somewhat shorter distances, Elon Musk has developed the so-called Hyperloop concept, where people sit in capsules that pass through a vacuum tube with minimal air resistance and speeds of about 700 km per hour: in other words, rather like an airliner. Meanwhile, fast trains are already more developed and will spread further. They sometimes use magnetic tracks that keep them soaring: allegedly one step ahead of the Hyperloop, but without the vacuum.

Another concept that is already making a huge breakthrough is the aforementioned drones and other flying machines that can be made as accessible as cars are today. Of course, drones etc. are already on the market, but their full potential is still far from being exploited, partly due to regulatory and technological issues.

Now they are here in the form of the quadcopter taxi. Dubai is leading the way with an autonomous, four-propeller drone. It is Chinese and called EHang 184. So far, it can transport a passenger for 30 minutes at 160 km per hour. The idea is for 30% of Dubai's traffic to take place in the air by 2030. It is not for me to judge whether this will work, but EHang 184 has been thoroughly tested and is also making its way to other parts of the world, Nevada, for example. Personally, I think that the option of flying directly from the roof of a building to an airport or to a meeting in another building will be in huge demand. I know business executives in Switzerland who do this almost every week, albeit in helicopters.

Of course, we can imagine deafening noise, if the air is full of quadcopters, but the noise is substantially reduced if they are electric, and there are already early types of electric aircraft as well that are extremely quiet.

In the longer term, the development of quadcopters will mesh with the modern phenomenon, in which airports are extremely important for growth. Areas with good airports usually evolve much more quickly than areas without them, and access to transport is an economic driving force like no other. The pattern is that you build the airport on the outskirts of the city, and then the city moves towards the airport (even though people complain about the noise) – simply because it is so attractive to have easy access to transport. However, quadcopter traffic will add a new dimension to this phenomenon by decentralising air traffic hubs. Quite simply, many places will see the emergence of a myriad of micro airports.

Medium distances and short distances

When it comes to new transport technologies, driverless vehicles are some of the most talked about, and also something that is very close to implementation. The concept is already quite widespread in metro systems.

The advantage is, of course, partly that driverless vehicles are safer than manually controlled ones, and partly that they will free up time.

The vehicles of the future will also be equipped with so-called Next-Gen GPS Devices, which, in addition to route planning, can take better account of weather, traffic, safety, and personal preferences than today. And, most importantly, perform real-time updates and, based on them, propose diversions. Concurrently, experiments are being conducted with built-in sensors in roads so that they can communicate with cars.

Hybrid and electric cars are, of course, an important growth area, and most analyses I have seen expect that, by 2040, we will have a car market in which about 5% of vehicles are hybrid cars that can be charged, and the remainder roughly equally divided between and petrol/diesel and purely electric cars. Personally, I expect that the switch to electricity will continue, but that petrol/diesel cars will still be common even way into the latter half of this century.

Speaking of plug-in electric cars, they may in fact not literally need to 'plug in'. An alternative is roads that facilitate the charging of an electric car via induction, when it drives above an electromagnetic field over a certain distance. This is referred to as 'inductive charging' and means that electric cars do not have to stop in order to recharge. When you drive over a charging area, your batteries are automatically charged – and your credit card emptied.

There is also speculation about making a kind of car–train hybrid. One example is personal rapid transit, or Podcars, where on a main road or motorway, your car runs on rails on a so-called BiModal Glideway, where the propulsion of all cars is computer controlled at very great speed – for example, 200 km per hour. An elegant parallel to this is the so-called Transit Elevated Bus – a new bus concept in which a guided bus runs on rails on both sides of the road above the cars. That means a two-storey road is occasionally created without having to build some big ugly cement structure, and coach traffic in the extremely large coaches (since they span a traffic lane) both avoids and counteracts traffic jams.

Short distance – micromobility

The most important new solution for short-distance transport is the aforementioned new forms of micromobility: mainly bicycles, kick scooters, and motor scooters. The obvious advantage is that they can greatly alleviate problems with traffic chaos, simply because they are much smaller than cars. At the same time, they contribute to a pedestrian street feel. And they do not require the huge parking multi-storey car parks in city centres that cars do. Because they can get anywhere, they are also a cheap, flexible way of transporting people the last mile: for example, from a car, bus, or train to the final destination, such as an office, flat, shop, or restaurant. Currently, work is being done on solutions to the problem of people strewing them all over the place, which many people often do (also with bicycles in some cities, by the way), when they are not the owner. But I expect this will gradually be solved or at least mitigated.

The transport solutions of tomorrow will make a huge impact on where and how we want to live. I could easily imagine that in the future, many buildings will have landing pads for quadcopters on their roofs, not just for drone delivery of goods, but also for flying cars/drones. Won't we also see the emergence of lots of so-called fly-in communities, where people have their microplane and share one of the take-off airstrips approved by the aviation authorities or a helipad? Will cars have built-in scooters that can be taken out? I think it's all pretty likely. So now let's take a closer look at the housing and urban environments of the future.

Innovation in the construction sector

Imagine the following. You own a plot of land and want to build a property on it. So, you upload the land drawings to a server from the municipality, which then automatically matches them with local building regulations and provides you with an illustration of where on the plot you can build and some scenarios for volume and height combinations. However, you have access to a software service that then displays a field in which you can list all your functional desires: 'Three bedrooms, one playroom, open kitchen, two car-garage, landing pad on the roof . . . '. The computer then displays a list of more than 60 different types of style – everything from country house to contemporary, minimalist etc. – and you select the type or types you prefer. Click, and it brings up images of a large number of houses, interior details, and garden plans that correspond to these styles. Now you embark upon a process in which, in the course of about an hour, you are presented with two different images to compare every 10 seconds – 360 times in total. Each time, on a scale, you have to indicate which of the two most appeals to you, or whether you find them equally attractive. On the basis of AI and the experience of tens of thousands of users, the adaptive system gradually identifies what you really like best.

Once you are done, you click on 'Make Plan', and a couple of minutes later you are presented with 10 alternative designs for your house, all of which meet both your criteria and local building regulations. Each of these designs comes with a computer-generated estimate of time schedule and costs.

Having later discussed the matter with your family for some weeks, you select a design and upload it to the sites of seven construction companies that provide their services on a building portal. Each of them has an AI computer, which submits a quote that takes into account both the estimated costs of the project and their own capacity situation.

That is how some of the architectural design and construction work of the future may look. Let's delve a bit deeper into the topic.

New technologies to assist building construction

Building technology is rapidly evolving, since technical science constantly scales new heights. A good example in the building industry is self-repairing cement to enhance quality and extend the life cycle. The technology involves incorporating a bacterium into the cement, which is activated when the cement strikes cavities or takes in water, after which the bacterium produces the cement to repair the cavity. The result will be lower maintenance costs and fewer repairs.

Less exotic is making surface materials with building-integrated photovoltaics, or BIPV. At its simplest, BIPV consists of solar-absorbent flat roofs or solar cell roof tiles and, in more advanced cases, entire building surfaces that can utilise energy from sunlight. Even glass windowpanes can be used to capture solar energy. Surplus power can then be used for light and heat, and for charging the likes of an electric car and quadcopter. We will witness an increasing transition from normal buildings to low-energy buildings and then to net-energy-producing houses. As a result, energy will be increasingly tackled in the cloud like digital services and human labour, and thus become part of the sharing economy. Moreover, such a short-range distribution of power will pave the way for the option of maintaining it in DC as it is produced. The purpose of converting to AC is the fact that it is the cheapest method of transmitting power over long distances, even though it must then be converted back to DC for many of the devices that eventually consume the power. Both conversions cost energy. But if there is no long-distance transport involved, you can save on these conversions.

In traditional construction, the value chain has been geographically split up in the sense that building materials and building components are often produced away from the actual construction. However, 3D printing technology facilitates the 3D printing of parts of a building on site, using either super printers that can produce entire walls or more specialised printers for smaller components. The technology also paves the way for a renaissance for building details. The castles and manor houses of the past had an abundance of intricate, detailed decoration created by craftsmen. However, over time, equal pay, VAT, and taxes made this financially unfeasible for just about everyone. This resulted in a simpler style of building, which then became modern. However, we still admire, for example, Renaissance or Art Nouveau and Art Deco, and this makes them veritable tourist magnets. 3D printing makes it possible to create something similar at prices that more people can pay, and that could create a renaissance for more complicated stylistic forms. Finally, we should mention that, if a builder cannot get hold of a special gizmo from a supplier, he can print it himself.

Another technology that will gain ground in the construction sector is augmented reality. This means that construction workers will no longer have to always look at a floor plan when doing a job. Instead, augmented reality will enable them to see what the project is supposed to look like when completed.

And, of course, we must not forget robots in the construction industry. For example, they are great at helping to install windowpanes – a task that is heavy, frequently demanding, and rather dangerous. Drones also offer a unique opportunity to make real-time aerial scans of construction sites and buildings to create an overview and generate 3D images and maps of buildings and related activities.

Smart buildings and digital control

More sophisticated hardware and software technology paves the way for smart buildings based on the IoT–big data–AI trinity, which can provide control of light, extraction, heat, ventilation, security, etc. For example, I recently had an evening meeting with the company Trifork in the canton of Schwyz (whose founder Jørn Larsen is a contributor to this book), where they demonstrated how the office was voice-controlled with Amazon's virtual assistant, Alexa. Curtains, lights, and ventilation were also voice-controlled, and when the last person left the office in the evening, a single voice command closed it. Conversely, when the first person turned up for work in the morning, she or he was welcomed with facial recognition, after which the door opened automatically, and the office lights, curtains, and ventilation were automatically adapted.

AI can also ensure that an alarm gets automatically triggered if an unknown person walks around the walls at three o'clock at night with a crowbar in his hands. Or if such a person walks around in a multi-storey car park trying several car doors. If some person can see whether or not a person should be there, so can an AI computer.

In addition, the future house key could be an app which is used to let strangers into a building selectively and for a limited period of time: for example, if you want to grant a tradesman or supplier access while you yourself are at work. You could also issue digital keys to employees and discontinue them online in an instant, as many companies already do. And private post boxes in smart buildings could perhaps become two-way boxes, where you can both place things to be sent and receive the likes of groceries delivered by a robot with code access, which then collects whatever needs to go the other way.

Office communities and cohousing

Just as we have a sharing economy in the field of computer power (server parks in the cloud, shared cars, etc.) we also have an increasing number of partly shared, coworking office communities such as those offered by WeWork, where companies can move in and out with quite short notice and otherwise share many common facilities. A private parallel to this is cohousing, a practical, economical hybrid of apartment building, hotel, and collective, which again contains various common facilities. Both phenomena provide flexibility and save money. Moreover, they bring people together and counteract loneliness. What both concepts have in common is that experiments are being conducted with themed versions, so, for example, there are office communities aimed at entrepreneurs.

In the cities of tomorrow, with the use of a variety of sensors, big data, and AI, we will increasingly see buildings, traffic lights, parking meters, and other objects communicate and optimise the course of events. So, imagine that an army of autonomous shared vehicles automatically flock to a stadium just before a soccer game ends. If a public bench or a lamp is broken or a wall has been painted with graffiti, you can also imagine citizens filming it and uploading it to an app, which tenders the repair task on a crowdsourcing platform, if a robot does not automatically repair the damage.

Tomorrow's jet-set nomads

Jeju is a Korean island just south of the mainland, and the capital is also called Jeju. On nomadlist.com, we learn that it is safe, has very clean air, and is easy to get around in – even as a pedestrian. And then of course the most important aspect, the Internet, which is not simply rated with broad terms such as 'OK', 'Good', and 'Great', but is evaluated on the basis of figures: in this case, 104 megabytes per second. The total score is 3.92 out of 5. Then, when you browse and read more about Jeju on the site, you come, for example, to a city map, where the districts are referred to as 'Hipster', 'Rich', 'Students', and 'Suits'.

Nomadlist.com and a large number of other platforms serve global nomads – often at the well-heeled end of the scale – people who could lead a quite ordinary life in one place, but who instead have chosen to live throughout the world. There are increasing numbers of these modern luxury tramps. The most important explanation for this phenomenon is of course also digital, since more and more jobs can be tackled from your computer. All you need is a fast, reliable Internet connection, so you can receive, send, and, if necessary, conduct video conferences. That is how I personally have been working for the past 20 years.

Many trends interrelate when it comes to global luxury nomads, and not everyone prefers those cities and areas that are already considered the smartest and most expensive. For some people, the freedom to live and work wherever you want is also synonymous with not having to work so much, if you choose to settle somewhere where the cost of living is cheap. Accordingly, the city of Ploiesti in Romania is now number 10 on nomadlist.com with total monthly living costs of $1244.

However, no matter where the global nomads are on the income scale, they reflect the same trend, which we see in many other contexts: people are mobile. In the middle of his life, my own father told me that all wise people should live where it is possible to produce wine, because the climate is always pleasant there. So, he moved from Denmark to Chile. I would add that skiing is another attractive factor, and you can do that in Chile too. But I chose Switzerland.

Just as people rate restaurants and wine online, the Internet now overflows with users' reviews of what it is like to live in every conceivable place on the planet. What is also becoming increasingly prevalent is that it is no longer your job that determines where you live, but instead where you prefer to live that determines where you will work.

In other words, we are generally becoming increasingly mobile, there are fewer norms, and curiosity is growing. Many people also choose to study abroad. From there, living abroad is not such a giant leap. 'Where is the greatest security?' the nomads may ask, and then move there. Or: 'Where is there a good leisure life, a good climate, a low tax burden, some good airports, or great freedom?' These kinds of questions can be important, because these mobile people often have a fantastic can-do spirit and strong competencies in sought-after fields.

Over time, it also leads easily to a network effect, where the most industrious and competent come together. Also, because one of the questions many of them ask is actually: 'Where can I find other people like me?' Meaning people with the same temperament, the same lifestyle, or working in the same industry. Since these people come together not only because they have the same lifestyle, but also because they have common professional interests, this produces hyper-creative ecosystems focused on special sectors. Some are small-scale business clusters. Others are more broad-spectrum economic centres of excellence such as Silicon Valley (for tech start-ups), the City of London (finance), Singapore (finance, biotech, etc.), Shanghai (software and hardware), central Switzerland (finance, software, commodity trading, biotech, etc.), Dubai (you name it), etc.

In many cases, such a centre of excellence sees the evolution of what is known in the United States as 'the triple helix': a trinity, in which public organisations, education, and private companies are all pointed in the same commercial direction. In my opinion, however, it takes more than a triple helix to create the magic. It requires the combination of (1) good access to excellent commercially relevant education, (2) good regulatory and tax-related framework conditions, (3) research and development centres of international companies, (4) venture investors, (5) easy access to good airports, and (6) the opportunity for an attractive lifestyle. However, the interesting thing is that powerful network effects easily arise out of such a centre. People are first drawn to them because of good framework conditions, including the six aforementioned factors, but later also because they offer a huge mass of talent and many like-minded people to get along with. In other words, success breeds success:

38. Open and mobile societies create social and economic network effects and thereby self-reinforcing economic centres of excellence.

A radical version of the modern nomad's life pattern will also be 'seasteading', where you move into a large ship that constitutes its very own society. Many ultra-libertarians have been playing with this idea for years. Don't you think it will happen one day? The question is then, where will they obtain a valid passport to travel to other lands? But there are many countries where you can buy passports.

What is more, the jet-set nomads will only represent a small part of the total travel activity, which also includes business travel, tourism, etc. Tourism will be a huge growth area, because one of the benefits that almost all people want more of when they get richer is great holidays. And, as in many other contexts, we will find – in fact, it is already the case – that holiday services will improve. And so, the supply is constantly increasing.

Growth in global tourism

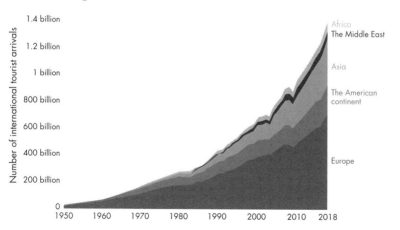

9.
THE NEW LIFESTYLES – EXPERIENCES AND SELF-REALISATION

Lars Seier Christensen, co-founder of the very successful Saxo Bank and later serial entrepreneur, debater, and venture investor, is one of my good Swiss-based acquaintances and, when it comes to politics and social development, he and I agree on most things. There is, however, a single issue on which once, during a discussion, we took different sides. That is the question of whether or not artificial intelligence and robots will create mass unemployment. Lars Seier feared yes, while I tended more to no, even though neither of us felt 100% sure. My lower degree of concern is basically justified by

Say's Law, which states that supply creates demand: if companies in a free market economy produce more, wages and other payments for productive inputs will create sufficient demand for structural unemployment not to occur.

This law has resisted one technological wave after another, ever since the economist, Jean-Baptiste Say, formulated it a few hundred years ago. Neither the Industrial Revolution, the green revolution, computers, the Internet, nor any of the other technological breakthroughs created systemic unemployment. In the early nineteenth century, for example, about 90% of the American population were farmers. Now the figure is less than 2%. Nonetheless, as I write, the United States is close to full employment and experiencing huge demand for the goods their business community is producing. However, Lars Seier argues that AI and robots will surpass human capabilities in so many parameters that this time many people will have difficulty competing with anything.

But in this context, I get faith in the future by looking at Lars Seier's own activities. He made his first fortune by creating Saxo Bank, a player firmly placed in the service economy. But what has he been focusing on since moving to Switzerland and later selling his Saxo shares? Largely on excellent restaurants (world class, in fact), ice hockey and football teams, Formula 1, cycling, wine production, and the like. And that is where I see a big part of the solution.

The experience economy - all the world becomes a stage

I think that, in the future, many of the jobs that will be lost to AI and robots will go towards creating experiences. Let me explain. Some optimists say that the Industrial Revolution meant that people ended up working like machines – uniform and routine and with no creativity or freedom. Then the service economy added a lot of routine work in offices. The advent of AI and robots, on the other hand, makes it possible to bring emotions back into production, like when a local carpenter knew the people who were going to eat at the dining table he was about to make. You see, when only machines do the work of machines, people can revert to what they are best at – working as people.

That is the way I see it. But we can also look at the issue more broadly. In the first few hundred thousand years of human history, people lived as hunters, gatherers, and craftsmen. Then huge growth in prosperity and employment came from agriculture, followed by industry and the mining of metals and fossil fuels etc. And in the past few decades, it has been services that have been creating much of the wealth, at least in the richest nations.

I find it interesting how the service economy has gained ground. Initially, providers of industrial products such as cars or computers sometimes offered free service and, for example, several financing options to better sell their products. But gradually, one supplier after another learned that there was actually more money and especially more customer loyalty to be gained by turning the business model upside down, so that it was the *service* the customer paid for, and the physical product that was now included. So, cars were now increasingly leased instead of purchased, IBM bought back corporate computers and instead set up a service scheme for them. Meanwhile, Xerox offered companies the option of photocopying on machines which Xerox still owned and serviced. So, the customer no longer paid for the photocopy machine, but a price per copy. Similarly, phone companies more or less started giving away phones in return for customers renewing their service subscriptions. These were all service models aimed at creating loyalty and user-friendliness.

But, in recent years, what Lars Seier has been particularly interested in is not so much traditional services as experiences. These are elements of what has been called showbiz, the entertainment industry, or, more generally, the experience economy.

The experience economy has been growing rapidly for quite some time. With their films, magazines, amusement parks, etc., the Disney group, for one, has shown to what extent it is possible to make a lot of the money along the way.

Today, experiences come in the shape of restaurants, sports teams, night clubs, etc. The travel industry features diving, hiking, sailing, skiing, cultural, and countless other types of holidays, such as wine picking in Tuscany, salmon fishing in Scotland, binges in Prague, gambling tours in Las Vegas, trekking on Mallorca, and medical tourism in Switzerland or Thailand. Or truffle hunting, flying in hot air balloons, swimming with whales, sleeping in ice hotels or under water – and golf tournaments on the moon.

Well, maybe not golf tournaments on the moon – yet – but perhaps one day? Speaking of the car and restaurant industries, experience shows that people are more likely to drop their façades if they are engaged in something else while speaking. That is why, for certain discussions, business lunches can be more successful than more formal business meetings. We also know the phenomenon from the now popular technique of filming people's conversation while driving. But this is also evident in the likes of TechBBQ, where businesspeople discuss start-up projects and venture investments while grilling steaks together – a charming phenomenon by the name of 'social dinners'. I think that in the future we can expect even more concepts where people mix work and leisure in ways that generate new creativity and energy.

There are still enormous opportunities when it comes to spreading the experience economy. A floor in a multi-storey car park does not have to be a mere cement shell. Instead it could have themed decoration and associated sound effects. So could corridors in airports. Everywhere in my day-to-day life, I see unattractive, sad, anonymous spaces just waiting to be swept up by the experience economy and turned into fascinating experiences.

One of the best new examples of how the experience economy can grow, however, is e-sport – electronic sport. I mean computer games. Growing prize pools for e-sports tournaments, live streaming, and improved infrastructure for professional leagues have all paved the way for the fact that, in just a few years, e-sport will have almost as much interest from the public as recognised sports: for example, the NFL. It is estimated that in 2019 around 380 million people will watch or take part in e-sport. In terms of revenue, the e-sports industry will also hit the $1-billion mark in 2019, and is expected to grow to $1.6 billion by 2021, which is a sizeable amount compared to the German Bundesliga's huge $2.8 billion. That is why an increasing number of investors are flocking to the e-sports industry. Back in 2018, Cloud9 became one of the most valuable e-sports teams in the world after raising $50 million in a major round of funding, which gave the team an estimated value of about $310 million. Wealthy individuals such as Mark Cuban have also entered the e-sport sector, and traditional sports clubs such as Premier League soccer teams are starting to buy e-sports players to represent them in competitions that combine traditional sports and e-sports – yet another example of the hybrid experiences that are constantly being created in the entertainment industry.

In their visionary book, *The Experience Economy* (1999), Pine and Gilmore give an illustrative example. In 1999, the commodity price for the coffee beans needed to make a cup of coffee was ¢1–2. After industrial processing and distribution, the price rose to ¢5–25. However, in a restaurant the coffee was sold as a service, so generally cost $2–4: in other words, 20–40 times more. But if you bought it in the form of a cappuccino on Piazza San Marco in Venice, which I actually did at that time, it cost $15, or more than a thousand times the price of the unprocessed commodity, several hundred times more than the price of the processed commodity, and 3–7 times more than what a cup of coffee would cost in a less attractive setting. The difference, which plenty of people, including myself, found worth the extra cost, was the amazing *experience* of drinking a cappuccino in such a place as Piazza San Marco in Venice.

However, the experience economy is still at an early stage compared to the service economy, and its breakthrough as a (or *the*) leading economic growth area will probably be characterised by the fact that companies will include both products and services in packages, which will generally be sold as experiences. Because that is where they see the major opportunities for avoiding commoditisation and brutal price wars.

The experience economy is labour intensive and features services we largely do not wish to see provided by robots or machines. For example, it is all about supreme craftsmanship or visits to off-the-wall restaurants like the popular Swedish Punk Royale (where I have had vodka served from a petrol canister and food served on plates that had first been smashed on the floor). It is about Swiss hand-assembled mechanical watches for sometimes astronomical prices, fireplaces that serve no purpose other than to be cosy, limited-edition luxury cars launched on the basis of the principles of haute couture, designer gardens, zen interiors, massage accompanied by beautiful scents and lounge music – and a thousand other things.

Incidentally, I also believe that internal combustion engines will have an enduring role in the experience economy. For people like me – and there are a lot of us! – there is a charm in the roar of an internal combustion engine with gearshift, vroom, clunk, bang, which in comparison makes an electric engine about as charming as an East German parking meter. If you do not get what I mean, imagine a Harley-Davidson without sound and gear changes. See what I mean? So, I still think there will be active petrolheads in 100 years, although it is uncertain whether their fuel will be fossil or created by, for instance, genetically modified algae or extracted form the air with direct air capture technology.

During this process, we also see lots of sectors, which had been dominated by mass-produced standard products, now featuring increasingly more superb craftsmanship. Just think about the many new varieties of coffee that have emerged in recent decades and the enormous growth of microbreweries that make countless new forms of beer and lately, for example, gin. Does this create jobs? You bet! In fact, there can also be a lot of money in it. In 2019, Bernard Arnault, CEO of LVMH, who make low-tech luxury products, took over the rank as the third-richest man in the world.

The changeable idea of prestige

The desire for prestige is a big driver of human behaviour and economic phenomena. People want sympathy or admiration, but how do you get it? Over the past few centuries, in many people's opinion, the ultimate achievement was belonging to the nobility – or, best of all, a royal family. The next-best thing was to know and befriend such people.

With the growth of the industrial society, economic and intellectual success became more recognised. They were things people had created themselves. Now you could get rich without being noble, and it became prestigious to live in luxury.

Personal development then became a third source of prestige, and people with higher education then often referred to themselves with titles such as Doctor Smith or Professor Brown.

Of course, there are still many people who associate significant respect with the nobility, being rich, or being highly educated, but all three elements seem to be losing some of their prestige. Instead, today, status is increasingly associated with what you *do* rather than who you *are* or what you *own*. If you live an adventurous life, promote good causes, or do some meaningful and demanding job, you can gain prestige and respect, and increasingly people communicate these things on social media.

Self-realisation – the service in which you are the product

The experience economy stands for fun and charm. Many people have heard about Maslow's Hierarchy of Needs (1943). It described a hierarchy of five human needs, which he expanded to six in the 1970s. Since then, others have made countless variations of this pyramid, but a recurring feature in all of them is the fact that we first prioritise immediate physical needs such as food, sleep, and sex. Then come safety and security in the form of being healthy, having income, a roof over our head, etc. Love, friendship, and intimacy follow, and then self-esteem – the feeling that you are doing something that gains other people's respect etc. Next comes self-realisation via the likes of aesthetic experiences, creativity, higher purpose in life, etc. At the very top of Maslow's revised, expanded model, he placed transcendental experiences such as spirituality, altruism, or what I guess we refer to today as 'mindfulness', in which we learn to sense the world profoundly. The major international trend of people turning to vegetarianism and veganism also belongs to this category.

Research has not been able to confirm that the needs in Maslow's and similar models are structured so hierarchically always and for everyone. People's priorities are different and complex. That said, business historians will recognise that the distribution of work forces in more primitive societies more or less reflected the shape of Maslow's pyramid, with the large majority of people working to supply Maslow's basic needs. Indeed, 200 years ago, the job of providing food and a roof over one's head constituted an overwhelming proportion of the labour market. That is what average people spent most of their working hours on. Of course, some very wealthy or otherwise powerful people were preoccupied with the likes of self-esteem and spirituality and, frequently, had the poor to build palaces and cathedrals for them, not to mention the many wars that poor people have been forced into against their will, so kings and dictators could realise themselves and bask in admiration. But, overall, in terms of work, the vast majority were at the bottom of the Maslow hierarchy.

However, what we have seen since is that the top of the hierarchy has gradually become wider in terms of employment, while the bottom has become correspondingly narrower. For example, now there are fewer farmers (bottom of Maslow's pyramid) and more ski instructors (top).

There are two reasons for this. Firstly, it is easier to mechanise the activities at the bottom than at the top, and secondly, our increasing abundance of basic services frees up time and money for more activities at the top, where it is human work we prefer.

While the experience economy is flourishing, and hopefully once again (cf. Say's Law) will help save us from more potential mass unemployment, I expect that another major growth sector in our economies will be assisted self-help and transcendental activity. This could be anything from fitness instructors to psychologists, couple therapists, nutrition counsellors, mindfulness coaches, gurus, yoga teachers, cosmetologists, plastic surgeons, various spiritualists, etc. Interestingly, what is being developed in this context is neither a physical product nor a service. It is *ourselves*.

Innovation and entrepreneurship – self-realisation that gets cheaper

In my opinion, a third major growth area will be innovation and entrepreneurship. I see two reasons. Firstly, starting a new, innovative company, which I myself have experienced, is an extreme form of self-realisation, which is clearly high up in the Maslow hierarchy. Secondly, it has become much cheaper to start new projects and companies, thanks to technologies such as cloud computing, video conferencing, open software APIs (Application Programming Interfaces), crowdsourcing, highly focused and thus affordable advertising options, smartphones, tablets, and, for example, global payment systems, in addition to a host of smart as-a-service provisions. Moreover, using the Internet and network effects, you can often achieve incredibly fast growth if you find the right model with your start-up. Even today we are witnessing the start of a global entrepreneurial boom, supported by the likes of TV programmes such as *Dragons' Den* etc.

Do-it-yourself and maker movements – working for fun

Self-realisation can also come in the form of craftsmanship. Given that new tools make it easier for people to create software and physical objects themselves, so-called maker cultures have emerged, producing physical objects, and hacker cultures for coding etc., which can be termed collectively as do-it-yourself (DIY) cultures. These are promoted by social media, open-source hardware and software, 3D printing, robots, etc., and digital DIY subcultures on social media support many of them. For example, somewhere in the world a maker can develop a new product and then upload the 'recipe' for it in the cloud, after which other makers, anywhere in the world, can replicate the work, for example, with robots, computers or 3D printers – and then improve on it. Similarly, much of what we see on social media is, in fact, DIY media production made by millions of digital makers.

A point of intersection between gig, microworks, and DIY is also referred to as co-creation, where companies collaborate with their customers to create the products. A simple example is co-constructed houses. Or restaurants where customers help with the cooking. However, it can also be via an app/store or as when LEGO gets user groups to develop new LEGO sets.

The benefits of co-creation can be both better user experiences and the fact that a company gets its products renewed by those who are passionate about them and need them. And, of course, these customers probably become excellent ambassadors for the company in this way. To a large extent, I regard co-creation as part of the self-realisation near the top of the Maslow hierarchy, parallel to people wishing to brew their own gin, go hunting, collect their own truffles, or make their own artisan products. They do it because they like it, even if the outcome or something that resembles it or tackles the same basic tasks could be bought for a fraction of what it costs to make it yourself. This is also a growth area in affluent societies:

39. **Increasingly, machines, robots, and computers meet the demands described in the lower end of Maslow's pyramid of needs. Meanwhile, a growing part of the human labour produce products and services belonging to the higher levels of the pyramid.**

One of the most fascinating phenomena we already see here and want to see more of is how we take elements from different silos and mix them in new ways: for example, in fusion music, where you mix several genres of music or in the amazing Cirque du Soleil, which combines theatre, concert, circus, sports, restaurant, drone shows, and more in impressive fusion experiences. For some time now in the restaurant business, lots of venues have emerged that combine restaurant visits with a cabaret and/or discotheque experience, or with unique architecture, nature, design, humour, or art. And in the car industry, the dealers-offer-dinner concept is growing, where you eat surrounded by luxury or sports cars. This is certainly something you can sometimes do in Zug, where I live. There are also book cafés everywhere: hybrids of bookshops and cafés.

Such trends will only accelerate in the future, and with the spread of wall-to-wall OLED screens (quite thin, flexible, or transparent video screens) or similar technologies, we will see, say, restaurants offering psychedelic audio-visual experiences.

Incidentally, the retail trade will have to reconnoitre these opportunities more and more, since physical shops have to compete with the in many senses more efficient electronic ones. The best way to do so is to offer total experiences.

To get a sense of how great the opportunities are, just take a look at the following (highly uncomprehensive) list of 40 areas that I believe will evolve in the lifestyle sector:

Adventure	Coaching	Healing	Mindfulness	Self-diagnosis
Altruism	Co-creation	History	Fashion	Sculptures
Architecture	Design	Luxury	Music	Social media
Bars	Debate clubs	Sound effects	Nightclubs	Screen art
Body-shaping	DIY	Food	Nature	Sport and
Body-tracking	Retail shops	Maker labs	Travel	fitness
Housing	Scents	Paintings	Restaurants	Theatre and
Shops	Gardens and	Mentoring	Collectables	film
	parks			Wellness
				Workshops

Just think how many options there are to combine them, and you will see where a lot of future jobs will come from.

Ultimately, I imagine a scenario in labour markets in which agriculture, commodity extraction, standard services, industry, and administration are largely handled by robots, AI, and other machinery, but in which the theatre-like experience economy, assisted self-help, transcendental experiences, and labour-of-love activities such as entrepreneurship, DIY, and maker activity along with the likes of hunting, collector activity, and commercial handicraft will be the province of lots of people. In other words, a Maslow hierarchy in which most human employment is at the top, where lots of fun is to be had, and most of the mechanical activity is at the bottom, where many people would prefer not to work. Accordingly, I will describe the labour market of tomorrow, as I see it, as follows:

The labour market of the future

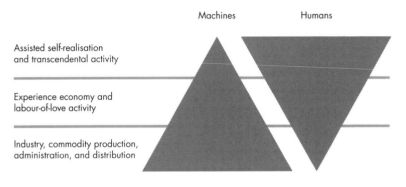

Machines   Humans

Assisted self-realisation
and transcendental activity

Experience economy and
labour-of-love activity

Industry, commodity production,
administration, and distribution

The human cloud – total transformation of the labour market

Just as we have witnessed a breakdown in types of family from the classic nuclear family to everything else, we are now also witnessing a more diverse, informal working life. What I believe we will see more and more of is:

- people do not work for a permanent employer;
- they have no fixed working hours;
- they do not have a permanent workplace;
- they do not have a fixed retirement age.

And in tandem with this, the concept of work–life balance will often be replaced by work–life fusion. As it happens, my own life matches the latter description. The boundaries between my work and my private life are fluid.

Ongoing interview studies reveal that on average, we are reducing the time we expect our current employment to last. This also relates to the fact that more people opt out of an abrupt transition to retirement, instead preferring a slow scaling down in the autumn of their life, but perhaps without ever completely letting go of their working life. Not only that. Increasingly we will see people who have periods when they are fit for work, where they hardly work, and other periods when they invest their all into their career. And we might even see people who do not stop working until they are 100.

Another issue: industrial society created giant companies with huge numbers of employees. I expect that this will also be the case in 10, 20, or (maybe) 50 years' and 100 years' time. But I believe that the net increase will be in smaller companies and among independent freelancers engaged in the experience economy, assisted self-realisation, transcendental activity, and labour-of-love activity.

In the labour market, there is increasing demand for flexibility from both employers and workers. On the one hand, employers can save money by not having employees permanently employed during periods when there is not so much to do and, on the other hand, they see that, because the world is becoming more changeable, it is an advantage to have freelance staff who gets inspiration from other jobs. And finally, they may be forced to make such big ongoing adjustments that it will be hard to see through, if they cannot flexibly replace the work resources they draw on. Similarly, employees seek the freedom to work where and when it suits them.

Working life past and present

The past

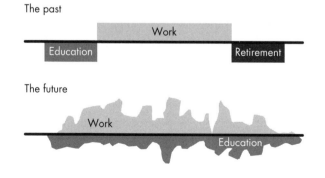

The future

Gig economy, microwork, and officeless work

The word 'gig' is urban slang for the live performance of an orchestra or other artistes, who often go from gig to gig with no long-term plan or predictability. So, the expression 'gig economy' describes how the same form of work is now spreading to other lines of business. Alongside this concept, other concepts have emerged: *find your own nook* and *bring your own device* (BYOD) or the alternative version, *bring your own technology* (BYOT) etc. where employers accept and even encourage employees to bring their own hardware and find their nook to work in.

The same is true of the previous concept in that many workers have to come to an office to work. Increasingly more people work 'from home', but the fact is that, often, they do not literally work from home. For example, in San Francisco and many other trendy places, there are an increasing number of cafés where you can pay, not for what you consume, but an hourly rate for the time you spend there. This is because people use the cafés as workplaces, where they pop on their headphones to block out the sound and get down to work. The reason is that they do not like sitting at home alone. In cafés and in flexible, temporary office hotels, such as those organised by WeWork, workers can be surrounded by other people who, like them, work 'from home', without working for the same company. Recent research has shown that open offices are rarely efficient, while closed offices can make people feel lonely. On the other hand, working in a café with 'ear flaps' combines concentration with the feeling of not being alone, so for many people it is the perfect solution.

Funny fact: in 2017, Nordic Eye invested $3 million in Weblife in California. At that point they had seven employees and no office. Seven months later, the company was sold for more than $60 million, and we got $20 million back from our investment. The funny thing was that, even at that point, the company did not have an office.

It can work fine, particularly as long as *nobody* has an office. However, I have found that if some people work at the office, while others do not, the situation can lead to tensions. The best solution is often either that everyone works at the office, or no one does.

In any case, generally speaking, all these issues are symptoms of the following rule:

40. **As societies become more digitised, the boundaries between private life and work, between home and workplace, and between work time and leisure time tend to dissolve.**

Of course, the movement has both advantages and disadvantages. Some enjoy being able to work wherever and at any time, even sometimes far away from an office, on their laptops, tablets, and smartphones. This type of work can often be categorised as microwork, where a working process can be regarded as an assembly line, in which each of several actors is responsible for a small task, and together they tackle the entire project. Examples of microwork tasks can include creating logos and slogans, solving scientific mysteries, or designing digital presentations. This form of work replaces much of the traditional company structure with flexible 'work swarms' and SWAT teams. In fact, you could call it a human cloud, a parallel to the computer cloud we use in the cloud or the energy cloud that will emerge when many buildings become net energy-positive.

Overall, it can be said that the trends in the future labour market will very much resemble the trends in other markets. There will be an 'un-bundling' of services, so we will more often trade not with the total of an employee's time but only with small chunks of it. In other words, a fluid, object-oriented labour market will be generated, in which you work – often in small chunks – anywhere, anytime, and for (almost) anyone:

41. **As societies become more digitised, an increasing number of services, including products, services, and labour, are broken down into smaller objects and offered in fluid markets – sometimes referred to as 'clouds'. Such markets will often have real-time price fluctuations, transparent competition, and ratings.**

For work providers, the gig economy often means higher productivity and less stress – because they will not experience being fired and going from full time to zero work from one day to the next. Instead, they have periods when there is a little too much or too little work, but without the threat of real unemployment hanging over their heads. Conversely, as part of gig economy, for some it may be difficult to scrape enough money together, as gigs are typically offered in intense competition, which pushes prices down. It can also be stressful for some people to be on trial every day, as opposed to having the comfort blanket that a permanent job represents for many people.

Overall, however, the gig phenomenon is growing, since many providers and many clients appreciate it. Together with the likes of AI, robots, and ExOs, the gig economy facilitates lighter-staffed companies, which is why, in the past few decades, we have already seen the average size of companies in the United States drop sharply. All of this is logical, for the dynamics of tomorrow will require a larger number of small and flexible companies, which will draw on external labour to varying degrees, depending on their correspondingly varying requirements.

More backsourcing

Since World War II – and especially since 1980 – migrations, increased trade, and relocation of production, under the collective moniker of 'globalisation', have been a strong, worldwide trend. There are plenty of reasons why it can continue, but some are beginning to argue that, in some cases, commerce and outsourcing may be rolled backwards. The reason is the aforementioned phenomenon called backsourcing. A factory or warehouse employee is often much cheaper in Eastern Europe and Asia than in Western Europe and the United States. But a robot costs the same anywhere. The same is true of an AI machine. And when robots and AI become cheap enough, backsourcing will increase. Therefore, it will be increasingly common for manufacturers in the wealthiest countries once again to have their production bases in their own countries, where it will be easier for them to maintain the innovation that comes from managing their own production.

Bespoke media

Media plays a major role in the experience economy, self-realisation, and innovation. An important element of tomorrow's media will be individualisation – a trend that is actually well underway, for example, via Flipboard and social media. But the trend will be far stronger, and each of us will end up being able to design exactly the type of media we prefer.

But it is not without its challenges. The fear of fake news and systematic, deliberate misinformation is widespread – and justifiably to some extent. For example, today we can already use so-called 'deep fake' technology to produce videos of people who, in an exceedingly lifelike way, appear to say something that they never actually said. The Internet gives every person immediate access to virtually any information. But, given that there are no well-trained editors to separate crap and fact, many people end up choosing completely distorted representations of the truth. Conversely, the Internet has the advantage that bad journalists and poorly established media – and there are lots of them – are immediately contradicted online.

Bespoke media and the formation of groups on social media mean that people increasingly live in echo chambers, where most participants agree with one another. Consequently, they easily overestimate how many people like themselves exist.

Despite the new forms of media, I think there is no doubt that traditional top–down media, in which professional journalists and experts inform people, will persist. But the predominant trend will be for information to flow every which way, and for the traditional journalist roles to be challenged by young, quick, and talented people, who are the ones that really make things happen and understand the essence of the stories:

42. **As the world becomes more digitised, the creation, communication, and curation of information and entertainment becomes more decentralised, networked, and interactive.**

One development we are likely to witness is so-called lighthouse media, where groups of particularly perceptive people, often not journalists, select or curate the best online content and pass it on to interested parties –perhaps with explanatory notes.

A basic condition that will contribute to a changed media picture may be that we will start to 'wallpaper' with OLED screens, maybe as large-scale collaborative video walls for video conferencing and VR simulations etc. In other words, perhaps video art will be the world's fastest-growing art and design phenomenon.

The screens can alter the entire ambience and external appearance of a building. This also means that you will not just create media for the screens we see today, but also for some that are far bigger and intended to create ambience. This will reinforce the following trend:

43. Global OLED screen area output grows around 30% annually.

Multi-identities are more acceptable

A growing trend that will continue is the acceptance and celebration of multi-identities. Traditionally, a banker would always be expected to come across as a banker, and a professor of economics as highly professorial, and there are still many exponents of that attitude. In reality, though, people are naturally more complex. For example, the banker might actually love motorbikes, and the professor hard rock. Fortunately – and not least because of social media – we are already increasingly readier to accept that, even publicly, a person can have two or more identities: for example, being a banker in a suit and tie at one point, and a biker in leather gear and boots at another. And, once we get used to it, people will start to realise that it is not only acceptable to have multiple identities, but actually a sign of health. So, we unbundle identities so to speak: one need no longer follow the other, which means that each individual becomes more free to live a whole and honest life:

44. As people get more used to showing their full identity on social media, they become less willing to hide it in their workplace.

Intelligence amplification – better, more flexible education

In the past few decades, there have been very high expectations that digital technology could significantly supplement education, but they have rarely been met. On the contrary, it has been found that the digital platforms often fail to engage students as much as was hoped for, and that the physical presence in the same room as the teacher is a key component to an efficient programme of education. This is especially true in elementary school, and perhaps the ideal model would be for AI and other technologies such as VR and AR gradually to take over only part of the teaching process in the course of schooling. Incidentally, Christopher Dede, a professor of learning technologies at Harvard, recently underlined the benefits of using intelligence amplification: the computer-assisted person in the learning situation.

Technology, on the other hand, is an unmatched assistant when it comes to propagating education and making it available to many more people. This can be done via open digital learning: particularly the so-called Massive Open Online Courses or MOCCs. In addition to being cheap and efficient, MOOCs also mean that you can learn something exactly at the moment you need to use it.

The prevalence of these online courses also has another advantage: they provide millions of people with the pleasure of being taught by some of the very best teachers in the world. Furthermore, online educational programmes provide perfect opportunities for experimenting with formats. Some people, for example, have discovered that the most effective learning method is on average seven minutes of instruction, followed by a small mini exam, before proceeding to the next seven-minute module, and so on.

Other evolving formats include education via education apps, computer games, and international online competitions (gamification), in which, in a manner of speaking, you play your way to knowledge. For example, my youngest daughter taught herself a lot of arithmetic by entering international online mathematics competitions, which worked brilliantly. When all is said and done, in the future education will play with far more tools, approaching a kind of mass-individualisation that we have already witnessed in retail. In addition, I believe that there is still a huge, unrealised potential in the fact that, for the majority of people, the most effective learning lies in tackling concrete tasks that they may find really fascinating as opposed to just learning about theory all the time. This focus on real-world problems as a way of learning is called discovery-based learning.

It should be noted that a general advantage of using open digital learning is that, by adding AI and big data analyses, we can get the electronic systems to improve constantly based on experience. The system that teaches will thus be a learning system in itself.

The very idea of everyone having access to education, simply by having a connection to the Internet, is a paradigm shift. In the distinction between those who have and those who do not, education is one of the most significant elements; and to the extent that we can adapt on a vast scale to individuals, so that each person receives precisely the education that is perfect for his or her brain, we will radically improve the lives of so many people. The combination of being able to attend lectures via video, tackling assignments and getting them marked (increasingly assisted by AI, when it comes to more complex answers), and access to counselling in the form of advanced FAQ formats will mean that even young people in the furthest-flung corners of the world can suddenly get qualifications and make their talents visible to potential customers.

It is actually a huge democratisation movement featuring the dissemination of knowledge and the opportunity for many more people to acquire knowledge and the qualifications to participate in democratic processes on a well-informed basis. The global level of education is improving and, thanks to increasing prosperity, AI, gamification, and the continued prevalence of the Internet, this development will continue. It will contribute to an increase in prosperity and, what is more, to a limitation of population growth – and is probably far more effective in addressing overpopulation issues than doling out condoms!

Technologies driving changed education in the future

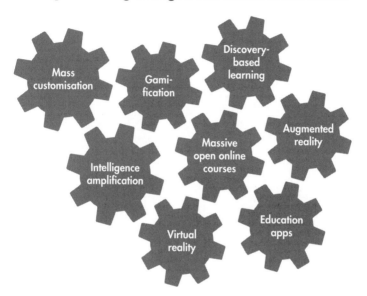

10.
BUSINESS MANAGEMENT IN A MORE DYNAMIC WORLD

In 2014, the economist and former McKinsey consultant Frederic Laloux published the bestseller Reinventing Organizations, *which I, and several hundred thousand other people, then bought. In this book, Laloux explains how over the years, people have changed their dominant forms of organisation. He divides them into five groups: (1) impulsive, (2) conformist, (3) achievement, (4) pluralist, and (5) evolutionary.*

Impulsive organisations

'Impulsive' is how Laloux describes the oldest form of organisation that has existed since the groups of hunters and gatherers of the Stone Age, governed by an alpha male. This (almost always male) figure makes most, if not all, important decisions, often leads through fear, and usually lacks long-term planning. He often thinks that the organisation's revenue – the fruits of everyone's labour – mainly belongs to him, after which he selectively distributes some of it to buy loyalty.

This form of organisation has prevailed for approximately 10 000 years, if not longer. What now differentiates it from Stone Age organisations is the fact that it often has a somewhat more advanced division of labour and lines of authority, which means it can be scaled up to more than the 20–40 people that typically belonged to a Stone Age clan.

We see elements of this form of organisation in the political leadership of many dictatorships outside the Western world, where it generally functions really poorly. We can also see examples in the more modern world: not only in small, family owned companies, whether a local restaurant or a young start-up company, but also in many religious sects, criminal street gangs, terrorist organisations, and criminal, mafia-like syndicates. In small organisations like this, this form of organisation can actually be highly effective, and in many start-ups that I have founded, worked in, or invested in, it's been great – at least in the early days.

Conformist organisations

The next level, which incidentally emerged in Mesopotamia approximately 4000 years ago, is the 'conformist' organisation. This involves a regulated, hierarchical pyramid structure with more stable processes and several fixed routines – in other words, what we could call 'method control' – and typically people are entirely rewarded according to fixed rules on the basis of seniority and title.

While the management style is usually quite authoritarian, because there are formal roles and processes, it is no longer essential to discuss everything with the top leader. In conformist, regulated organisations, for the most part employees follow written rules rather than their own insight. In this form of organisation, people are very often expected to wear a uniform: for example, suits, white lab coats, police uniforms, and the like.

Precisely because of the fixed roles and processes, this form of organisation can scale up to very large structures. Similarly, it creates a certain degree of predictability and gets people to exercise self-discipline vis-à-vis living up to their defined roles and routines.

Today, conformist leadership dominates most public institutions, including, to varying degrees, the armed forces. It is also common in authoritarian religions such as the Roman Catholic Church, which is extremely top–down and hierarchical with employees in distinctive uniforms.

However, conformist leadership tend to raise problems, of which the most important are: (1) the way of thinking and responsibility are quite often at some distance from insight and consequence; (2) pay does not always reflect differences in effort; (3) their intended conformity counteracts innovation; (4) their centralisation demotivates employees; and (5) they tend to continually build up ever-increasing staff functions.

Achievement organisations

During the Renaissance and at the start of the Age of Enlightenment – and particularly during the Industrial Revolution – a new form of organisation emerged, in which the very formal control was replaced by target management.

A good example is the reorganisation of the German army introduced by the Prussian General Gerhard von Scharnhorst in 1810–1812. Previously, German warfare had been very methodical and top–down, but now so-called *Auftragstaktik* – mission command – was introduced. It entailed dividing an army into small units intended to move in isolation, only coming together for large battles. Each unit and soldier were given both very clear instructions on *what* to achieve and great freedom to decide *how* to achieve it. In other words, the approach was more decentralised and flexible: what we call 'agile' today. It reflected the phenomenon, which, in 1834, the German war strategist Klaus von Clausewitz called *Nebel des Krieges* – 'the fog of war'. Because plans almost never worked in this fog, the idea was to operate agilely in small units, in which insight, responsibility, and consequence were closely associated. Fortunately, the British and American forces had their own mission command, which helped them win the war.

This form of organisation prevails in most of today's large modern companies, where people are often governed by KPIs (key performance indicators) and budgets, and where they refer to 'management by objectives'.

Pluralist organisations

Frederic Laloux's fourth form of organisation is the 'pluralist', in which the focus is on a company's culture, staff motivation, and on the higher purpose of the organisation. In this context, expressions such as coaching, teamwork, stakeholders, and empowerment prevail, and in general there is more of an attempt to involve employees in overall decisions and values. There is also a responsibility that exceeds merely enriching the shareholders. A company of this sort will often aim deliberately to benefit society as a whole.

Lots of companies have moved in this direction, even though very few are entirely pluralist. One reason for this may be that pluralistic companies can be difficult to manage. For example, there may be internal disagreement about the overall interests the organisation should be promoting. What is more, there can sometimes be so many discussions that necessary decisions are postponed for far too long. For instance, staff can work against innovation and rationalisation, as when staff representatives on boards in German car factories opposed the transition to the manufacture of electric cars, because they are easier to produce and therefore require less labour. So, in this specific case, the involvement of employees damaged the long-term interests of both the company and society.

Evolutionary organisations

In *Reinventing Organizations,* Frederic Laloux indicates that each of the four above-mentioned forms of organisation has its strengths, and that each may be ideal when it comes to certain issues. But he believes that in the future we will see growth in something different: what he calls the 'evolutionary' organisation.

Here, employees work in small teams, in which insight, responsibility, and consequence are inextricably linked. All the teams help each other, but mainly make their own decisions. Employees are no longer expected to leave their personality at home. Instead, they are accepted for who they are, and have no need to conceal their private habits and attitudes. Nor do they have to wear uniforms, unless strictly needed for some reason.

Frederic Laloux's five organisational types

Evolutionary
- Self-organising
- Dynamic matrix
- Clear shared values
- Agile and decentralised planning
- Real-time information
- Flexible
- Self-management
- Self-motivation
- Whole humans
- Decentralised planning

Pluralistic
- Democratic
- Fair
- Including
- Broad stakeholder focus
- Group oriented
- Coaching and team-work
- Idealistic/value-driven
- Empowerment
- Like a family
- Collective reward/the objectives bring their own reward

Achievement
- Hierarchic pyramid
- Accountability
- Key performance indicators
- Management by objectives
- Materialistic
- Meritocratic
- Reward for results
- Owners are the key stakeholders

Conformist
- Hierarchic pyramid
- Long-term stability
- Management through rules
- Fixed roles and processes
- Authoritarian
- Formality/status orientation
- Rules, manuals, uniforms

Impulsive
- Alpha leader
- Intuitive leadership
- Short-term oriented
- Agile

In evolutionary organisations, making mistakes is far more tolerated than previously, just so long as the organisation and the parties involved learn from them. Planning resembles what is typical of modern start-ups, so no detailed, long-term plans get made. Instead, everyone expects a partly unpredictable journey, on which employees are driven by passion and competence, while they continuously adapt to constant changes in the outside world. There are almost no staff functions, planning is very simple, fluid, and decentralised, and information is shared transparently and in real time. Consequently, overall the organisation is agile, creative, and spontaneously self-developing. That is why Laloux calls it evolutionary.

New technologies create new forms of management

I believe that Laloux is totally spot on when he claims that the future will lie increasingly in the hands of organisations along the lines of his evolutionary model. I believe that one of the reasons for this is that the technological development, which used to promote conformist and achievement organisations, is now increasingly favouring evolutionary ones. Our digitised society needs companies that can not only motivate people who have many choices in life, and who must navigate quickly and flexibly through a rapidly changing reality, but also mobilise huge coordinated forces to win the big battles that are worth fighting: for example, battles to create network effects.

In general, small businesses have an easier time tackling change than large ones, so the small ones often fare pretty well in a changing world. In recent years there have been positive accounts of how effective entrepreneurs usually work – primarily quickly, but most of all *flexibly*. Their plans are often just lists of bullet points: a so-called 'business model canvas'. They also make simple, minimalist product drafts, which they test regularly in the market, even before they are half finished. On that basis they regularly and quickly change their business model canvas and products in accordance with the mantra: *fail, fast, forward*. Sometimes they even –repeatedly – change their plans drastically – that is what is known as 'pivots'. In other words, they dribble their project like a professional football player elegantly and quickly navigating a ball around a large number of defenders, and in flexible cooperation with his or her team, towards the goal. Without a manual, of course, and with no clear plan – but with great agility and constantly with the goal in mind. This is an expression of an effective evolutionary organisation in action.

The new information paradigm: seek-sense-share

A rapidly changing world requires new methods for developing our insight. In this respect, I believe that personal knowledge management (PKM), as described by the Canadian, Harold Jarche, is a good approach. An important element is a distinction between (1) seeking information, (2) thinking about information, and (3) sharing information and thoughts about it.

'Seeking' covers many activities, such as targeted Internet search, literature search, various kinds of subscriptions to physical and digital news sources, reading books and magazines, and following the right people and organisations on platforms such as Twitter and LinkedIn etc. The next step in the PKM model, 'thinking about information', helps ensure that you can prioritise, apply parts of the material, and provide feedback on the search process. And the third step, 'sharing information and thoughts about it', is about activating the best parts of the knowledge and insight you have accumulated. Sharing knowledge and insight can send good signals about which topics you are interested in. Personally, at the time of writing, I have about 30 000 friends and followers on various social media, and when I post about topics that interest me, I get back an incredible amount of information, thoughts, introductions, ideas, and sources from my network. So, my seek–sense–share process becomes a creative loop that fits in well with an evolutionary form of working. And that is a part of the way in which information is generally emerging:

45. **As the world becomes more digitised, personal information gathering evolves towards grassroots-structured multipoint-to-multipoint interactive loops rather than pyramid-shaped point-to-multipoint dissemination.**

What should be kept permanent and what should be done flexibly?

In my opinion, the first step towards a more evolutionary management style for larger and more mature organisations is to distinguish between what needs to be flexible and what does not. Let me start by saying that the values of an organisation should preferably not be changeable and certainly not unclear. Precisely because the world is very changeable and an organisation evolutionary, it is both more important and more difficult to ensure that everything that the organisation does actually reflects these values. A military analogy is the question: 'What are we fighting for?'

Derived from these rules comes a moral code of conduct, which must also be well-conceived and well-communicated, since together the values and code must form the solid foundation. In the military, this would be 'rules of engagement'.

But what about the 'changeable' aspect? Previously, changes were often something that occurred in particular projects and were tackled in a discipline known as 'change management': maybe involving an off-site weekend, during which the top management discussed a problem such as: 'Shall we use that new Internet thing for something?' However, the shift from a situation where change was mostly an *exception* to one in which it is mostly the *rule* challenges management and the whole way of understanding change, whichever of Laloux's five forms of organisation you come from. So how can a company increase its agility and become spontaneously evolutionary?

The answer is that agility must be institutionalised. It has to be incorporated into everyday working methods. Let me give you some examples of how to do this vis-à-vis staff. I like to call the method 'DII' – Delegation, Involvement, and Inclusion.

Delegation – activate the staff

Let's start with delegation:

- Divide the organisation into smaller, autonomous units, where insight, responsibility, and consequence are united closely in each unit.

- Switch to mission-control management, in which *what* needs to be achieved is clear, but *how* it is to be achieved is more flexible.

- Organise internal *Dragons' Den* events, in which employees compete for budgets for new ideas.

- Organise internal innovation competitions.

- Allow members of staff to spend part of their time on their own projects.

- Allow 'skunk works': development teams who work outside the organisation's normal routines.

Again, these are just some examples of how to delegate initiative and responsibility in an organisation. None of them work everywhere, and some places will not be suitable for any of them.

Having said that, an analogy may shed light on the difference between classical leadership and the way forward as described here:

traffic control at a crossroads. Classic management corresponds to the use of traffic lights. Drivers simply have to respect the signals and otherwise give the matter no more thought. In this analogy, a more up-to-date management system is a roundabout. A roundabout controls traffic by means of a code of conduct, which allows each driver to exhibit situational behaviour.

Involvement – make use of your meta-organisation

An additional approach is to make more use of the surrounding world in your project. Here are some examples of how it can be done when we start with a meta-organisation: in other words, an expanded team of people with a looser affiliation to the company:

- Set up various advisory boards consisting, for example, of young talents, experienced entrepreneurs, senior managers, scientists, or the like.
- Organise conferences, at which representatives of new and promising phenomena are invited to give presentations.
- Create a high level of visibility on social media, in the hope that this will reveal new contacts and ideas.
- Create a digital forum on the organisation's lines of business. Or find other ways to turn your organisation into a hub for inspirational traffic, people, or ideas.
- Mobilise user groups to develop applications based on your core technology. In other words, open the door to more collaboration.
- Use software and lightning-fast test methods among customers, suppliers, or others to gain an understanding of the needs of your meta-organisation.
- Use crowdsourcing platforms to find solutions to your challenges.

- Hold innovation jams.

- Host coding boot camps and software hackathons or the like.

Inclusion: mobilise the whole world for your project

Now we have looked at methods both of (1) delegating among staff and (2) involving people from the meta-organisation. A third initiative might be to include the outside world:

- Create a corporate incubator or accelerator.

- Set up a corporate venture capital fund.

- Make co-investments with venture funds or other skilled investors.

- Systematically acquire innovative organisations operating in the company's field.

- Practice systematic business model cloning: copy what others have done that works.

- Create an app store based on the company's core technology, just as Apple and Samsung have done for smartphones.

- Enter into collaboration agreements with digital giants.

- Establish systematic joint ventures with partners who need applications featuring the company's core technologies.

- Use open architecture: in other words, sell not only the company's own products but also others.

- Establish systematic spin-offs, so the whole organisation becomes a kind of incubator.

So now you have a total of 25 examples of practical methods that can help make a mature organisation permanently creative and agile – even if management is not in on everything. At the heart of such an organisation there would be a core team, a kind of military command centre, whose role is much more that of a football coach than of a player. Also bear in mind that if management succeeds in delegating tasks to – involving – and including countless individuals both within and outside the organisation, the whole structure will no longer be a conformist command pyramid but a multidimensional network. In other words, network management.

Network management entails a flatter structure, but with a myriad of tentacles extending into the surrounding world. This means that management control and management power, in the classic sense, will often have to give way so that a number of smaller units do the work, each unit possessing the vital trinity of insight, responsibility, and consequence. One practical example of this is when small local teams, rather than a central HR department, are in charge of recruitment. As mentioned previously, Frederic Laloux described how staff functions almost disappear in highly evolutionary companies.

Once you have realised that, within your business area, you cannot seriously command either what should or will happen and, as a result of this realisation, you have institutionalised the permanent creativity and agility of your organisation by deploying methods as just described.

There is a huge fact you are going to have to come to terms with. You may be in charge, but actually you have no firm plan. At least not one that will be sustainable in the heat of the battle. Your values and code of conduct may be carved in stone, but your business plan may begin to resemble the business model canvas of a start-up. A situation like this takes humility and the abilities to listen and relinquish approaches that once worked but no longer do. Plus, a willingness to take risks. And curiosity. In fact, the total opposite of 'do as I say, because I know best'-style management. You see, network management presupposes that the network as a whole 'knows best'.

Algorithm-based management versus human management

Then there are the autonomous parts of a company. In this context, Stafford Beer's management theories from the 1950s are particularly relevant, because they later led to concepts of autonomy known as cybernetics.

Cybernetics is all about regulatory mechanisms: for example, those parts of the human body that function unconsciously, including blood circulation, respiration, digestion, etc. Similarly, by deploying combinations of, say, IoT, big data, robotics, and AI, large parts of a company can sometimes operate totally 'on reflex' – actually like an inner DAO. At the same time, the company's performance can be monitored via standard dashboards. The cybernetic concept of making part of a company instinctive has influenced the likes of management theorists and advisers such as Peter Drucker and Fredmund Malik and is becoming more relevant in tandem, for example, with the exponential development of electronics. What is more, umpteen 'cyber' concepts are constantly emerging: cyberspace, cyber security, cybercafé, cybercrime, and cyberwar. They are all offshoots of cybernetics.

You could call the autonomous part of a company its 'algorithm'. In that sense, a modern company might consist of a combination of value-based management, network management, and cybernetics or algorithm.

Business as unusual

To sum up, I would say that you can certainly equip your business to tackle the extremely changeable world described in this book by combining:

- Seek–sense–share loops: information and insights are created through decentralised interaction.

- Value-based management: acute awareness of values and codes of conduct, and efficient communication of them.

- De-uniforming: members of staff are increasingly accepted for who they are – warts and all.

- Increased tolerance of error: members of staff may make mistakes, as long as they and the organisation learn from them.

- Network management: delegation, involvement, and inclusion, and fewer staff functions.

- Business canvas planning: overly detailed planning is replaced by something simpler and more fluid, and information is shared transparently and in real time.

- Cybernetic management: functions based on automation and tracked with real-time dashboards, possibly combining IoT, big data, and AI.

On the one hand, the agility and creativity of the company will then be *institutionalised*. On the other hand, management will have more time to devote to what they are best at: the intuitive, human aspects, including work on visions and strategic/core innovation, assessment of future scenarios, personal deal making, team building, communication with the outside world, and ensuring that the company's actions reflect its values.

In a more future-proof organisation, all the teams help each other, but mainly make their own decisions. Employees are no longer expected to leave their personality at home. You are accepted for who you are and have no need to conceal your personal attitudes, sexuality, or weaknesses, which is why you probably no longer need to wear a uniform to erase your private self. Mistakes are tolerated, as long as you learn from them.

The idea is not to plan either your life or the future of the company in great detail. Instead the whole process should be regarded as an unpredictable journey, on which you and your staff are driven by passion and competence, while you continuously adapt to internally generated ideas and to constant changes in the outside world. There are almost no staff functions, and planning is very simple, fluid, and granular. Decision-making is very much decentralised, while information is transparent and provided in real time. Overall, the organisation is agile and interwoven inextricably with the surrounding world. And overall, the direction is this:

46. **As the global speed of innovation grows, the predominant corporate management styles will trend towards Laloux's evolving organisations, where spontaneous innovation is institutionalised.**

11.
THE POLITICAL IMPLICATIONS OF TOMORROW'S TECHNOLOGIES

Just as technological development has led to new forms of management in private *companies, across the ages it has also influenced* political *development. Just think of the political effect of the Industrial Revolution. Industrialisation generated unprecedented increases in prosperity, which had an infinite number of positive effects for both states and their citizens. However, the new technologies also generated long, inscrutable value chains. These led to increased specialisation, so people no longer understood one another's lives and jobs to the same extent as before. Under these new framework conditions, three new principal philosophies emerged: Liberalism, Socialism, and Fascism – besides their many spin-offs, including Anarchism, Communism, and National Socialism. These societal models clashed and led to a great deal of violence and suffering.*

The reason for mentioning this, of course, is that the technological and commercial predictions I have tackled in this book will also have political implications that we must include in our thoughts about how the future may proceed. This chapter is my take on the subject.

Three social standard patterns that often undermine civilisations

Before really going into the specific political implications, I would like to underline three permanent phenomena in civilisations, which I will believe will have a significant impact on political development in the decades to come: (1) the Karpman drama triangle, (2) over-institutionalisation, and (3) shifts in dominant moral instincts.

The Karpman drama triangle

The Karpman drama triangle relates to an irrational, and often very destructive, psychological game between people who assume three different roles:

- The Persecutor, who typically conceals his or her own weaknesses, and who exerts excessive control, criticism, anger, humiliation, violence, authority, condescension, etc.

- The Victim, who has opted for an often lifelong loser role. Everything is the fault and responsibility of other people.

- The Rescuer, who typically feels guilty, indifferent, or weak deep down inside, but who wants to compensate for this by constantly working on rescue projects on behalf of other people or the whole world and by making that mission very clear to the outside world.

An important feature of this is that people who want to play a role in this game actively seek out other people and cast them in the two missing roles. For example, someone who wants to play the Victim may look for someone else to play the Persecutor, while a Rescuer may look for Victims. It is often the self-proclaimed Rescuers that trigger the game, clearly conveying their Rescuer status via 'virtue signalling'. Through statements, attire, or actions they make it clear to the outside world that *they* are the goodies: which, of course, implies that the others are *not*. Then they appoint Victims and Persecutors. In order to gain absolution – particularly if you have been cast as a Persecutor – you can then hand over power to these Rescuers and maybe buy indulgences in various forms.

There are many problems with this phenomenon, including the fact that it often prevents people from taking responsibility for their own lives, and it often impedes voluntary win–win transactions.

But it is extremely widespread. Consequently, through the ages, the drama triangle has constituted a philosophical foundation for many religions, each of which, in its own way, divided the world into devout Victims, unbelieving Persecutors, and proselytising Rescuers. In the Middle Ages, for example, Europe experienced countless wars and conflicts between Protestants and Catholics, both of whom regarded themselves as the devout Victims of abuse by others. So, one Karpman drama triangle reinforced the other. Additionally, in recent times, the often-violent conflicts between Protestants and Catholics in Northern Ireland were a full-blown manifestation of the drama triangle. The same is often true of modern-day conflicts between Shia and Sunni Muslims.

Not only has the Karpman drama triangle played an important role in many religions, but in addition to theocracy (priesthood), it has also been the backbone of totalitarian movements such as Socialism, Fascism, National Socialism, and Communism and at the very core of various vendetta cultures throughout the world.

Admittedly, much of it disappeared in Europe as Christianity became gentler, the Iron Curtain fell, and national wars in Europe largely disappeared. However, already in the 1980s, it started to gain ground again in the form of the more extreme forms of eco-fascism, which wanted to rescue the world from avaricious humanity. And, more recently, it has reared its head in today's budding culture of persecution, or offence culture, in which various sections of the population cast themselves in the role of chronic Victims, while pointing their fingers at the Persecutors they want to be saved from by Rescuers.

Over-institutionalisation

The second, and frequently very destructive, repetitive pattern of civilisations is over-institutionalisation: a phenomenon that results in insight, responsibility, and consistency being increasingly removed from one another, while an ever-increasing proportion of society's activity is no longer made up of voluntary win–win transactions but is imposed. However, it is important first of all to note that over-institutionalisation is a spontaneous phenomenon that is extremely difficult to combat in conformist organisations, since their natural tendency is to create ever more of it. Secondly, it is so strong that it has not only ruined countless civilisations throughout the ages, but is also a recurring phenomenon in private companies. Thus, modern companies with conformist organisations spontaneously become increasingly bureaucratic and rigid until they often perish for that very reason.

But it is more serious when it destroys civilisations than when it causes individual companies to fail. And it certainly does destroy civilisations. In fact, for example, the anthropologist and historian Joseph Tainter, the historian and evolutionary theorist Clay Shirky, and, particularly, the historian Carroll Quigley (all three American) have indicated that over-institutionalisation has been the very factor that destroyed numerous civilisations.

Over-institutionalisation has often taken the form of religious tyranny. However, I believe that today's path towards over-institutionalisation in secular societies usually consists of the following five phases:

- Phase 1: The Minimal State. The state is in charge of people's security and handles practical tasks only in cases where these clearly are best addressed collectively.

- Phase 2: The Social Security State. The state to a greater extent helps the sick, the young, the old, and the unemployed.

- Phase 3: The Welfare State. The state also helps people of low income, regardless of whether they are jointly responsible for their own situation.

- Phase 4: The Equalisation State. The state's added objective is to level out income and prosperity through the transfer of money.

- Phase 5: The Total State. The state has a dominant role in media, education, production, freedom of expression, and people's private economy.

Whether the fifth phase – the Total State – ends up being actual totalitarianism is a matter of definition. However, the important thing to realise is that the future we are attempting to look into will, in my opinion, encounter major problems as a result of over-institutionalisation.

The collapse of norms and moral decadence

The third important phenomenon, which will also affect the future, as I see it, is a drift in people's prioritisation of moral instincts. In his groundbreaking book *The Righteous Mind* (2012), the social psychologist, Jonathan Haidt described six moral instincts, all of which have been important throughout millennia for the survival of cave people:

- Protection against violation (traditionally to ensure the survival of offspring).

- Fairness (to escape parasites and facilitate collaboration, including trade).

- Loyalty (to be able to support each other in adversity).

- Faith in authority (to get collaboration and lines of command to work).

- Cleanliness (to avoid infections).

- Freedom (to remove constraining leaders).

Personally, I would also say that diligence, willpower, and willingness to take risks are important moral instincts for the majority of my friends and family, even though they are not on Haidt's list. In any case, one of Haidt's well-founded theses is that we are all born with an individual symphony of instincts that significantly affect our choices in life, including our political attitudes. But Haidt also demonstrates how, in modern society, these modern social instincts are exposed to new situations, with which our distant ancestors were not familiar. One example that springs to mind is how we project our instincts of loyalty and belief in authority onto our affiliation with sports teams. And the fact that, in today's extremely clean world, our innate instinct for cleanliness often turns into food hysteria, where we suddenly think we are being poisoned by things that are really quite healthy and harmless. Or, in the Karpman version, we are Victims of poisoning by Persecutors in the evil food industry, but we can be healed by good Rescuers. So 'detox' has become the new buzzword.

However, moral instincts not only guide individuals in directions that are not always appropriate; they can also contribute to destructive, collective mass movements. For example, I believe that the first five of Haidt's above-mentioned six moral instincts may well be – and often have been – abused as driving forces in the Karpman drama triangle: as when non-believers are described as 'unclean' or when people with their instinctive faith in authority cast themselves at the feet of self-appointed Rescuers, who are actually dreamers and charlatans.

However, there may also be a shift in a society's relative prioritisation of the various instincts if it has long been spared from obvious threats. For example, statistics show a correlation between the roll-out of welfare societies and so-called norm degeneration. In tandem with increasingly better welfare services, funded by an increasingly higher and more progressive tax burden, we often witness an erosion of the work ethic. When incentives to work are reduced, some people will work less or attempt to avoid work altogether. Of course, this can be thought of as a free choice, but it becomes problematic when the same people make use of society's common, and very expensive, services. In addition, a moral decline can set in, in which increasingly more people attempt to help themselves to public funds, simply because they see other people doing it. It is somewhat similar to problems in corrupt societies, in which everyone is corrupt because everyone else is.

Any competent historian knows that this phenomenon is nothing new. There is an excellent example in the TV serial about the second president of the United States *John Adams,* in which Adams and Benjamin Franklin visit the all-out decadent court of Louis XV, where the men wear ultra-feminine clothes and thick layers of mascara, and live lavishly off the people's money. Meanwhile, John Adams is a down-to-earth, practical man of humble background who wants a minimal state in his own homeland. Adams is overwhelmed by the decadence and comes across like a dog in a game of skittles.

In fact, the phenomenon of increasing decadence is aptly described by the Arabian historian Ibn Khaldun in his book *Muqaddimah* (1377), in which he divided dynasties into four stages:

- Stage 1: Entrepreneurial leadership that builds values through diligence and thrift.

- Stage 2: A fairly efficient generation who has seen the first generation at work and understands staple societal values.

- Stage 3: A less efficient third generation operating on the basis of the now-established, efficient traditions, but without fully understanding or appreciating their deeper reasons. As a result, they are less efficient.

- Stage 4: A fourth generation that is completely lacking in the necessary virtues and understanding of – or interest in – how value is created, so they simply squander everything.

For generations now, the West has largely been spared from war on its own territory, plague, cholera, or famine. That is exactly why, in my opinion, there have been violent shifts in the prevailing moral instincts. As a result, large sections of the population have severely reduced knowledge of – and interest in how values are created and protected. So, as I see it, we are experiencing a moral decadence that does not sufficiently equip nations to tackle threats, or even to maintain the momentum of previous generations to create an increase in prosperity. In fact, I believe that, while this phenomenon is very strong, its rise is blurred by the benefits we gain from the development of exponential technologies. But the underlying threat is the fact that we may perhaps be a little too similar to the generation in Stage 4 of Ibn Khaldun's model, recklessly squandering the trusted talents.

47. Due to negative self-organisation, society has spontaneous tendencies to disintegrate cf. the Karpman drama triangle, over-institutionalisation, and decadence. All three of these tendencies are spontaneous and very difficult to counteract.

It should be noted that such disintegration does not only involve money and power. When travelling around the world, I have often been amazed to see older buildings and art bearing witness to former cultures that – apart from lower technological stage – were far more sophisticated than the ones now inhibiting the same areas. And whenever I see this, it is clear that the only thing that has progressed in the area – technology – was not developed by themselves but imported from other more advanced civilisations. I suspect that the single most common reason for such cultural decline is excessive separation between insight, responsibility, and consequence, which can happen as a consequence of excessive enacting of the Karpman drama triangle as well as of over-institutionalisation and decadence.

The future welfare society – pyramid states or agile app stores?

As far as I am concerned, the aforementioned phenomena constitute general threats to our civilisations. But there are also more specific problems in modern mixed economies, where the public sector is predominantly, in Frederic Laloux's terms, conformist: method-driven and hierarchical. I believe that these organisations carry the seeds of their own destruction.

The first is the so-called Baumol effect, or 'Baumol's cost disease', named after the American economist William Baumol. One can easily raise wages in one sector if productivity per employee increases accordingly. Great. But then take a string quartet, which is one of Baumol's favourite examples. String quartets have not experienced any increase in productivity for hundreds of years. Nevertheless, like other people, musicians expect pay rises. That means that consumers see their services as increasingly more expensive when compared to all sorts of other things. That is why professional classical music also requires large amounts of public subsidy for its survival.

Now, string quartets are not a major factor in global economy. But the big problem is that public sectors throughout the world suffer from the same problem. Unlike private companies, they do not work under competitive pressure so have limited incentives for innovation and productivity improvements. Nor do they reward them. On the contrary, because if the public sector rationalises, some of their staff will simply get fired. In fact, as a result, over time they have nigh-on zero productivity gains, so they feel increasingly more expensive and engulf increasingly larger amounts of the GDP – even though the quality of these services does not improve. And if, as an alternative, we freeze the public sector's budgets' GDP share, due to the Baumol effect, their quality will be ever poorer.

One of the main reasons for the lack of productivity growth in public services is the use of monopolistic method management, which is a feature of Laloux's conformist organisations. This means that those who decide what to deliver, even at retail level, through laws and directives, determine *how* the tasks should be solved – in other words, the exact opposite of *Auftragstaktik*.

Method management can be justified in certain contexts – both in the public and private sectors. McDonald's, for example, is very method managed, because uniformity here is a big priority. However, there are also a number of disadvantages associated with it, because when you take away responsibility from people, they easily become irresponsible, and when you deprive them of power, they often feel powerless. In addition, method management creates an atmosphere of distrust, because it shows that those who make decisions do not trust those who work. Method management also stifles creativity, because it puts a stopper on experiments.

Similarly, over time, method management leads to such complex regulatory jungles that increasingly fewer people can find their way through them. On top of that, administration costs constantly grow – partly because, as Laloux pointed out, conformist organisations generate very large staff functions. And finally, it should be noted that method management freezes organisations or societies in states that totally hamper them from keeping step with an ever-evolving reality. In other words, excessive method management amounts to over-institutionalisation and, the faster technological development proceeds, the more hopeless the states' lead-footed method-management model becomes.

Another reason for the Baumol problem is that, in general, we manage other people's money less responsibly than we manage our own. One example is the so-called budget-maximising model in public sectors, which was scientifically described for the first time in 1971 by the researcher and university professor William Niskanen. Public servants typically attempt to increase their own organisations' budgets in order to gain more subordinates and more power. This is a lot different from private companies, in which managers typically try to maximise their profits by *reducing* costs and thus headcount and generally improving performance.

We also have Mancur Olson's Non-Work Law. Large bureaucracies typically produce a myriad of working committees and sub-committees, each of which works increasingly more slowly, creating unproductive work for each other. The sum of all this is rather disheartening:

48. **Public institutions tend to gobble up increasingly larger amounts of a society's economy, while their efficiency lags increasingly further behind.**

Due to the combination of Baumol's cost disease and norm degeneration, modern welfare states have often had a steadily increasing tax burden, which I regard as a major problem in itself. In fact, the aforementioned Ibn Khaldun had already described at as follows: 'It should be known that at the beginning of a dynasty, we get substantial tax revenue from low tax rates. When it ends, we get poor tax revenue from high tax rates.' I can elaborate on this with some obvious examples of the harmful effects of too high a tax burden:

- It is mainly detrimental to creative enterprises, since many artists, athletes, entrepreneurs, and others, who work with great uncertainty and variable earnings, have very uneven incomes. They often alternate between being top taxpayers and being in financial distress, when they then apply for social security. The distress is very much a result of the fact that, because of their sporadically massive tax bills, they were not able to save in good times for the subsequent bad times.

- Excessive taxation destroys division of labour and jobs. If Mr Smith, a tradesman, offers to paint a wall for a homeowner, Mr Brown, and if both pay a marginal tax rate of 50% plus 25% VAT, Mr Smith has to be about five (five!) times better at painting than Mr Brown before it makes sense for Mr Brown to pay for Mr Smith's services. And, if the marginal tax rate is increased to 70%, the requirement for greater efficiency increases to 14 times. This phenomenon pressurises many people to leave the labour market, and they become welfare recipients instead.

- It leads to more undeclared work, since the temptation for this increases with the tax burden.

- It causes more social fraud. People who live off undeclared work seek social benefits to justify the fact they do not have an official job.

- It increases the brain drain. The most talented, risk-taking, hard-working professionals flee from countries with excessive taxation.

- It results in less physical mobility. Particularly high car taxes reduce people's willingness to work, where there is no easy access to public transport.

- It leads to unproductive saving. Instead of investing their savings in productive companies (shares), where the money is taxed, people conceal their profits in unproductive things such as gold, jewellery, or home improvements, which the tax authorities have a harder time spotting. This is especially true if the money comes from undeclared work or crime.

- It hampers innovation. It makes less sense to take risks as an entrepreneur if any winners are taxed to the hilt.
- It counteracts job mobility. Heavy taxes prevent people from saving. Therefore, they dare not change jobs or industry, let alone start their own business.
- It costs a fortune in administration. The more punishing taxation becomes, the more resources are deployed on administration, collection, optimisation, punishment for evasion, etc.

While public administration continues to be based on Laloux's conformist management model, the overall consequence of the above-described challenges is a tendency for tensions to get even worse over time.

There is also a threat that a so-called 'welfare coalition', most of whose income is from the state, and who can vote to get the money of a minority, which could also ultimately lead to collapse.

Forces that lead to chronically low growth or stagnation in welfare states

The sum of the aforementioned societal problems is, as mentioned, that modern mixed economies contain the seeds of their own potential destruction. The Karpman drama triangle, persecution culture, over-institutionalisation, moral decadence following crisis-free periods, Baumol's cost disease, negative norm degeneration, and sky-high taxation can lead to persistently relative, and finally maybe absolute, deterioration. That is what happened, for example, over many decades in Argentina and is often somewhat similar in the second, third, or fourth generation of successful families.

The battle for top-down management and decentralisation

In my view, there is a huge underlying tension in society between those who are mainly advocates of public power concentration and a hierarchical society, and supporters of more decentralised, grass-roots communities.

When it comes to the public sector, hierarchical models took over a long time ago. In my native country Denmark, for example, until the 1970s just over a few thousand parishes were important power entities, but then most of that power passed to the municipalities, which were then merged, just as the counties had been merged to form regions, which were then again merged. And while all that was happening, more and more power was channelled to parliament, which then forwarded increasing parts of it to the European Union, the United Nations, and other international organisations. In other words, the power was continually moved further away from individuals and local communities and concentrated at the top of increasingly larger entities. Arguments on behalf of this trend have often relied on the benefits of 'common solutions' and 'harmonisation'.

As we have seen primarily in China, centralisation can be promoted with technologies such as IoT and big data to monitor people via sensors and behavioural analyses, and AI to locate threats to the system. It is thus possible to take centralisation far.

So, the public sector has predominantly *centralised,* which is a natural tendency for Laloux's conformist organisations, whereas the private sector – as we saw, for example, in Chapter 11, predominantly through apps, crowdsourcing, blockchain, MOOCs, the sharing economy, the rating economy, 3-D printing, and DAOs – has *decentralised.* This is an often profitable opportunity which we see in Laloux's achievement organisations, and which is key to his pluralist organisations and essential for the evolutionary ones that are now emerging.

Technologies that can promote decentralisation

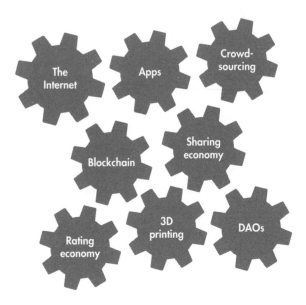

In this context, it is important to understand that a decentralised market economy is at the heart of creativity. For example, it has a built-in sorting mechanism, in which ideas are constantly filtered through the ability to attract the right team of entrepreneurs, to convince financiers like me, and appeal to commercial customers like us all. Overall, a market economy is thus evolutionary, even if its companies are not individually so.

This is supported by the fact that today information flows much more freely. Traditional media such as books, radio, and TV were all based on top–down methods to spread information from the few to the many. But the Internet enables information to flow up, down, and sideways – you name it – completely freely, based on grassroots models and through millions of interlocked seek–sense–share loops. Thus, the information flow has become evolutionary, undermining the assumption in conformist organisations that the elite knows much more than the rest of the people.

Currently, ground zero for the debate on centralisation versus decentralisation is perhaps the European Union. Here, two very different views are confronted. Germany and especially France – albeit with considerable internal resistance – are pioneers of the view that the European Union must be centrally controlled like a kind of Roman Empire with common solutions and harmonisation. Conversely, a number of peripheral countries are more in favour of becoming an EFTA for free, autonomous nation states: free trade and political diversity. This tension also involves a clash between a conformist and an evolutionary societal model.

If this conflict is not to end up as a very bad marriage, it may be necessary to divide into two or more EU membership provisions, ranging from large-scale to small-scale centralisation. If this does not happen, I predict that the bad marriage may get really ugly, as such marriages often do.

Openness or closedness?

We have seen that, unless there is immigration, people in wealthy nations have too few children to stabilise their populations. At the same time, there are prospects of major population growth in the poor parts of the Middle East and large parts of Africa. This will of course continue to support mass migrations, which again will cause many countries to restrict immigration. One argument for this is that welfare states would soon go bankrupt if they had open borders and offered welfare to every Tom, Dick, or Harry that came in. Conversely, inhibiting migration can be costly when it comes to people who could play important roles in the labour market. Indeed, some of the most creative and economically well-functioning regions in the world have highly international populations.

In this context, I think that countries – for example, EU countries – will gradually come up with models in which borders are *conditionally* open, the conditions being that immigrants can support themselves and abide by the rules. This is, for instance, the basic model in Switzerland, which, besides having a relatively evolutionary social model, is one of the most international countries in the world. But it is also pretty good at preventing immigrants from draining public funds or making a living from crime. I can imagine a future in which that kind of 'smart openness' will gain ground.

The information problem in public management

Public sector management also has a growing information problem, since the difference between the population's vast collective knowledge and the state elite's comparatively limited insight is increasing. It is fair to say that a clan leader in the Stone Age probably shared a significant part of his clan's overall knowledge with others, but this is, of course, not the case in highly advanced modern societies with extreme division of labour and much larger entities.

Two of the first people to highlight this central theme – and at a time when it was a lot smaller – were the Austrian economists Ludwig von Mises and Friedrich Hayek, both of whom described how information in a society is spread everywhere. Every day, every single person – the schoolteacher, the craftsman, the businessman, the researcher, and everybody else – collects and processes complex information from his or her own world. Assuming that an elite is supposed to control the behaviour of all these people on the basis of the hierarchical model, it is unlikely that it can possess more than a fraction of a percent of an entire society's overall knowledge and insight. So, supposing optimistically that it has 0.1% of the total knowledge, on the basis of that 0.1% of society's knowledge, should it have the right to tell the people, who have the remaining 99.9%, what to do about most things in life?

Hardly. And that is why decentralised systems tend to perform best. Decentralised systems also gain in the long term, because they have far more experiments and much more competition; and since the trinity of knowledge, responsibility, and consequence is united in decentralised systems, they motivate people to a much greater extent. Incidentally, Nassim Taleb presented this theme very nicely in his book, *Skin in the Game* (2018). The book's main point is that, if people will not live personally with the consequences of decisions, then they should not be making them. Consequently, I will take the liberty of naming this book's penultimate law after him:

49. Taleb's Law: The systems in which insight, responsibility, and consequence are closest to one another usually do best in the long run.

When client–server computing made it big, it outperformed many companies, who still advocated master–slave computing. And that has also been the case with every subsequent computer paradigm. The strong philosophies of decentralised intelligence and information, which form the basis of recent computing paradigms, such as client–server computing and later personal computing, network computing, edge computing, and cloud computing, also annihilated companies that did not keep up with the progress, and they continue to do so. But, in my view, the really striking phenomenon is that states are allowed to base their behaviour on conformist organisations, who not only resemble the master–slave computing model of mainframe computers, but who also increasingly do so. So, my prognosis is partly that, going forward, power and prosperity will be concentrated in those countries that best understand how to convert from a master–slave societal model to personal network–edge–cloud-like systems divided into countless discreet, logical entities, each with a fusion of its own insight, responsibility, and consequence: cf. Taleb's Law. In other words, the future will be dominated by states that depart from conformist organisation in favour of achievement, pluralist, and – last, but not least – evolutionary organisation forms.

Laloux compares impulsive organisations to packs of wolves, conformist organisations to military ones (without *Auftragstaktik,* I would add), achievement organisations to machines, pluralist organisations to families, and evolutionary organisations to living organisms.

Yes, living organisms. In this respect, it is interesting that Taleb's Law also works in nature. Just think about how nature is organised: in a myriad of small, rational, and autonomous cells, each with its own chemical algorithms for making useful decisions. A human body, for instance, consists of billions of cells that together create organs etc. And each cell of every single organ is programmed to filter what is going in and out, and to respond logically to external impulses. Biology, which could not be more evolutionary, is thus very much based on edge computing. It is this organic decentralisation principle that we elegantly copy in a predominantly market economy society or in a technology such as IoT and a business model such as the sharing economy – and in evolutionary forms of organisation. In other words, from the outset, nature has dangled this in front of our noses, and now we see its principles deftly applied to electronic ecosystems and increasingly to private business models too.

That is the next thing for states to learn. Thus, in the public sector management of the future, we must seek more evolutionary and hacker-friendly societies, which consist of smaller autonomous entities, each of which can easily be substituted with others via an open platform, and in which money to a greater extent follows the citizens, who can then choose their providers in publicly sponsored 'app stores'. This could be done, for example, by offering people certain amounts of crypto money, which could each be used specifically for special purposes such as education. Originally, economists called this phenomenon a 'coupon economy'. But, if it were based on blockchain, 'token economy' would be a more appropriate expression.

The Roman Empire

So, what is my actual prediction in this case? Unfortunately, it is that states – especially the larger ones – will be bad at converting from conformist to more agile models. Those who do manage to will become magnets for migrations of dynamic people and for growth-oriented, profitable companies. The formation of the evolutionary state is perhaps one of the most underexploited opportunities in our society.

In reality, maybe the fall of the Roman Empire and what came after might be a good reference vis-à-vis what we are starting to experience. The Roman Empire in Western Europe existed from 27 BCE to 476 CE. Its fall came pretty quickly. It took just 71 years from being close to the peak of its greatness until it was brought down by Germanic tribesmen. Subsequently, the next 500 years or so saw the emergence of a belt of thousands of city states stretching from (and including) present-day Northern Italy to Switzerland, Germany, Eastern France, the Benelux, and parts of Northern Europe. As I mentioned before, these city states witnessed tremendous creativity, and this *decentralised* structure led to experimentation, enabling inhabitants to migrate to wherever the best opportunities were. A major analysis of this period's migrations by the US institute of analysis, NBER, concluded, for example:

> As measured by the pace of city growth in western Europe from 1000 to 1800, absolutist monarchs stunted the growth of commerce and industry. A region ruled by an absolutist prince saw its total urban population shrink by one hundred thousand people per century relative to a region without absolutist government. This might be explained by higher rates of taxation under revenue-maximizing absolutist governments than under non-absolutist governments, which care more about general economic prosperity and less about State revenue. (Long and Shleifer, 1993)

That is what we are already seeing, and I believe it will intensify. So, I think that what we are going to experience politically in the West might be reminiscent partly of the final stages of the Western Roman Empire (the Eastern Roman Empire was conquered by Muslims in the fifteenth century), and partly of the creativity and voting with feet which later occurred among the numerous smaller city states.

Government as a platform: small government - big services

One way to mitigate the risk of systemic political crises is to pursue government as a platform.

In this context, think of smartphones. These provide access to millions of apps, all of which have been tested to meet certain legal, security, and quality requirements, but which were developed externally. In other words, smartphone providers crowdsource the vast majority of their services, which users then rate. This creates a huge range of different services at very competitive prices (many services are even free) and promotes incredible innovation.

One prerequisite for this has been the fact that smartphone providers offer Application Programming Interfaces (APIs): in other words, well-defined software interfaces that facilitate the easy integration of foreign software with theirs. Similarly, in a government-as-a-platform model, you could imagine that public data and services would be very open, so that individuals could work with them and make extensions, plugins, etc.

But that is not all. Imagine a state that says: 'We want to offer all citizens tax-funded access to a range of services such as education and health insurance, and we will ensure that they comply with certain requirements. But each citizen can choose his or her own providers.'

This is the platform concept in a nutshell, abandoning method-managed monopolies and instead promoting competition and choice, and thereby generating innovation and productivity gains. In such a system, insight, responsibility, and consequence will also be more closely linked in a number of local units, which corresponds somewhat to converting from master–slave, mainframe computing to networked and edge computing. The consequence is that service providers spend less time fulfilling the requirements of public method-management systems, instead focusing more on their customers.

But how would customers choose? Through rating systems, which would emerge spontaneously. However, in addition, the state may require any service provider on the public platform to disclose certain information, such as average grades in a school or current waiting times at a clinic. Smartphone providers and other modern companies almost always have online dashboards, which display in real time their most important target figures such as sales, complaints, revenue, data flows, etc. In other words, they know precisely – here and now – where the proverbial shoe pinches. But if public services are offered by private or autonomous companies, customers must also know where the shoe pinches – here and now.

Another development in public services may be that an increasing number of approvals etc. can be booked online via small smartphone apps and websites, which provide immediate answers to most of them, similar to how people get order confirmations and delivery estimates in seconds when ordering online from private providers like Amazon.

And when the state itself provides services, it can offer real-time tracking of case handling. It is rather like having packages shipped by private providers, where you can usually see online exactly where in the system your package is at any moment, or where, in the case of Uber, the car you ordered is in real time and when you can expect it to arrive.

Moreover, such real-time feedback is not only useful for the customers/citizens, but also for the providers. Politicians and public sector administrators will also become much more efficient if they see how well the systems are working via online, real-time dashboards. And when something does not work, it will be clear to everyone who is responsible.

The growing attraction of basic income

Another aspect of technological development may be an increasing argument for basic income. As mentioned earlier, I am personally not so concerned about mass unemployment as a result of new technologies, but it seems likely that welfare states in the West, in their current forms, will run into some major problems. First, experience shows that welfare states create incredibly expensive management and control regimes. Welfare, machinery-related administration costs for both a state and its citizens combined can easily reach 20–25% of the revenue collected in taxes. Secondly, welfare states can maintain clients in inactivity, because even the slightest sign of willingness/capacity to work can lead to loss of benefits: a relationship that ends up attracting some people to assume chronic client roles, akin to the perpetual Victim in the Karpman drama triangle. This is why basic income may be chosen to replace lots of the traditional elaborate welfare system.

In fact, there have been experiments with this in several places in the world with limited success. See, for example, Rutger Bregman's book *Utopia for Realists* (2017) for a description of such attempts.

However, the success criterion for introducing a basic income must be, partly, that such a system only ensures a quite limited lifestyle and, partly, that any work can actually be worthwhile, so the basic income in no way becomes unnecessarily passivating.

It is also interesting that basic income has advocates from all parts of the political spectrum. For this reason, too, it seems likely to me that different countries will experiment with it again and perhaps eventually find a model that works. If I have a single major fear vis-à-vis such a project, it is that it will make it easier for parts of the population to live like totally pacified screen zombies, sinking into the digital world and becoming totally cut off from real life.

Value-based public management – good or bad?

In Chapter 11 I described how, more than ever before, in a turbulent future, private companies will need to have, and communicate, clear values. Value-based management in a company means you only hire people who agree, and that is what you then try to do.

But does the same apply to future states? In this context, the answer is somewhat less black and white. Every nation has a set of basic values expressed in its constitution, and I believe that most people in most nations support their constitutions. However, major migrations mean that increasing numbers of population groups are migrating to countries whose constitutional values are not theirs, and to which they are sometimes directly opposed.

The basic problem is that you can only have value-based public management if there is overwhelmingly common support for these values in the country's population – and that requires a certain degree of internal homogeneity. This particular issue, by the way, is described excellently in the last chapter of the classic book *State, Anarchy, and Utopia* (1974) by the philosopher Robert Nozick. If states are, or become, too large or multicultural to meet this criterion, the tasks of that state should be reduced to the purely practical. If this does not happen – if the state pursues core values that large parts of its population disagree with – you will lose trust and coherence. And that is happening in quite a few places.

If I have to draw a general conclusion about how technical development both challenges and offers new opportunities to public management and administration, the overall task must be to gradually reduce the use of conformist organisational models with their vast legislative jungles and frequently unrealistic leaders, and to arrive instead at something that combines achievement, pluralist, and evolutionary forms of organisation. In this context the keywords include 'government as a platform' and maybe 'basic income'.

12.
THE FINAL RULE

We are approaching the end of this story, so I guess now is a good time to ask if there is one simple common denominator – do the accounts of all the different topics lead to one overarching conclusion? In the very last line of this chapter, I will attempt to formulate one, but before doing so, here are a few highlights that strike me as particularly important.

There is no end to innovation. As we saw with Ziman's Law, human scientific activity seems to double every 15 years and grow 100-fold every 100 years. It appears that this can continue as far as the eye can see, since computers will handle increasing parts of it at an ever-faster pace. Furthermore, since innovation is essentially about recombining what already exists, the more we have developed in the past, the more new things will be possible to create in the future. For these very reasons, innovation is, to all practical intents and purposes, endless and only limited by the extremely generous laws of physics plus the existence of liberal societies that permit free thinking. And whereas often the first market response to new core technologies may seem disappointing, over time people figure out new business models and applications, which trigger endless cascades of new business opportunities and technologies. Infinitely.

On that note, we have lots of technologies with exponential or hyperexponential growth. An increasing number of technologies exhibit exponential or hyperexponential growth. This includes, for instance, the sequencing and synthesising of DNA, global growth in the number of IoT devices, the amount of digital data produced and stored, the amount and speed of bandwidth available, the global OLED screen area output, the number of usable radio frequencies, the performance of LEDs, batteries, hard drives, etc. While I have provided numerous examples of these throughout the book, in reality, there are countless more. In particular, whenever a new technical field moves from analogue to digital, the rate of innovation and performance tends to move from linear to exponential, and more exponential phenomena pop up. By the way, there is a lot of this amazing progress that official calculations of GDP growth do not capture.

Among the most radical changes is the fact that we can now program biology. We very recently began to learn how to code life with great precision. With this technology we can eliminate existing species (specicide), make extinct species reappear (de-extinction), change species, and create new ones *en masse*. And we can also re-code our own species, and I have no doubt we will. Increasingly, we will also code cells as if they are robots at our service so that they can perform magic for us. In short, we are the new programmers, and nature is our new computer.

AI and quantum computers will lead to recursive superintelligence. In an increasing number of disciplines, computers beat the human mind, and increasingly this includes areas involving intuition. In this context, AI plays a huge role. Furthermore, quantum computers are breaking through with powers to tackle certain kinds of calculations billions of times faster than the fastest supercomputers today. All of this will have wide implications, but perhaps the biggest is that computers will become increasingly brilliant at formulating scientific hypothesis and writing software, and soon even better than any humans, which will stimulate run-away scientific discovery and technical innovation.

There will be sensors and Internet everywhere. Far more than ever before, we will – through IoT – equip the non-organic part of the world with artificial nerve fibres, organs, and small brains. So, a huge number of worldly objects will be able to do things that insects do – and will sometimes even look like them. In other words, we will create a completely non-biological ecosystem that will expand collective intelligence and capability, and, unlike biological ecosystems, this one will be constantly analysed with big data and AI. This will certainly make the world a whole smarter, but also less private.

We will never run out of resources. The ultimate resource is innovation, and since this is not running out but rather evolving exponentially, the expectation that we will soon run out of resources will remain an unrealised fear as it has been for centuries. Indeed, over the last 200 years, the real prices of all main categories of commodities have declined substantially and rather consistently. This happens because of innovative (1) synthetisation, (2) compression, (3) virtualisation, (4) recycling, (5) sharing, and (6) substitution. Oddly, since our ultimate resource is innovation, the more people we are on Earth, the faster the rate of innovation – and the greater the abundance *per capita*. In the future, this increased abundance will play out through the launch of new super-materials, smart genetic engineering, new nuclear energy, including perhaps the use of thorium plus nuclear fusion, synthetic meat, vertical farming, and much more.

Environmental problems will not be solved through light or dark environmentalism. However, bright environmentalism (growth, wealth, and innovation) will eventually do the job. Experience tells us that the introduction of new and smarter technologies almost without exception resolve environmentally unsustainable practices, and that, overwhelmingly, these technologies are developed and first deployed in the richest of nations. Furthermore, the most efficient birth control is growing wealth. For this reason, we cannot solve environmental challenges by limiting growth, wealth, or consumption. On the contrary. The way forward lies in more growth, wealth, and innovation. Fortunately, a myriad of exceptional technologies to address environmental challenges are either rolling out or in the pipeline.

Labour markets are turning Maslow's Hierarchy of Needs upside down. Increasingly, machines, robots, and computers meet the demands described at the lower end of Maslow's Hierarchy of Needs. Meanwhile, human labour increasingly makes products and services that belong to the higher levels of the hierarchy – including the theatre-like experience economy, assisted self-help, transcendental experiences, and labour-of-love activities such as entrepreneurship, do-it-yourself, and maker activity.

Digitalisation is not only about bits and bytes, but also about new granular markets and flexible lifestyles. Digitalisation facilitates real-time dataflows, which again provide the information needed to break markets down into smaller tradeable units such as we see in crowdsourcing and the sharing economy. This includes granular markets for labour, data storage, software use, electricity, and much more. Such granular units of products and services become available in clouds and at prices that fluctuate in real time, and are subject to ratings and transparent competition. This rating and cloud-based exchange of granular products and services, whether big, small, or tiny, constitutes a significant refinement of our market economies and also one that counteracts inflation. Furthermore, when it comes to labour markets, these trends lead to the growth of a flexible gig economy, in which people increasingly have no fixed workplace, working hours, holidays, or even pension age. Instead, they become more prone to live their adult lives in fluid combinations of work, leisure, and learning – but perhaps never retiring.

New technologies stimulate new forms of organisation. Just as mainstream computing migrated from a master–slave setup towards a client–server setup, followed by networked and edge computing, new technologies will drive leading management styles towards distributed, autonomous networked organisations, or what Frederic Laloux has called 'evolutionary organisations'. In this respect, the sharing economy and rating systems are vital and will continue to develop explosively. In other words, we are no longer talking only about smart objects, but also about smart ecosystems, in which both humans and machines will do business with each other in new, improved ways. However, in public management, the predominant management style will remain the hieratic conformist organisation for far too long, which will create tensions and problems.

We will gain access to more exciting experiences. Some of them will come from new computer games and associated e-sports, new types of media, and the likes of virtual and ambient computing: in other words, from electronics. We will also be offered fascinating new, hybrid experiences that will enrich all of our senses and play on all our feelings, not to mention new combinations of physical and electronic experiences as in augmented reality. So much of this is going to be amazing.

Along the way, all sorts of startling things will occur. Some of these we can predict with a fair degree of certainty, others we can only conjecture about, while still others will materialise like a bolt out of the blue. Examples of the probable, which are now being worked on, are nuclear fusion, quantum computers, cultured meat, super-intelligence, deexcitation, cancer vaccinations, and radically life-prolonging technologies. But we must also expect the unexpected. For example, did you so much as envisage blockchain before it appeared? I doubt it. And how many people foresaw vaccines and anaesthesia before they arrived? Err . . . not many.

Future challenges will largely be met with future technologies. Thanks to the staggering innovation of the future, we will inevitably discover that common assumptions that the challenges of the future will be solved with today's technologies will often be wrong. For instance, in my opinion, it is obvious that within the next 100 years the world will have access to extreme amounts of comparably clean energy. But do I think that most of it will be generated by solar panels and wind turbines? Actually no. I think it will largely come from something that does not work today.

And now, for the last rule. Overall, the future sounds pretty peachy, and my belief is clear. The future will be better than the present, just as I believe that the present surpasses the past. And that brings me to the 50th and final key rule of this book:

50. Overall, the world is going to be a better place.

What do you think?

APPENDIX: SOURCES AND INSPIRATION

In addition to the small Bibliography, I decided to upload sources to my website www.larstvede.com under the *Supertrends* section, from where many of them can be clicked to lead directly to the information. Apart from that, it should be noted that there is a constant flow of new sources on many of the topics described, which is why I would encourage readers who wish to learn more to simply Google the relevant subjects.

I would also like to describe briefly how *in general* I keep myself informed, and mention some of the writers I have found particularly inspiring.

On the subject of writers, I read or listen to (as audiobooks) about 30–50 books per year – particularly when I am travelling. For example, I like audiobooks when I am driving, and printed books when sailing in the summer or flying. Some of the writers I have found particularly inspiring are: David Deutsch, Craig Venter, Nicholas Wade, Stewart Brand, Jonathan Haidt, Thomas Sowell, Nassim Nicholas Taleb, Steven Pinker, Bjørn Lomborg, Niall Ferguson, Matt Ridley, Charles Murray, Richard Dawkins, and Paul Collier. But of course, there are countless others.

I prefer to buy books online, because then Amazon, where I buy them, gets to know me and gets better at recommending other books. After 20 years' of intensive use of this service, Amazon's algorithms know pretty well what it takes to make Lars Tvede happy!

I also receive large amounts of analytical material from various major banks, which is generally of high quality. In addition, from the age of 18, I have been subscribing to *The Economist* and also use the app Flipboard for information. However, it is background information and analyses that interest me. I do not have much time for so-called 'breaking news'.

In accordance with the aforementioned principles of Harold Jarche's personal knowledge management, I am also a very active user of social media for reading, sharing, and debating information. Facebook, LinkedIn, and Twitter are my most important platforms, even though currently I am on six others. My experience is that Jarche is absolutely right. If we share information and thoughts about the topics we find interesting on social media, we get huge amounts of inspiration in return – particularly if like me you have about 30 000 friends and followers and follow a very large number yourself. The fact that most people occasionally share a bit of private or non-professional material on these platforms too just adds a bit of fun. I do this as well.

Generally speaking, it is a good idea to start your activity, particularly on LinkedIn and Twitter, by following people you find professionally inspirational. Then the algorithms will regularly suggest others of the same category or calibre. After that, you are up and running.

The last-but-one point I want to make about information is that, as Jarche points out, you should spend some time reflecting deeply. For my part, this rarely happens in the office, but when I am practising sport or sailing – you name it.

And, finally, in most people's networks, there are some who are predominantly givers, and others predominantly takers. I am not talking about whether they invite you to dinner or never pick up the tab (well, maybe just a bit), but about whether you get something positive back when talking to them. For example, if you come up with an idea, do they come up with a reciprocal one, so things progress? Do they offer to put you in touch with people they know that are relevant to what you are talking about? Friends and acquaintances who do so are inspirational, so naturally you should try to reciprocate. And, just like knowledge and understanding, inspiration will be essential when it comes to tackling the wild future. With knowledge, we can create great results in our ever-changing world. But without knowledge, we will easily get blindsided, scared, and bewildered.

BIBLIOGRAPHY

Beckerman, W. (1996) *Through Green-Colored Glasses: Environmentalism Reconsidered.* CATO Institute.

Booker, C. and North, R. (2009) *Scared to Death: From BSE to Global Warming: Why Scares are Costing Us the Earth.* Continuum International Publishing Group Ltd.

Brand, S. (2009) *Whole Earth Discipline: An Ecopragmatist Manifesto.* Viking Books.

Bregman, R. (2017) *Utopia for Realists: And How We Can Get There.* Bloomsbury Publishing.

Buckminster Fuller, R. (1981) *Critical Path.* St Martin's Press.

Collier, P. (2007) *The Bottom Billion: Why the Poorest Countries are Failing and What Can be Done About It.* Oxford University Press.

Deutsch, D. (2011) *The Beginning of Infinity.* Viking Books.

Ehrlich, Paul R. (1968) *The Population Bomb.* Ballantine Books.

Ehrlich, Paul R. (1975) *The End of Affluence.* Amereon Books.

Festinger, L., Riecken, H., and Schachter, S. (1956) *When Prophecy Fails: A Social and Psychological Study of a Modern Group That Predicted the Destruction of the World.* Harper-Torchbooks.

Franklin, D. (ed.) (2018) *Megatech: Technology in 2050.* Economist Books.

Gore, A. (2007) *An Inconvenient Truth.* Perfection Learning.

Haidt, J. (2012) *The Righteous Mind: Why Good People are Divided by Politics and Religion.* Pantheon Books.

Hawkins, J. with Blakeslee, S. (2005) *On Intelligence: How a New Understanding of the Brain Will Lead to the Creation of Truly Intelligent Machines.* Times Books.

Ibbitson, J. and Bricker, D. (2019) *Empty Planet: The Shock of Global Population Decline.* Robinson.

Kaku, M. (2012) *Physics of the Future: The Inventions That Will Transform Our Lives.* Penguin.

Khaldun, I. (1377) *Muqaddimah.*

Laloux, F. (2014) *Reinventing Organizations: A Guide to Creating Organizations Inspired by the Next Stage in Human Consciousness.* Nelson Parker.

Long, J. B. D. and Shleifer, A. (1993) Princes and Merchants: European City Growth before the Industrial Revolution. NBER Working Paper No. 4274.

Mackay, C. (1841) *Extraordinary Popular Delusions and the Madness of Crowds.* London: Richard Bentley.

Meadows, D. L., Meadows, D. H., Behrens, W. W., and Randers, J. (1974) *The Limits to Growth: A Report for the Club of Rome's Project on the Predicament of Mankind.* Universe Books.

Nozick, R. (1974) *State, Anarchy, and Utopia.* Basic Books.

Paddock, W. and Paddock, P. (1968) *Famine, 1975! America's Decision: Who Will Survive?* Little Brown.

Piketty, T. and Goldhammer, A. (2014) *Capital in the Twenty-First Century.* Harvard University Press.

Pine, B. J. and Gilmore, J. H. (1999) *The Experience Economy: Work Is Theater & Every Business a Stage.* Harvard Business Review Press.

Pinker, S. (1997) *How the Mind Works.* W. W. Norton and Co.

Ridley, M. (2010) *The Rational Optimist: How Prosperity Evolves.* Harper.

Roslin, H., Rosling, O., and Rosling Rönnlund, A. (2018) *Factfulness: Ten Reasons We're Wrong About the World – and Why Things Are Better Than You Think.* Flatiron Books.

Simon, J. (1981) *The Ultimate Resource.* Princeton University Press.

Sundararajan, A. (2016) *The Sharing Economy: The End of Employment and the Rise of Crowd-Based Capitalism.* MIT Press.

Taleb, N. (2018) *Skin in the Game: Hidden Asymmetries in Daily Life.* Allen Lane.

Tvede, L. (2016) *The Creative Society: How the Future Can Be Won.* LID Publishing.

Venter, J. C. (2007) *A Life Decoded: My Genome: My Life.* Viking Books.

Wade, N. (2006) *Before the Dawn: Recovering the Lost History of Our Ancestors.* Penguin.

INDEX